A View from the Cosmic Mirror

Reflections of the Self in Everyday Life

Gary Gemmill, Ph.D.
George Kraus, Ph.D.

authorHOUSE®

AuthorHouse™
1663 Liberty Drive
Bloomington, IN 47403
www.authorhouse.com
Phone: 1-800-839-8640

First published by AuthorHouse 10/20/2010

ISBN: 978-1-4520-3284-9 (e)
ISBN: 978-1-4520-3283-2 (sc)

Library of Congress Control Number: 2010908777

Printed in the United States of America
Bloomington, Indiana

This book is printed on acid-free paper.

To order A View from the Cosmic Mirror or learn more about it, visit www.TheCosmicMirror.org

Contents

REPARATION AND HEALING

Dedications

To my daughters, Paula and Wendy, who are my guardian angels on my life's journey.

—Gary

To Lori, who continually helps me see what I do not.

—George

Acknowledgements

The people in our lives are our own cosmic mirrors that keep us in check. They help us better understand who we are. And we are eternally grateful to them.

To all our remarkable colleagues who have lovingly and courageously revealed their shadows and auras to us—Eynav Accortt, MA; Joyce Appell, LPC; Victoria Baker, PhD; Emily Baldwin, LSW; Phyllis Berman, PhD; Angela Branch; Pat Copas, LPCC; Melinda Costello, PhD; Michael Elmes, PhD; Bobbie Fussichen, APRN; Bruce Heckman, PhD; Michael Hewitt, PhD; Casey Kelliher, PsyD; Jim Kane, LPC; Lorena Kvalheim, PsyD; John P . Layh, PhD; Melissa Layman-Guadalupe, PhD; Katie Malone; Marlene Rodenbaugh, PhD; Fulya Sari; Robert Sheitoyan, PhD; Joyce Shields, LISW; Charles Smith, PhD; Julie Upchurch, LSW; Solange Vasques; Casandra Watson; Matt West, LPC; Michael Wilson, LPC; Ruth Willfong; Cal Wynkoop; all our graduate students—and especially to Kathi Lewis, PsyD; Marci Rogers, PhD; and Kate LeVesconte, PsyD for their learned insights on the presence of the mirrors in their lives and the ones in our own.

We also wish to express our gratitude to the mentors who have inspired us—K. Arnold Nakajima, PhD; Elizabeth Mintz, PhD; Erving Polster, PhD; Ed Klein, PhD; Walter Stone, MD; Celeste Sinton, MD; and Jack Layh, PhD—

each of them has immeasurably enhanced our lives and our development, and we are very grateful to them.

From Gary: George, words are inadequate to express my indebtedness to you. You have helped rekindle a passion for writing about the important things in my life. Working with you on this book has been a wonderful learning experience. It has led to many insights into what it really means to be colleagues as well as friends.

From George: Gary, the time with you working on this book has been the most meaningful, rewarding, and worthwhile of my career. Thank you for your presence in my life. I am also so very grateful for the presence in my life of my children, Miles, Michael, and Aurianna. You are the dearest people, and I love you so. Finally, I am eternally grateful to my wife, Lori. You have not only been an inspiration to me in creating this book, but you have generously offered your wisdom and insights throughout the editing process.

We have made every attempt to trace copyright holders. If any have been inadvertently overlooked, we do apologize and will be happy to acknowledge them in future printings. Special thanks is given to the many fine photographers whose work we have used with permission from iStockphoto.com, including mlenny (Alexander Hafemann) whose photograph of the German autobahn appears on the front cover and to Mario Tarello whose photograph of the solar eclipse appears on the back cover. Special thanks is also given to the following artists and photographers–Benny Lasiter, Giacomo Rizzolatti, Bob Mcleod, Kevin Schoeninger, Derek Chatwood, Sarah Pants, Bidwiya, Vanessa Andres, Chris Lipman, Alexmixi, PoppyW, and Massimo Merlini–whose fine work we are grateful to use. All the drawings involving animals were illustrated by Bob McLeod, and we are grateful to him for them. Special thanks is also given to Harcourt, Inc. for their permission to reprint the book cover from Le Petit Prince by Antoine de Saint-Exupéry, copyright 1941 and renewed 1971 by Consuelo de Saint-Exupéry. We are especially indebted to Tom Tuttle for the use of his fine photography. And we are grateful to Sidney Harris for the use of his clever and poignant cartoons.

Preface

"The universe is the mirror of the people,
and each person is a mirror to every other person."

—*A Cheyenne tribal lesson*

Recently, we were riding in a car with a friend who asked us to tell him what our book, *A View from the Cosmic Mirror,* was all about. We replied that it was a tool that could help him look deeply within himself to discover what he may conceal from his own awareness. We told him that what he keeps hidden from himself distorts his view of others. We also told him that what he mistakenly perceives in others distorts his view of himself. Laughing, our friend said, "Life is like a mirror. What we see out there may be a reflection of us."

This is the central theme of this book. Our outer world, which we label "reality," is linked to the inner world of our thoughts, feelings, attitudes, perceptions, wishes, and fears. The view we have of ourselves mirrors what we see in the world. The view that we form of the world, with all the people and objects in it, is a reflection of all that we carry inside ourselves. To resolve the personal and interpersonal struggles we face in our everyday lives requires learning how to penetrate our own defenses and cultivate knowing ourselves in deeper and more profound ways. Doing so enables us to see ourselves more clearly in the reflections surrounding us. It is our reflections in what we are calling the cosmic mirror that can provide us with a more complete view of ourselves. And how we see ourselves affects how we see and treat others.

It is our premise that we cannot really know ourselves without an awareness of how others in our lives function as mirrors to us. Often without our knowing it, others reflect back to us submerged and concealed parts of our self. It takes learning how to see these reflections to really know ourselves in depth. It takes others to help us find the parts of ourselves that are unknown to us and hidden in their reflections. Using examples from history, pop culture, and from our everyday experiences, *A View from the Cosmic Mirror* takes you on a journey of self-discovery. It is a journey that we hope awakens your unseen but life-affirming reflections in the world around you.

How do we discover the hidden parts of ourselves? How do we find our gateway to real vitality and engagement in life? What drives us to repeat over and over again unhealthy patterns in our relationships with others? *A View from the Cosmic Mirror* describes how to better understand how the unseen parts of ourselves influence the choices we make in our personal growth. It shows how to look deeply at our self in the emotional mirror to better understand our self. It also explains how we can relate to ourselves and others more profoundly and in healthier ways.

In the first section of the book, *The Foundation of the Cosmic Mirror*, we define the structure and processes of the cosmic mirror: the shadow, the aura, polarities, projection, and magical thinking. We explain the origin of the cosmic mirror and how we developed it. We demonstrate just how pervasive the cosmic mirror is. And finally, we describe its central role in our perception of the world. *Everyday Illustrations of the Cosmic Mirror* is the second section of the book and begins with the role of the cosmic mirror in our relationships with our parents and our children. Next, we use the cosmic mirror to unravel our identity as men and as women. We also talk about its effect on our romantic relationships. We discuss the dynamics of scapegoating, the creation of leaders and icons, the role of the cosmic mirror in how we define mental health, in the complex dynamics of corporate work groups, as well as the contentious relationships that can exist between sects within a society and between nations.

Finally, we discuss the process of *Reparation and Healing* of the self. Here, we explain how to find the hidden half of our inner polarities; how to discover, take back, and move beyond our disowned projections; how to uncover the unseen emotional side of the cosmic mirror; and finally, how to use our feelings to guide us to a place of renewal, to a place of endless possibilities, and to a new and more self-fulfilling emotional life. We hope you enjoy your journey.

The Foundation of the Cosmic Mirror

1

The Nature of the Cosmic Mirror

"A man sees in the world what he carries in his heart."

—*Johann Wolfgang von Goethe*

There is a Japanese folktale that portrays the power of the cosmic mirror. The folktale takes place in a small village in a place known only as the "House of 1000 Mirrors."

> Long ago in a small, far away village, there was a place known as the House of 1000 Mirrors. A small, happy little dog learned of this place and decided to visit. When he arrived, he bounced happily up the stairs to the doorway of the house. He looked through the doorway with his ears lifted high and his tail wagging as fast as it could. To his great surprise, he found himself staring at one thousand other happy little dogs with their

tails wagging just as fast as his. He smiled a great smile, and was answered with one thousand great smiles just as warm and friendly as his. As he left the house, he thought to himself, "This is a wonderful place. I will come back and visit it often."

In this same village, another little dog, who was not quite as happy as the first one, decided to visit the house. He slowly climbed the stairs and hung his head low as he looked into the door. When he saw one thousand unfriendly looking dogs staring back at him, he growled at them and was horrified to see one thousand little dogs growling back at him. As he left, he thought to himself, "That is a horrible place, and I will never go back there again."

The happy dog sees the reflection of his warm and friendly attributes in the one thousand mirrors. The second dog sees the reflection of his mean and unfriendly attributes. The wisdom embedded in such allegories and Zen-like stories is profound. Yet, it is not easy to grasp how to make use of it in our daily lives. It is one thing to recognize the wisdom and quite another to constructively apply it to ourselves.

The idea of a cosmic mirror that reflects our unseen image has been around for centuries. The most literal interpretation of the word mirror is that it is a surface capable of reflecting an image of something that is placed in front of it. But when we look at ourselves in the mirror, how do we know that what we are seeing is a clear reflection of our complete self? Throughout the ages, learned scholars, philosophers, and sages have advised us to search for our innermost self in the reflections of those we encounter in our daily life. For example, the Siddha yoga guru Muktananda declares, "There is a great mirror in the Guru's eyes, in which everything is reflected."[1] But in and of themselves, memorable remarks like this one do not provide the guidance needed to apply their insights to our everyday lives.

Benny Lasiter

Seeing Who We Really Are

The people, objects, and symbols in our daily face-to-face world comprise what we have chosen to call the cosmic mirror. And we can learn how to use it on a daily basis to find our reflection in it. As noted psychiatrist Carl Jung has said,

> One is always in the dark about one's own personality. One needs another to get to know oneself.[2]

When we feel strongly about someone (either positively or negatively) it can tell us a great deal about ourselves. It can provide us a clear mirror into our unacknowledged self and our heartfelt inner struggles. People, objects, and symbols that elicit intense attraction, admiration, repulsion, or fear usually indicate that we perceive something about them that we may be having trouble acknowledging in ourselves.

Mirroring is not simply a metaphor for a mental process. It is a physical process as well. Scientists who study nerve cells in the brain have uncovered the physical basis of mirroring. They call these specialized cells *mirror neurons*. And they have found these unique neurons in monkeys, birds, humans, and other species. These nerve cells fire when we watch other people performing an action and when we imitate the same action. These neurons are located in the part of the brain that controls thinking and action.[3] Studies of human infants suggest that the system of mirror neurons develops in the first year of life. And it leads infants to imitate and understand the actions of others.[4] For

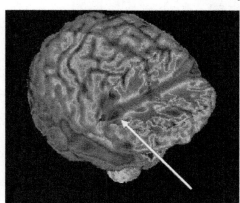

Giacomo Rizzolatti

The Location of Mirror Neurons in the Brain

example, a one-day-old infant will stick out his tongue in response to a parent sticking out *their* tongue![5] Another everyday example of mirroring takes place when someone yawns; inevitably, their yawn is contagious, and like a mirror image, we yawn back. Scientists also believe that mirror neurons are the physical source of empathy. It seems we do not simply learn to be empathetic. We are hard-wired to be emotionally reflective of others' feelings.[6] In fact, neuroscientist Marco Iacoboni argues that the concept of "self "and the concept of "other" are meaningful only as they interrelate. Without a concept of the other, there would be no concept of self and vice-versa. He theorizes that mirror neurons in infants are formed by the interaction of self and others. As he puts it, "In other people, we see ourselves with mirror neurons."[7]

The core idea of the cosmic mirror is that we unknowingly populate the world around us with our denied inner attributes and struggles. For a variety of reasons, we have a great deal of difficulty seeing these attributes and struggles as our own. We also form a view of ourselves by unknowingly filling our inner world with the attributes, thoughts, and feelings from outside of us—we unknowingly develop opinions about ourselves by taking in what opinions others try to place in us.

We are using the term *cosmic* to convey a sense that such mirroring is universal—it is all around us in our daily experiences. It is vast and extends across people and cultures. It is also part of an orderly system of processes within ourselves. Mirroring is cosmic in the sense that it follows a predictable pattern of development and fits into a larger system of thought and action. But most of us know very little about mirroring processes. Mirroring is cosmic in the sense that to see in others our own hidden reflections requires an ability to temporarily step outside our self and reflect on our own experience. It requires seeing more clearly what has not been seen or only dimly seen. To do this involves exploring our hidden and unknown self.

We are not using the term "cosmic" to refer to an other-worldly or even religious experience. We are talking about an experience that simply goes beyond our usual ways of thinking and habits. To look into the cosmic mirror allows us to identify and evolve undeveloped parts of ourselves. To learn how the cosmic mirror operates allows us to grab hold of one of the most powerful personal growth forces in the universe. Philosopher Alan Watts captures well the idea of the cosmic mirror when he states,

> Underneath the superficial self, which pays attention to this and that, there is another self more really us than I. And the more you become aware of the unknown self—if you become aware of it—the more you realize that it is inseparably connected with everything else that is.[8]

Underneath the surface and conscious self lie the undiscovered parts within us that are waiting to be given a voice. They are the parts of ourselves that we discount, deny, disown, or place into other people or objects. By doing so, we do not readily acknowledge them and do not recognize their reflections when we might see them in others. It is the set of these unseen reflections that we call the cosmic mirror. From within themselves, our primitive ancestors attributed "evil" spirits and "good" spirits to objects and animals outside of themselves. Today, we, too, cast out into our outer world the "dark" and "illuminating" parts of our innermost self. We see the "evil ones" and the "angelic ones" outside ourselves but often fail to see how they may be a reflection of our own unknown self.

Jack and Jill, a married couple, illustrate how the cosmic mirror works in our daily lives. Jack considered himself a rugged, adventuresome, strong, silent type. Rambo was one of his heroes. Like Rambo, Jack often felt wary of others and preferred to go it alone. But he also feared losing his independence by being engulfed or emotionally devoured by other people. He feared they might get "too close" to him. The friends he made did not seem to last. Jack loved Jill but could tolerate only so much intimacy from her. When Jill wanted emotional closeness Jack became irritated and described her desires as "touchy-feely, mumbo-jumbo psycho-babble."

Jill loved Jack. She loved his boldness and physical toughness and strength. However, she often saw him as quite aloof, distant, and even cold. She was frightened of the idea of losing Jack's closeness and of being abandoned. Her cell phone was always with her; she considered it her "life-line." Being unable to enjoy times of solitude, Jill frequently made phone calls or visited other people to fill the void inside her. It angered Jill that Jack wanted to go out jogging on his own. It threatened Jill when they wouldn't hug or share their emotions. To distract her from dealing directly with her loneliness, she often pushed herself into compulsive and unhealthy interactions with others.

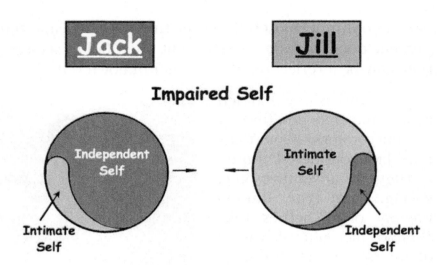

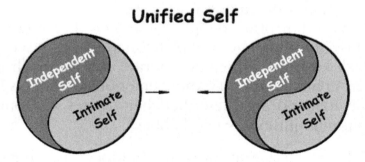

Looking at their relationship in terms of reflections in the cosmic mirror, Jack was mired down in his excessive need for independence. He used this to minimize and deny his need for intimacy. Avoiding intimacy allowed him to mask his deep fear of engulfment by others. Jill reflected the intimate side of him. She was focused only on her need for intimacy and buried her need for independence. Avoiding independence allow her to mask her deep fear of abandonment by others. Jack reflected the independent side of her. This is labeled in the figure above by the term "Impaired Self." In reality, both Jack and Jill possessed within themselves what seemed to be missing in each of them. This unacknowledged part of themselves was placed into and displayed by their partner. The truth of the matter was that Jack did, indeed, have an intimate self as well as an independent self. And Jill did, indeed, have an independent self as well as an intimate self. We call the integration of these parts of one's self the "Unified Self." The strong negative charge in their relationship was contained in their cosmic mirrors. What they saw reflected in each other was the disowned and unacknowledged part of themselves. And at an unconscious level, this was what attracted them to each other—each had something to which the other person needed to connect deep within their self.

Like many couples, Jack and Jill were initially but unknowingly attracted to their disowned parts. And this was reflected in their partner's most apparent characteristic. In most relationships, the most desirable characteristic about the other person frequently mirrors what we cannot see in ourselves. We can only see it in others. In the 1996 comedy-drama *Jerry McGuire*, Tom Cruise is attracted to Renée Zellweger's tenderness and sensitivity—a sensitivity that he does not see within himself nor does he share with others. In one of the key scenes of the film, he tells her, "You complete me." But as most couples can attest, in due time, this honeymoon period ends. Each partner begins to sense the other's flaws. The idealized partner loses their luster. And as this new phase unfolds, the idealized quality that was believed necessary to complete each partner is often later seen as a failing in them—admired independence often begins to feel like emotional distance; caring sensitivity often begins to feel like insecure dependence.

In a sense, too much of "a good thing" is not always a good thing. Each person begins to sense that they cannot have exactly what they had wished for in their partner. They feel trapped with the awareness that along with the "good" they must unexpectedly live with the "bad." Such deep and hidden mirroring must be brought into awareness and owned before each partner can see the other in a more whole, complete, and authentic way. Two people, each who see only half of themselves and only half of the other person, do not make one whole person or a whole relationship. The hill that Jack and Jill need to climb is to become more fully aware of the advantages and disadvantages of their own independent and intimate qualities. They also each need to learn to see that they have within themselves what they both desire and dislike in the other person.

Externalizing the Wizard Within

Frank Baum's *The Wizard of Oz* is another illustration of how the multitude of self-images that comprise our inner world becomes reflected in the cosmic mirror. As the story unfolds, the Scarecrow, the Tin Man, and the Cowardly Lion are each alone and isolated. But they join together to search for their disowned mind, heart, and courage. Eventually, they find the Wizard of Oz who tells them that they already possess the qualities they seek. Nevertheless, they feel that these qualities are outside of themselves and something only he can provide. At first, they simply were unable to authorize themselves to acknowledge it. Believing that only someone else could give them what they needed, the Wizard performs a magical ceremony for each of them. One by one, they find the disowned parts they had formerly obscured from their own view. The Scarecrow finds his brain, the Tin Man finds his heart, and the Cowardly Lion finds his courage. In the end, each recognizes that they had within them what they had been looking for all along.

By the end of the movie, Dorothy realizes that she has been awakened from a dream that she has populated with all the important people in her life—her "good" witches and her "bad" witches. Baum's theme reveals that all the good and evil that Dorothy sees in her outer world were reflections of parts of her inner self. Her fears, her aspirations, her heroes, her loves, her enemies, and her ambitions were within her all along.

The Cosmic Mirror on the World Stage ...

Our world seems to be headed on two paths. On one of them, we are moving toward an ever-advancing technological future. It's filled with marvelous devices that create ever-increasing ease in staying connected to others and to what is happening in our outer world. On the other path, we are unintentionally creating a world with ever-widening polarizations of human and social extremes. We are a nation at war with "evil doers" but ourselves divided into "blue states" and "red states."

We seek enlightenment, and yet we segregate ourselves and others into "Rambos" and "Barbies"; "Blacks" and "Whites"; "gays" and "straights"; "young spoiled brats" and "old geezers"; "the greedy rich" and "the lazy poor." As a society, many of us hold belittling and derogatory views of other societies and other sects within our own society. We try to neatly package others into oversimplified and stereotypic labels. The "fickle moderates" disparage the "bleeding heart liberals" who vilify the "right-wing conservative war mongers" who attack the "deadbeat anti-American tree huggers" who denigrate the "sanctimonious Christian Coalition." The "Real Americans" battle the "Anti-Americans."

But what really divide us from one another are neither national nor state borders. Nor can it be solely attributed to religious, ethnic, gender, or age differences. We are losing our focus on our common goals and desires. There is widespread social dissent and discord. Even in the most sacred of all human commitments, almost 50 percent of marriages end in divorce. And yet, we are a culture of people longing for an enlightened view of ourselves and others. How, then, do we end up creating the human divisions that we wish to avoid? Given our desire for greater wholeness, what makes us so divisive? What keeps us from having the peaceful and constructive life we so desperately seek? The cosmic mirror answers these questions this way: we see the conflicts in the world happening "out there"—we do not see them also going on inside of us. We see the dissonance around us as somehow separate and distinct from who we are. We mistakenly believe that if we simply change our external world then our internal world would become peaceful and calm. However, the opposite is actually true—finding peace within affects those around us.

No one can dispute that the world has its enmity and antagonisms—there is hostility and evil action in our world. But *A View from the Cosmic Mirror* suggests that whether we feel we are directly responsible for it or not, we all make our own contribution to it. Here's how:

1. What we "see" going on in our outer world is also a reflection of what is happening inside ourselves.

2. What we see in ourselves is distorted by the way we perceive the world.

A View from the Cosmic Mirror is a description of a process continuously ongoing in our inner life about which we are only dimly aware. It explains how our inner life inevitably affects the actions we take in our outer world and how our perceptions of others shape who we perceive ourselves to be.

Applying the principles in *A View from the Cosmic Mirror* can take place in an almost limitless number of ways. They relate to leadership, romance, and psychiatry. They apply to scapegoating, magical thinking, and hero worship. They can be applied to our relationships with parents, children, and spouses, and to many other common problems of everyday living. The cosmic mirror can be seen in literature, films, television, and songs. It reflects both the darkest and the brightest aspects of what we keep hidden within us. Seeing its reflections more clearly and completely allows the masked parts of us to shine through, to be understood, and to be more fully and constructively utilized.

On the Importance of Developing a Common Conceptual Language

Many of the building blocks needed to understand the cosmic mirror may be familiar to you. Some may not. In either case, it is quite helpful to have a common language and terminology to describe the concepts used to construct them. To this end, we have made an effort to define words that may be unfamiliar or unclear or that may have been used in other writings where other meanings were implied. To avoid any interruption in the rhythm and flow of your reading experience, though, we have placed many of these definitions in a glossary located at the end of the book.

On the Importance of a Good Theory

It's been said, "Nothing is more practical than a good theory."[9] To explain mysterious and complex events requires integrating what may be old, unfamiliar, and novel ideas in new ways. A long time ago, we believed that the world was flat. But, basic theories from astronomy revealed how this belief was false—a new theory explained that the earth revolved around the sun. It also demonstrated that the earth was round. It is now common knowledge and a very *practical* thing to know. We no longer need to fear sailing off the edge of the world.

Complex ideas can only be made practical by understanding the simpler ideas that comprise them. This is why we have begun this book with this section entitled, *The Foundation of the Cosmic Mirror.* We want to provide you with the necessary building blocks to understand and make practical the idea of a cosmic mirror. For many people, theory building is helpful, fun, and answers many questions. But for some of us, theory development can seem boring, tedious, and time-consuming. For those of you who dread reading about theory, we would like to encourage you, nevertheless, to begin by reading this first section. We think it will be well worth your effort.

2

Reflections of the Shadow

"If you have not seen the devil, look at yourself."

—*Rumi*

Invariably, we run into someone who tries our patience. We feel intolerant of them. Their behavior irks us. They rub us the wrong way. Other people may agree with us that the person's qualities are irritating. But for some reason, others are able to tolerate them better than we are. This person just seems to "push our buttons." The "buttons" that get "pushed" are the very qualities that we find difficult to manage in ourselves. If we react strongly when seeing arrogance, greed, lust, rage, resentment, hostility, envy, awkwardness, cowardice, crudeness, self-indulgence, or insincerity in another person, it is because it is uncomfortably resonating with something deep inside us. We are unable to tolerate or empathize with these negative attributes because we have not learned to identify and acknowledge the possibility that we ourselves may possess these attributes—that what we are seeing in the other person might also be inside of us—that the undesirable quality seen in another may be a denied part of our self. When this is occurring we have buried those attributes outside our awareness. This is the cosmic mirror in action. When our emotional reaction is strong, what we are seeing in the other person is a reflection of our unknown and repressed self. To disown those attributes does not cause them to leave us. Whether we acknowledge them or not, what is unwanted is nonetheless alive within us—residing below the threshold of awareness. Carl Jung called this dark part of us *the shadow*.[1]

The Shadow Side of Our Nature

Jung believed that we see in others all the evil, sinful, crass, and dark qualities that we do not like to recognize, much less acknowledge, within ourselves. He viewed the fear of strangers and creation of enemies as largely mirrored reflections of our own unrecognized and unacknowledged inner self. The shadow side of our self contains feelings, thoughts, and attributes that are out of our awareness. And they are potentially destructive to us and others. The shadow resides in our undiscovered self. It is the under-defined part of us—the part of us that is unexpressed and undiscussable.

We have met the enemy, and "They" are "Us"!

If you can think of the characteristics you are most intolerant of in others it is probably a fairly accurate picture of what is hidden in your own shadow. We often operate under an illusion that we truly know ourselves and have resolved our own problems. We may erroneously believe that we are free of flaws; therefore, it is only "others" who populate the world around us with negativity. The more we deny our own shadow, the more likely we are to be blind to our own flaws—seeing them only in others. The darkness buried deep inside us is evident in our fascination with the darkness in the world. It's what attracts us to television, film, and literature dealing with crime, war, and monsters.

What we repress in our shadow starts early in our lives. Child psychologist Melanie Klein describes how, from a very early age, we mentally

"Many of the things that are too uncomfortable to acknowledge we bury in our shadow."

split off our inner world into two distinct polarities. Our thoughts, feelings, memories, and internal images of our outer world are separated into mutually exclusive categories: objects that are viewed as purely "good" and objects that are considered purely "bad".[2] She used the term *objects* to refer to the contents of each category (like we might refer to "objects of love" or "objects of hate"). A "good object" is someone who the child believes can do no wrong. It is someone who is idealized, perhaps even idolized— someone or something that has only good qualities and not bad ones. At birth, a mother who dutifully holds and feeds her child becomes the child's first good object.

A "bad object" is someone who is believed to do only wrong or harmful things. It is someone who is devalued or scapegoated—someone we might hate or for whom we have no regard or no respect—someone (another person) or something (another group, organization, country, or culture) that has only evil qualities and holds no redeeming value. When a child is belittled in a way that makes them feel ashamed of who they are, they begin to see *themselves* as a "bad object." Their view of themselves along with the strong and uncomfortable feelings that are associated with their view of themselves are often choked off from awareness and placed in their shadow. Their shadow holds their anger, their fear, and their shame. Just as important, their shadow contains a sense that the feelings themselves are bad and wrong—in other words, their shadow also contains their darker emotions. As Carl Jung expressed it,

> Everyone carries a shadow, and the less it is
> embodied in the individual's conscious life,
> the blacker and denser it is.[3]

On a daily basis, the news media reports on the flaws and indiscretions of politicians and celebrities. State governors Elliot Spitzer of New York and Mark Sanford of South Carolina are portrayed as hypocrites when what is seen as their dark sexual side has become publically known. The infidelities of Tiger Woods are viewed in stark contrast to his image as an "all-American boy". It was as if we believed that these men were not capable of such actions. Their shadow side exposed for all to see, the scandals surrounding these men mirror the collective shadow surrounding infidelity and sexual impropriety.

The internet fills with websites that tout the absolute discretion of introduction services for married people looking for extra-marital affairs. And yet, we continue to believe that others can be placed on moral pedestals. When celebrities are caught the longing and urge for extra-martial sex hidden in the collective shadow come roaring out. But the exposure of celebrities represents the tip of an iceberg. By mistakenly believing we lack the capacity to do likewise, the public ridicule of such figures allows us to bath ourselves in the self-righteous belief that it could not happen to us.

The Cosmic Mirror on the World Stage ...

Ever-present on the world stage, the shadow revealed itself in the New York Post's cartoon depicting two police officers shooting and killing a monkey then oddly quipping, "They'll have to find someone else to write the next stimulus bill." The cartoon was widely interpreted as likening President Barack Obama to a chimpanzee. People around the world demanded the New York Post apologize for its senseless racial and political thoughtlessness. Not only were New York Post employees bewildered and angered, the paper was inundated with complaints of racial prejudice.

While at first defending the cartoon, New York Post chairman Rupert Murdoch eventually stated,

> Last week, we made a mistake. We ran a cartoon that offended many people. Today I want to personally apologize to any reader who felt offended, and even insulted. Over the past couple of days, I have spoken to a number of people and I now better understand the hurt this cartoon has caused.[4]

Contained in their shadow, the editors of the New York Post initially denied considering how the cartoon could be interpreted as offensive. What was obvious in hindsight was the part of themselves they could not see. The hostility implied in their racial insensitivity was both denied and projected into the content of the cartoon itself. One way of looking at it was that the editors distanced themselves from the disowned feelings contained in their shadow by placing them out into the world. Once, denied, the outward expression of their passive and denied hostility took the form of the racially insensitive cartoon.

The power our shadow can have in our daily lives is clearly seen in the life of Linda, one of our workshop participants. She was an avowed pacifist who was seen by those who knew her as "the sweetest and kindest person ever." She was active in groups that supported nonviolent ways of handling problems. She also avoided watching any movies or TV programs with violent themes. As her marriage fell apart, though, she developed severe migraine headaches. She also told us that she had been haunted by a recurring nightmare. In the nightmare, she was herself, screaming and running away from a large dark monster that was trying to capture and devour her. Her doctor ruled out any medical explanation for her headaches. And at his suggestion, she entered therapy to sort out why she was feeling so frightened and uncomfortable. When asked by her therapist how she dealt with her anger, she replied, "I can't answer that question because it implies that I get angry. I never get angry. I have never been angry at anyone in my whole life."

As Linda's therapy progressed, the wall of denial around her anger dissipated. She realized that she had been angry with many people in her life, especially her father. She recalled how he mentally and physically abused her during her early teens. Until she reached this point in her therapy, she had blocked it out. The rage she felt at her father was intense to the point that she wished he were dead or that she could kill him for hurting her. There was no real risk to her acting on her wishes. She would never do so. It was all she could do just to think about them. For her, those thoughts, along with her legitimate feelings of anger, were taboo. Linda's therapy involved helping her see that when being abused by someone it was OK to feel angry.

She realized that hidden in her shadow was a deep rage that was frightening to acknowledge. She was frightened to acknowledge it, because she felt as if it might get so out of control that she might act it out. The devouring dark monster in her dream was her rage. And she could not separate having the *feeling* of rage from *acting on* that feeling. Eventually, though, Linda began to recognize that she did get angry. She realized that there were things in the world and in her life that it was understandable to be angry about. As she recognized this, the anger in her shadow began to be expressed and channeled in a constructive way—by talking about it. In releasing her anger in this way, she maintained her personal integrity and expressed more of herself. The monster she feared was her own denied inner anger. With this awareness, Linda's headaches and haunting nightmares disappeared.

It's hard to accept something about ourselves that seems negative. Bill, an executive in one of our workshops, provides another illustration of how to acknowledge and become connected to our emerging shadow. He began the workshop complaining of fatigue, low energy, and having lost his zest. He wrote the following description about a manager with whom he was working:

> I really hate John. When I see him he is often abrasive and cutting toward me. I find him to be a rather superficial person who lives life on a surface level. He seems distant and indifferent toward the needs of other people. I sometimes feel he is just pretending that he is interested in what we are talking about—only going through the motions. His heart really isn't in what he's doing. At times, I feel he is not there at all. He seems totally absorbed in himself.

Bill was asked to reconsider the comments he made about John as if they applied to himself. He was then asked to read his personalized comments to the group. Bill began,

> I really hate some things about myself. I am often abrasive and cutting toward people. At times, I find myself to be a rather superficial

person who is just living life at a surface level, distant and indifferent to the needs of other people. [At this point Bill sighed and nodded his head in agreement. He also realized how cutting he was being about John.] I sometimes feel I'm pretending I am interested in what I am talking about and I am just going through the motions. My heart really isn't in what I'm doing. When I'm with others I'm not always there. I am totally absorbed in myself, unable to find a way out.

Finishing his reading with a softened voice, tears of sadness streamed from his eyes. The message reflected in his cosmic mirror connected deep within him. He saw for the first time the shadowy parts of himself that were the basis of his intense dislike for John. He also faced his own pain around pretending and his own discomfort with being insensitive to others. By seeing for the very first time his cosmic reflection, Bill freed himself from having to use his vital energy to keep hidden these thoughts about himself. He also realized that he did not have to continue to project his thoughts about himself onto John. With this awareness, his relationship with John lost its strong negative emotional charge, and at the close of the workshop Bill felt more energetic.

Sadness
Fear
Rage
Disgust
Power
Intelligence
Humanness

Qualities Often Found Inside the Shadow

> *"My enemy said to me,*
> *'Love your enemy,'*
> *and I obeyed him*
> *and loved myself."*
> *-- Kahlil Gibran*

As Jung so aptly put it, "We meet ourselves time and again in a thousand disguises on the path of life."[5] The cosmic mirror helps us see through the masks, personas, and disguises that we may unwittingly wear. In the workshop, Bill found one of his disguises in the form of the thoughts and feelings he had about John. Until that moment, it was deeply buried in his shadow.

The shadow within us is our disowned internal enemy. As Kahlil Gibran states in his book *Secrets of the Heart,* "My enemy said to me, 'Love your enemy,' and I obeyed him and loved myself." We need both friends and enemies to understand ourselves fully. The internal enemy to which Gibran is speaking is our shadow.

The shadow often appears in our dreams. Dreams are considered to reflect bits and pieces of our everyday life. But dreams are also viewed as representing disowned or under-acknowledged parts of our self. We can access these parts by retelling the dream as if it were happening in the present moment—by describing our dream using present-tense verbs and adverbs as if the storyline of the dream were unfolding right here and right now. The next step in the process of revealing these disowned parts of our self involves asking the dreamer to select parts of the dream that standout for them. The dreamer is asked to play out these parts by giving each of them a voice and by encouraging a dialogue between the parts. This is how the shadow can be uncovered.[6]

Vivian, one of our workshop participants, shared a dream of hers. As Vivian told it,

> I am entering what seems like a kind of funhouse where I need to move through cramped spaces and manipulate objects in my surroundings in just the right way. I'm getting trapped in these tight spaces. It makes me feel like I'm suffocating.
>
> Now, I'm escaping and confront a man who is rude and abrasive. He's calling me a "fake," a "phony," a "manipulator." He wants to pick a fight with me, but I quickly tire of his provocations and walk away. He is following me, and I quicken my pace. As I have done in many dreams before, though, I feel my legs getting heavy. I feel like I am running through quicksand. I remember having felt this slowness before, and I don't like it. Just as I think this, I turn and face my pursuer. He's continuing his verbal attacks, but other people are appearing around us. I now tell him, "Stop it! Just stop it!" and turn to walk away. With satisfying relief, I am doing so without him. He is embarrassed and stays back with the crowd.

To help Vivian re-own and take back the shadow parts of herself, we asked her to describe in more detail each of the dream's major elements. We ask her to play the role of the funhouse, the man, the heaviness, and Vivian herself. She then begins to describe each facet of her dream.

> I am the funhouse in my dream. It seems like
> I am made for fun, but I will trap you if you
> enter.

After she said this, Vivian paused to discuss how much she presents herself to others with her "smiley, fun-face." She told us how she does not let on to others how often she felt trapped in her aloneness—hiding who she really was. She spoke to the other workshop participants about how fearful she was of letting others know this side of her. Something surprised her, though. Having told this to other people in the workshop, she paradoxically felt relieved. Vivian continued to give voice to each of her dream elements by stating,

> I am also the man in my dream. I am angry
> and want to hurt you, but I will only use words.
> I try to be threatening and scathing. I try to
> scare you. Deep down, though, I am lonely
> and not sure how to relate to others.

As she said this, Vivian became aware of just how much she kept others at a distance with her irritability. She saw the effect it had in creating her sense of isolation and exile. But one of her biggest insights was recognizing just how much she had treated herself with abrasive and scathing disregard. She sighed deeply and then said, "I am really *tired* of *doing* that to myself." She then went on,

> I am also the heaviness in my legs. I bring
> you down. I weigh you down. I keep you from
> escaping. But in a way, I am a help to you,
> though, because if you didn't have me you
> would just run away instead of confronting
> the bullies in your life.

> Last but not least, I am me. I cramp up and
> get scared sometimes, but somehow I make
> it through, because I wind up facing my fears
> head-on. By doing so, I somehow move past
> them.

She then began to reflect on what she had just done. She felt proud of herself for being so open with the group. She felt supported by them. But she also internalized their support and transformed it into a new form of self-support.

Vivian's dream became a cosmic mirror to the contents of her hidden shadow. She used the dream as a container for what she had not recognized in herself. This container held her prominent fears in life. It held her feelings of helplessness and her propensity for self-persecution. At the same time, though, her shadow obscured the budding awareness that she was a survivor. By more fully developing the characters in her dream, Vivian was able to reconnect with the paradox of her heavy legs. She realized that the heaviness was a guide to help her do what she most feared—confront the scary man inside her. Finally, Vivian was able to be the parent to herself she had so longed for in her life. She took on the role of the proud mother and father to herself. In this role, she encouraged herself to disclose her feelings to others and find her courageous side. She also was able to reward herself for doing so. For Vivian, her shadow was revealed, confronted, metabolized, and transformed into a more defined and whole self.

Personal Mirror Reflection

Make a list of three people that you immensely dislike. These people should be those that trigger feelings of anger, disgust, fear, or other similar but intensely unpleasant feeling. The list does not have to include people you personally know, although it can. After you have made your list, write down the three qualities you most dislike about each of these people.

The name (or initials) of Person 1: _____	Three qualities you most dislike about Person 1: 1. _____ 2. _____ 3. _____
The name (or initials) of Person 2: _____	Three qualities you most dislike about Person 2: 1. _____ 2. _____ 3. _____
The name (or initials) of Person 3: _____	Three qualities you most dislike about Person 3: 1. _____ 2. _____ 3. _____

After you have made your list, try to identify or take ownership with each of the qualities that you attributed to each of the people you dislike. To do this, choose a close friend to listen to you while you use the following sentence stem,

"I am _____ (insert the disliked quality),"

Say the complete sentence to your friend. What happened when you tried to take ownership for the quality? Share the experience with your friend.

Personal Mirror Reflection (Revisited)

Once you have completed the previous *Personal Mirror Reflection,* write down one of the names (or initials) of the person you listed who has a particularly negative charge for you. Place that name (or initials) at the top of the section below. Now, using the three qualities you listed above (and any other disliked qualities that come to mind), write the things you dislike about the person in Column 2. Now write all the things that you *like* about that person in Column 4. Even if we dislike someone, we can usually find *something* that is at least "OK" about them.

The disliked person's name (or initials)

1	2	3	4

After you have filled in columns 2 and 4, write the following words in Column 1: "I don't like myself when ..." Also, write the following words in Column 3: "I love myself when ..." Now, read each of the sentences you've created for each of the qualities you have listed. Process the experience with your friend. What did you discover?

It's hard to believe, but what we most *like* in ourselves often gets put out of our mind. For example, if someone compliments us our knee-jerk reaction might be to discount it. We do this because we may have learned that it is conceited, narcissistic, or prideful for us to do otherwise. We may not really believe the complement. Or we might think, "What do *they* know!" We often ignore or deny the hidden talents within us. Part of the reason we may do this is because to many of us, possessing those talents implies that we are then responsible for using those talents. Feeling such responsibility can place added and unwanted stress and pressure on us. We might come to believe that it would be better not to try at all if failing at living up to the complement seems too big a risk.

What happens to the unacknowledged talents and positive qualities that we deny or minimize in ourselves? We suggest that our denied qualities—both the desirable and the undesirable within us—get placed out into the world and into other people and objects that reflect their images back to us. Our coworker or friend or family member becomes the enemy when it was something disquieting about ourselves that was triggered. We idolize someone else while we discount our own strengths and unrealized capabilities. We populate our outer world with characteristics of our inner one. But while we attempt to rid ourselves of these concealed qualities, the unacknowledged inner darkness (and denied inner light) haunts and beckons us wherever we go. It does not disappear.

We are lured and repelled by people and things around us. We also attribute many of our denied positive and negative qualities to them. We do it to protect ourselves and others from what we fear about possessing those qualities. While in the short run it may feel less uncomfortable to deny it, developing a greater awareness of this process can be one of the most profound of our life's learning.

In this chapter, we have been discussing the shadow side of our personality. In this part of our self, we contain the "negative," undesirable, and unflattering parts of us that we feel we must keep hidden. But at the same time, we often keep hidden from ourselves the "positive," desirable, and constructive aspects of who we are. We might hide our power to lead others. We might hide our bravery. We might hide our intelligence, our creativity, and our sensitivity. How and why we do this is the focus of the next chapter: "Reflections of the Aura."

3

Reflections of the Aura

"My life is my message."

—*Mahatma Gandhi*

It goes without saying that the qualities we see and admire in others are also qualities we would like to see in ourselves. Some people see their own radiance; others don't. Many times, these admired and sought-after qualities are undiscovered parts of ourselves. They are parts of ourselves that we keep hidden, and they are contained in what we are calling *the aura*.

The shadow contains the darker side of us. As we discussed in the last chapter, when we are not aware of our shadow it can potentially be destructive to us. Like the shadow, the aura contains attributes that we do not recognize. Like the shadow, the aura's attributes are feared.

That's why we keep them hidden. By contrast, though, the aura is a container for the illuminating and potentially constructive and positive side of ourselves. Jung included all aspects of the unknown personal self in what he called the shadow. From the perspective of the cosmic mirror, though, the concept of the aura is used to differentiate the hidden constructive attributes from the destructive ones. In our experience working with clients, the dynamics of these distinct structural aspects of the self are quite different. As we did in Chapter 2, we would first like to look at Melanie Klein's concept of *splitting* to help us make this distinction.

A Manifestation of the Aura Within

Recall that the child mentally splits or separates their sense of people and objects in their outer world into purely "good" and "bad" compartments.[1] Into one of these categories, the child also places their view of themselves. Like two ends of a magnet, these *polarities* of "good" and "bad" are opposites of each other. To go beyond Klein's notion of the good-bad polarity, though, a child uses a variety of other polarities or opposites in order to make crude distinctions for themselves. For example, a child constructs and organizes their world around such polarities as "light" and "dark," "warm" and "cold," "love" and "hate," and so forth. Adults do this as well. But many of us get lost or trapped at one end of a polarity or the other. For example, we may see others in a predominantly or excessively good or bad light, when a more balanced blend of these qualities may be much a more accurate assessment.

We inflexibly believe that both the world and ourselves are either "black" or "white," "good" or "bad." People can narcissistically become lost to the light within themselves or they can nihilistically become lost in their own darkness. But there is no darkness without light, no light without darkness. They coexist. Each word implies the other. Achieving peace of mind and emotional wholeness involves integrating both ends of these polarities. It means understanding that each of us is a mixture of opposites. In this sense, if we have a shadow we must also have an aura.

Throughout art history, radiating auras and halos have often been painted above the heads of religious figures. They were used to denote their spiritual qualities. The luminosity around their heads might be a form of supernatural reality. It might merely be a perceptual after-effect from looking with awe at a charismatic figure. Some people believe that a person's aura can be "seen" or their "color" identified. The "truth" about this is not important. What is important is the fact that for centuries, these auras have appeared again and again in religious art from cultures across the world. Apart from suggesting that auras and halos may have physical or metaphysical meaning, they hold psychological meaning as symbols of a spiritual, transcendent, or higher self within us. And this is why we have chosen the word aura to describe the denied but transcendent qualities within us.

Many people believe in the existence of UFOs. In his book on flying saucers, Jung argued that it is not important whether they exist or not. What is important is that they exist in the beliefs of people from a wide variety of cultures.[2] He hypothesized that UFOs, flying saucers, and alien beings are symbols of a deep longing for a sense of wholeness and unity that seem unavailable to us on Earth. Many of us feel hopeless and alienated from our own creative life force. To hold on to our hope of reconnecting with this life force, many of us externalize or cast out for safe keeping any unrealized ability to tap into this creative force. We push it into outer space, where we see it coming back to us in an alien form. We have an alternative, however. We do not need to cast our creative life force into the emptiness of outer space. Within each of us, there is a fragile, gentle, and loving extraterrestrial within us— an ET of our own—capable of finding a meaningful and loving home in this world.

A Longing for Wholeness

The aura can be identified in many of the books and accompanying regalia on *guardian angels*. In a 2007 Gallup poll, 75 percent of American adults said that they believed in angels.[3] In fact, since 1994, five Gallup poll surveys have consistently found this. It makes sense why the TV show *Touched by an Angel*, was watched by millions of viewers. Guardian angels are containers for the "angelic" qualities in us. They are supernatural symbols in which we place the higher or spiritual qualities within us. Angels are mirrors that reflect our own divine inner qualities.

An awareness of the divine in all of us can be seen across many cultures. It is reflected in the Hindu word "namaste." This is a respectful greeting or parting phrase, which literally means, "I bow to the divine in you, which is also in me." It is usually accompanied by a slight bow with the palms of the hands pressed together over the heart and with the fingers pointing upward. It is not an expression of idolatry. It is a simple acknowledgment and appreciation of the divine within all of us. Similarly, in Siddha Yoga, the most powerful chant is "Om Namah Shivaya." In Sanskrit, it means to honor the God that lives in all of our hearts. The two basic beliefs of Siddha Yoga reinforce this. The first belief is that God lives within you, as you. The second belief is that God can be seen in one another.[4] The qualities we see and attribute to God also exist within us as parts of us.

Images of Angels and Demons Through the Ages

This way of thinking is quite different from the beliefs of religious or spiritual seekers who view God(s), goddesses, or spirits existing *outside* of themselves. They often do not see in themselves the spiritual qualities that they attribute to their divine figure. They often do not see their god reflecting back to them their own image. Instead, the spiritual qualities and wisdom are seen as residing only in a supernatural form. These seekers are often unable to fully take ownership for all the wisdom and guidance that is inside of them. Because the qualities are externalized, using and refining this wisdom in daily life can be quite difficult.

Things we consider to be supernatural cannot be verified with existing scientific methods. It is a fact, though, that, psychologically, they exist in the minds of many people. To take an example, we can't scientifically prove ghosts exist. But many people believe otherwise. In 2007, the American Association of Retired Persons conducted a survey of over a thousand of its members. Fifty percent of them believed in spirits or ghosts. Thirty-eight percent said that they had actually felt the presence of something they thought might have been a spirit or a ghost.[3]

In the language of the cosmic mirror, ghost figures are containers for both the aura and the shadow elements that we place in them. From our aura, we put into ghosts our wish for immortality. One of our greatest hopes is that we will become part of the divine and breathe eternal life. We materialize and personify this hope by placing it in ghost figures. From our shadow we place in ghosts our fear of death. Without the hope of a life eternal, we might be overwhelmed and immobilized by our fear of death and nothingness. Because of this, they serve an important function in our lives. The aura of divine immortality and the shadow of death are among our deepest hopes and our greatest fears.

Using the concept of the aura, as part of a week-long residential personal-growth workshop, we have designed a "guardian angel learning activity." The activity begins with participants randomly selecting a slip of paper from a basket passed around the room. On the slips of paper are the names of people in the workshop. And each person ends up with one of their names. Each participant then becomes a guardian angel to the person whose name they have selected. To do this, they are to closely observe the person during the week (both in and out of the workshop sessions). They are told not to reveal the name that they have drawn until they are instructed to do so.

The guardian angel is to observe the issues with which they see the person struggling. They are also to reflect on what they believe will be useful to the person to sustain or accelerate their personal growth. It is announced that at the end of the week, they will be asked, without revealing who they are, to write a letter of guidance and encouragement to the person that they picked. They are also asked to make a copy of the letter for themselves.

On the last day of the workshop, all the letters are collected by the workshop leaders and delivered to every participant. They then read the letter they have received from their unknown guardian angel. Each person is then asked to express their reaction and tries to guess which group member is their guardian angel. As you might expect, there is a great deal of excitement and intense emotion inherent in this process. After hearing their remarks, most participants believe their assigned guardian angel from the workshop clearly sees their struggles.

The identity of the guardian angel is eventually revealed. After this, the guardian angel is asked to pull out their copy of the letter they wrote. They are asked to read it aloud in the group with one important change. They are to substitute the words "I," "me," or "myself" for the word "you" or for the other person's name. Even though the letter itself may have meaning to the person who was observed, the letter is also a message to the guardian angels themselves. Guardian angels become immediately aware of the mirroring process. They see the importance of the words that they have chosen to describe the person they had observed. They learn how other people serve as a cosmic mirror that reflects their own discounted qualities. Taking on and enacting the role of a guardian angel to someone else allows a person to more clearly see their own spiritual and nurturing qualities. They realize that these qualities are often denied, under-acknowledged, or under-developed. Rather than placing them into someone else, they see their own denied reflection, often for the first time. This fosters greater ownership of these qualities for themselves.

Each person hears what others have done in their role as a guardian angel. In doing so, everyone's behavioral repertoire is enlarged. The process of guiding another person more deeply, spiritually, and lovingly nurtures themselves. Louis, one of our workshop guardian angels sent the following message:

> You are one of the treasures in my life, and you mean so much to me. To share your emotions and experiences is your greatest gift. To feel them is to love yourself.

When he read it aloud, personalizing it from his own perspective, he said,

> I am the treasure in my life and I love myself. To share my emotions and experience them is my greatest gift. To allow myself to feel them is to express my love for myself.

In the same workshop another guardian angel was assigned to observe the workshop leader and wrote,

> You have helped each of us grow. You have fed our hearts and souls. Our love for you grows, as we are guided by your wisdom to learn more about ourselves. The work you do is exhausting. I worry about how you replenish your energy. I want you to feel the same relief that you have allowed us to feel. Treat yourself well, and take in the caring that others have for you. I wish you peace and

harmony as you continue your work of love to the people of the world. May you find the love and happiness you long for.

When she personalized it, she reread it as,

I have helped myself to grow. I have fed my heart and soul. My love for myself is guided by my wisdom to learn more about myself. The work I did was exhausting, though. I worry about how to replenish my energy. I want to continue to feel the relief I allowed myself to feel this week. I want to treat myself well and take in the caring that others have for me. I wish myself peace and harmony as I continue my work in loving myself. May I find the love and happiness I long for.

The notion that there are guardian angels is not just a Christian phenomenon. Guardian angels are depicted in many religions, such as Judaism, Islam, and Zoroastrianism. They also are a vital part of New Ageism. They appear in the Hindu religion as "divas." And they can be seen in the ancient Egyptian culture as "griffins." The basic function that is attributed to angels is to guide us, protect us from harm, and provide a direct connection to God. Their purpose is to provide a sense of comfort and reassurance in a chaotic world. The word angel is derived from the Greek language where it means "messenger." In Christianity, the idea of guardian angels can be found primarily in Psalm 91:11, which reads, "For He shall give His angels charge over thee, to keep thee in all ways." The Zoroastrians believe that at birth, everyone has a guardian angel assigned to them. In the language of the cosmic mirror, guardian angels are our externalization of the wished-for life affirming qualities that are also within us but that we may not fully acknowledge or see.

At first thought, it might seem strange that we can deny a positive characteristic in ourselves. But many of us doubt our potential for success. We might discount a compliment. Or we might in some way obstruct our view of the "good" within us. Many of us fail to see the depths of the glowing radiance in our own eyes. When positive parts of our self are cast off into our aura, what results is a *de-skill-ing* of our own creativeness, constructiveness, and spirituality. We end up forsaking our own competence, potential, and divinity. Geraldine choices illustrate this process.

Geraldine was eighty-five and lived in a nursing home. She was irritable and fatigued. She had a cynical view of the world. She also excessively isolated herself. She thought that being eighty-five with failing health meant that

> *"Quite often, we fail to see the gleam in our own eye."*

she had little to offer others. So she kept to herself. She was keeping her aura hidden from her own view. As you got to know her though, you could see her witty sarcasm and how she playfully recognized others enjoying it. This was the glimpse she saw of her own denied aura. With encouragement, she took a risk and began socializing with others. As she did, others began to see her witty sweetness too. More importantly, as she began to see the glow in *their* eyes, she began to see more of the glow in her *own* eyes. Geraldine had Alzheimer's, but the disease didn't stop her from reconnecting with and transcending what was formerly denied and contained in her own aura.

The *Jonah Complex* is a concept that was used by psychologist Abraham Maslow when referring to the tendency to deny our own talents and perceive them only in others. The label is based on the story of the prophet Jonah who was trapped in the belly of a whale. God trapped Jonah in the whale, because Jonah was afraid to follow the voice of God within him. As Maslow expressed it,

> We fear our highest possibilities (as well as our lowest ones). We are generally afraid to become that which we can glimpse in our most perfect moments ... We enjoy and even thrill to the godlike possibilities we see in ourselves in such peak moments. And yet we simultaneously shiver with weakness, awe, and fear before these same possibilities.[5]

Like Jonah running away from the call of God to do the divine work of preaching to others, we often evade giving birth to our own constructive and creative qualities. Like Jonah, we run away from fully embracing our own god-given talents.

In *The Republic*, Plato uses a story to describe the subjective nature of reality, which further illustrates how we can discount our own greatness.[6] In the story, there are a group of prisoners who are chained from childhood to the wall of a cave. Plato suggests that we imagine one of the prisoners somehow freeing himself from his bondage, leaving the cave, and seeing for the very first time the sun illuminating the world. What were formerly merely shadows are brought into the light. In doing so, though, the only reality known to the freed prisoner is now shattered. Frightened by the new images he sees, the prisoner elects to return to the cave. He rechains himself to the wall and readjusts to the shadows of the world with which he was familiar. He could not handle something unknown, complex, and new. So he returned to the security of the world he did know. Being "outside the box" for the first time, the freedom was overwhelming. His only experience of life was living inside the darkness of the cave. And he was unable to overcome his fears or move forward despite them.

Although it may seem hard to imagine we have mixed feelings about experiencing personal freedom in our lives. It is an essential expression of our individuality. But it is also something that can frighten us. Creating our own path in life is something we must do on our own. And we can often feel alone, anxious, and unable to amply provide ourselves with the support we may need. This was one of the tenets of psychoanalyst Erich Fromm's landmark book, *Escape from Freedom*.[7] Fromm believed that it was much easier to deal with "freedom from" internal and external opposition than it was to deal with the "freedom to" construct a life that feels meaningful on a day-to-day basis. In fact, Fromm thought it was so burdensome a challenge to do so that he felt that this explained why many people were willing to fall victims to dictatorial regimes—like what gave rise to Nazi Germany. In some ways, people fall victim to the false promises of dictators to escape from the personal freedom necessary to grow and to solve what may seem like insurmountable personal and social problems.

To shatter our own personal myths and expose our vulnerabilities in the hope of being transformed into something different can be a terrifying prospect. Children—adolescents especially—are pushed to just this point when they are asked to adjust and adapt to new and ever-changing realities. How well they do so shapes their personalities as adults—but not always in functional and adaptive ways. As adults, we have the freedom to pursue our own personal growth—we are only limited by our imagination, cultural programming, and psychohistory. But the prospect of re-experiencing difficult feelings and dilemmas that were benchmarks in our earlier life can elicit great fear. This fear can preclude us from taking an honest look at ourselves in the mirror. It can also lead us away from attaining the very things we long for.

The process of discovering how we place our attributes into other people and other objects can be overwhelming. But the amazing reality is that an awareness of our own process simultaneously can free us from those fears and other constraints we may place on ourselves. Once we have become aware of this process, we have a choice. When we have a choice we then can truly create our own experience and direct our own existence. We no longer are trapped in our fears of experiencing something new. Julie and Sam provide a vivid example of how our aura can be reclaimed.

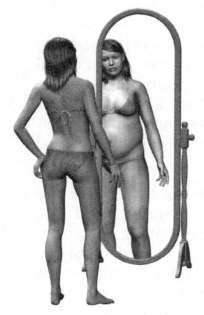

The Aura of Denied Positive Qualities

Julie lived an isolated life. Her adult son, Sam, had reentered her life and moved in with her. Authoritarian and domineering, her son slowly began to choke off Julie's self-esteem, her sense of purpose, and her vitality. She loved her son. But Julie and Sam shared a mutual overdependence on each other. She passively submitted to his demands. In doing so, she developed a servile role that entrenched her in a pattern of unhealthy accommodation to him. At the same time, it reinforced her son's dictatorial manner while also placing more responsibility on him. Julie unknowingly placed her own power and dominance in her son, and she disowned it in herself. She also passively swallowed yet denied her rage at his insensitivity.

At the same time, Sam could not tolerate his own sense of helplessness and purposelessness. He placed these qualities into his mother. Sam also felt angry but excessively responsible for taking care of his mother—as if his mother was incapable of helping herself. As Julie's therapy progressed, though, she better tolerated looking at her own pattern. She began spending more time out of the house. She started to enjoy the healthy and affirming companionship of others. Eventually, Julie began to take back the denied aura of her own power and control over her choices and actions. She began asserting herself with her son, and she began to see that she was much more capable than she had been giving herself credit for.

ScienceCartoonsPlus.com

To take another example, Luther, was a forty-year-old organizational consultant who participated in one of our workshops. He was feeling depressed and stuck in his career. He loved his work but had always carried with him the idea that he didn't measure up. He firmly believed he couldn't do what others could do. He also believed that others could see through what he called his "charade of competence." During the workshop, Luther wrote the following description of someone in his life whom he admired:

> Ryan has been an inspiration to me. He brings out the best in me. He is as skilled at human relations as anyone I've met. Even in the midst of highly emotional conflict, he uses his people skills to understand others. He demonstrates his respect while at the same time maintaining his own position. He is sensitive to others' feelings and needs. He is genuine in the way he comes across and the way he "walks the talk." He is honest with the people he coaches. He seems to be someone who has an unusually clear understanding of what people need and deserve from each other.

Luther was asked to read aloud to the group what he wrote but to personalize it as he read it. That is, he was asked to identify with what he wrote about Ryan as if it applied directly to him. Luther began by saying,

> I'm an inspiration to myself. I bring out the best in me. I'm as skilled at human relations as anyone I've ever met. Even in highly emotional conflict, I use my people skills to

try to understand and demonstrate respect
while maintaining my position.

At this point in his reading, he hesitated and tears streamed
down his face. He was gently encouraged to go on with his
reading, and he continued by saying,

> I am sensitive to others feelings and needs.
> I support others. I am genuine in the way I
> come across and the way I "walk the talk." I
> am honest with the people I coach and have
> an unusually clear understanding of what
> people need and deserve from each other.

As Luther read his statements aloud, he acknowledged
that while these admired qualities were also true about his
mentor, these qualities were true about himself as well.
This was the first time in his life he began to genuinely
feel the truth in his statements. In the process of reflecting
on his cosmic mirror, he was able to more clearly see his
own considerable skills and personal values. He stepped
outside the Jonah Complex, and found his concealed aura
in a new and life-affirming way.

The relationship between patients and their doctors provides
another example of the aura in
action. Many of us idealize our
doctors. We place our lives in
their hands and have the highest
expectations that they will heal us
almost without us needing to tell
them what's wrong. We rarely ques-

*The Early Externalization
of Our Own Fears*

tion their judgment. We have faith that they know exactly
what to do. In a way, we see them as all-knowing beings.
We rarely question their ability to heal us—even when we

feel they spend too little time with us. In the process of over-idealizing them we can deskill ourselves from our own healing powers. Who are the people, though, who take on the physician's role, and with it, all the trappings of our idealistic projections?

The cosmic mirror suggests that people who become physicians may be those who have difficulty accepting the idea of death. In many ways, this is adaptive for them. It also has its advantages for us. We do not want our doctors to give up on us. We do not want them to become consumed with the idea of death. We want to have the utmost confidence in their opinions. We want them to work hard keeping us alive, especially when we may feel hope is lost. We want them to help us cheat death. In a sense, the idealistic projections from our own aura that we place in physicians resonate with their fear of death contained in their shadow.

As close as physicians are, though, to the process of living and dying, why don't they attend the funerals of their patients?[8] Have you ever attended a funeral where the doctor of the deceased was there to comfort surviving family and friends? The cosmic mirror suggests this occurs because death may be something emotionally denied by doctors and projected out into their patients. It is something that other people experience. It is believed that physicians may not be able to bring themselves close to the emotions associated with death, because it triggers their own anxieties about it. As physician Sherwin Nuland writes,

> Of all the professions, medicine is one of the most likely to attract people with high personal anxieties about dying. We became

doctors because our ability to cure gives us power over death of which we are so afraid.[9]

In a similar vein, transplant surgeon Pauline Chen speculates on a process similar to those involved in the cosmic mirror when she states,

> We may be a self-selected lot who eagerly suppress those fears as we adopt a professional ethos that embraces denial.[10]

Prehistoric caves often contain drawings by shaman (ancient medicine men) that have been interpreted to represent the cave dwellers' attempts to conjure up magic spirits that could help them. Their actions were a means of finding an external place of safekeeping for their own hopes and wishes. Along the same lines, the ancient Greeks and Romans imbued their gods with the owned and disowned admirable qualities—qualities that

The Search for the Externalized Aura

came from within them. Their gods also mirrored their unadmirable qualities. Aphrodite (Greek) or Venus (Roman), the Goddess of Love, possessed the capability of great love. Yet she also was considered to be treacherous and malicious with a destructive and deadly power over men. Similarly, Zeus the supreme God and ruler of Olympus, was considered wise, kind, and powerful. Yet he also was imbued with a bumbling infidelity and a vengeful nature. He destroyed others with his mighty bolts of lightening. Poseidon (Greek) or Neptune (Roman), ruler of the sea, was considered wise, dignified, and powerful. Yet he also was considered to be quarrelsome, jealous, and belligerent. He was capable of unleashing his anger with a flurry.

"Relationships that are emotionally charged provide a mirror into our hidden and unacknowledged self."

The ancient Greeks and Romans made their gods in their own image. They did it so they could both admire and identify with them. At the same time, though, when the mortal men and women of the times experienced jealousy, anger, or fury, they tended to disown those feelings. They believed that it was the gods, operating through them, and not themselves who were causing their emotions and actions. In essence, they disowned those shadowy feelings and pushed them out into the cosmos. They did this to avoid personal responsibility for them. In this sense, the gods were scapegoated for a person's own flawed behavior. The people of that time also excessively attributed positive qualities to the gods by failing to recognize those qualities as emanating from within themselves. When something went well in their lives it was the gods who were smiling upon them.

In his classic book *Siddhartha*, Herman Hesse describes how the Buddha's aura may have first been revealed. Siddhartha was actually the family name of the Buddha. In one passage, Hesse looks at his own reflection in the river and begins to see something more. Hesse writes,

> Siddhartha made an effort to listen better. The image of his father, his own image, the image of his son merged, Kamala's image also appeared and was dispersed, and the

image of Govinda, and other images, and they merged with each other, turned all into the river, headed all, being the river, for the goal, longing, desiring, suffering, and the river's voice sounded full of yearning, full of burning woe, full of unsatisfiable desire.[11]

For Hesse, the river is a metaphor reflecting all the wisdom and understanding in the universe and our place within it. Siddhartha learns how to use the river as a mirror for attaining self-wisdom. He discovers how everything is contained in it just as all that is in the

The River: A Reflection of Ourselves

universe is reflected in every object, every thought, and every person. He realizes that all those he had ever known were reflected in the image he saw of himself in the river. As Hesse wrote, "A frightening emptiness was reflected back at him by the water, answering to the terrible emptiness in his soul."

Hesse's message for all of us is clear. The enlightenment available to us depends on how much of ourselves we are able to see and acknowledge in all that is mirrored around us. As Siddhartha did, we, too, can stay connected to the rivers in our lives that mirror all the good and bad that is in our own soul. When the Buddha was asked, "Are you a god or a man?" he replied, "I am awake."[12] What he meant by this was that he was aware of all that he was, his place in the world, and the world's place within him. The word Buddha refers to "one who is awakened or enlightened."

In this sense, we all become Buddha when we are awake to the mirrors in our daily lives. The self-enlightenment available to us depends on how much of ourselves we are able to see and accept in all that is mirrored around us—both in our shadow and in our aura. Alan Watts has commented on this very same idea when he said,

> We do not 'come into' this world; we come out of it, as leaves from a tree. As the ocean 'waves,' the universe 'peoples.'[13]

The study and practice of *transpersonal psychology* has a great deal to do with the aura. Transpersonal psychology focuses on our creative potential. It is the study of how it develops and how it can be channeled. It is also considered the study of those psychological processes where we experience a deeper connectedness to others and to our self. We experience our transpersonal self when we feel connected to our "higher power." We feel the "divine" in us. We feel "awake." We feel we have had an "epiphany" or a "peak experience." These and similar descriptors are all used in referring to the shift to such a transpersonal sense of self.[14]

Carl Jung studied Eastern and Western religions, alchemy, parapsychology, astrology, and mythology. He did so in an effort to identify the struggles, wishes, fears, desires, fantasies, and dreams that are common across people and across cultures. He believed that many of these experiences are not fully known to us because they are contained in our

Symbols in the Search for Transformation

unconscious—that is, beneath our own awareness. He called the unconscious themes that are common to all people the *collective unconscious.*

Originally, Jung called the collective unconscious the "transpersonal unconscious." He believed that all of us have an innate drive toward growth and wholeness. He saw this drive as a natural process in which these universal and collective images and experiences guide us and help us unfold our better nature. He called these universal images *archetypes.* He believed that we all have the power to lift ourselves to a more inner-connected and other-connected sense of sacredness and compassion. When this happens, we evolve as human beings.

Much of counseling and psychotherapy targets shadow issues. In this sense, the goal of therapy is to undo negative experiences from our past. This aspect of therapy is designed to help the client become aware of and master their own inner critic and the dark side of themselves. At some point in all effective therapy, though, aura issues must be examined and tapped. The client must go beyond the negativity of their shadow and give birth to their constructive and creative potential. Exploring aura issues, though, can feel as fearsome as they can seem enticing.

To feel most intensely alive, we must address both shadow and aura issues. If we over-focus on one side of ourselves to the exclusion of the other, we can't become fully whole or complete. Unresolved shadow issues limit us from reaching our authentic spiritual self. This is the danger in self-help approaches that stress the "power of positive thinking." In and of itself, "thinking positively" is not sufficient for growth. We can't fully realize our higher self unless there is sufficient resolution to the denied negativity contained in our shadow. John Welwood, a leading figure in bringing together Eastern and Western psychology, calls this *spiritual bypassing*. According to Welwood, spiritual bypassing is,

> ... using spiritual ideas and practices to sidestep personal, emotional "unfinished business," to shore up a shaky sense of self, or to belittle basic needs, feelings, and developmental tasks, all in the name of enlightenment.[15]

Over-focusing on our aura can lead to a type of spiritual narcissism. This occurs when a person constantly is trying to get high from more and more peak experiences with little regard for others and with little regard for their unresolved negativity. What seems like the development of one's aura becomes an avoidance of one's shadow.

Just how to identify what is in the transpersonal mirror and then apply it to our everyday world is not easy. In Somerset Maugham's penetrating book, *The Razor's Edge*, Larry Darnell goes to Tibet in search of a higher or truer meaning to his life. He goes to a monastery and speaks with a Tibetan monk. The monk tells him, "The path to salvation is as narrow and as difficult to walk as a razor's edge." Darnell mockingly says to himself, "It is easy to be a holy man on top of a mountain." He reflects how difficult it is trying to remain a holy man when surrounded by the trappings of our daily world. Despite its wisdom, the irony of this statement is that it is not easy to be holy on a mountaintop nor more difficult to be holy in our everyday world. The task is challenging yet attainable in either setting, because it's not the setting that matters—it is the mindset. This mindset is aptly captured by Cheyenne tribal member Hyemeyohsts Storm, who eloquently says,

In many ways this Circle, the Medicine Wheel, can best be understood if you think of it as a mirror in which everything is reflected. "The Universe is the Mirror of the People," the old Teachers tell us "and each person is a Mirror to every other person" ... Any idea, person, or object can be a Medicine Wheel, a Mirror, for man. The tiniest flower can be such a Mirror as can a wolf, a story, a touch, a religion, or a mountaintop.[16]

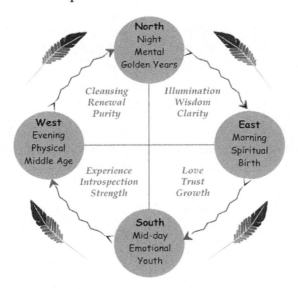

It seems clear that people and objects in our immediate surroundings can become powerful cosmic mirrors for all of us—reflecting all the greatness within us that may not be fully visible to us. In everyday life, the cosmic mirror consists of people, objects, and symbols in our world onto which we externalize attributes from our own inner self. In many ways our outer world is a social construction of our own mindset. It is a mirrored reflection of our inner world—with all the beauty and impressiveness contained within us.

Personal Mirror Reflection

Here's an exercise that will help you build a sense of your aura. Similar to the *Personal Mirror Reflection* you completed in Chapter 2, imagine that there is an article being written about you in the local newspaper. Contained in the article are three positive and admirable personality characteristics that are true about you. What positive qualities would you like to read about yourself?

To help you identify the three positive qualities you sense may be true about yourself, here's a list of words from which you can choose. Pay attention to which words have an especially strong emotional charge for you, and write down three of the words that are the hardest for you to own about yourself. Use the spaces at the bottom of the list to include words that come to mind that are not listed.

Accepting	Empathetic	Respectful
Adaptable	Friendly	Sensible
Bold	Humorous	Smart
Brave	Idealistic	Spiritual
Calm	Ingenious	Spontaneous
Capable	Logical	Sympathetic
Caring	Mature	Talented
Clever	Organized	Trustworthy
Compassionate	Patient	Warm
Creative	Powerful	Wise
Dependable	Relaxed	Witty

_____   _____   _____

Chose a trusted friend to involve as your partner. Take turns sharing the three things you would like hearing said about you. Identify each of the three things and say them out loud in a sentence that takes the following form:

"I am _____ (the positive quality)."

For example, if you identified "mature" about yourself, then say, *"I am mature."* For each of the positive qualities, your partner will then say to you "You are _____ (the positive quality)." For example, your partner would say, *"You are mature."* Pay attention to how you feel when you identify with the quality and how you feel when your partner says it to you. These feelings can tell you something about what might be contained in your aura that you may not have fully embraced.

The idea of a cosmic mirror in our lives is compelling. In one form or another, it has been discussed throughout the ages. In the last two chapters, we have described two fundamental components of it—the shadow and the aura. The shadow and aura are elements of the cosmic mirror that share a common characteristic. They are at the opposite ends of a basic polarity. The shadow contains the darker and more feared attributes like rage, sadness, and shame. The aura contains the creative, life-enhancing, and life-affirming attributes like our hopes, our ambitions, and our gifts. In the language of the cosmic mirror, the very structure of our internal world—with all its thoughts, perceptions, and emotions—can be understood as a constellation of interacting polarities. This idea is so essential to understanding the cosmic mirror that we spend the next chapter discussing it.

4

Polarities: Finding the Other Half of Our Self

*"Everything requires for its own existence its own opposite,
or else it fades into nothingness."*

—*Carl Jung*

In the natural world, all extremes are defined and opposed by their opposites. Opposing polarities—such as warm/cold, light/dark, conscious/unconscious, wellness/illness, and life/death—are in constant interplay. These polarities contain psychic as well as physical energy. Typically, though, we see only one side of any polarity at a time. Or we lean toward more clearly acknowledging one end of a polarity than we do the other.

Vanessa Andres

The Infinity Mirror

When we emotionally compartmentalize and split off our aura or our shadow our mind and body react to it. We cannot do otherwise. There is no way for us *not* to have a reaction to this splitting process. And this reaction affects both our physical and mental health. It keeps us from being our complete self. It diminishes and constricts us, and we become fractionalized. All of our inner life is regulated by the dynamics of opposition—becoming aware of this inner dynamic is essential to our personal growth.

In Robert Louis Stevenson's *Dr. Jekyll and Mr. Hyde*, Jekyll writes a letter to his good friend. In it, he describes his failed experiment to discover the dark side of himself. He tells his friend, "My devil had long been caged. Hyde arrives with a roar and a fury that I had not expected."[1]

Chris Lipman

Jekyll tries to predict when Hyde—the evil side of the human experience—will show itself. He designs an experiment to separate his two polarities—Jekyll and Hyde—by looking at what was good and evil in himself. But he underestimates the strength of his own evil side. His experiment careens out of control. The story of Jekyll and Hyde points out one of our deepest fears—the fear that connecting to the shadow side will release an uncontrollable monster within us. This is not an inevitable outcome, though. It is more an *imagined* fear. Looking into the cosmic mirror enables us to safely see both our Jekyll side and our Hyde side. When we see both sides of our polarities we become more evolved and complete as human beings.

One way that we defend against seeing our inner self is by trapping ourselves in a process where we deny one end of a polarity and exaggerate the other. This process begins when we get a glimpse of one of our objectionable behaviors, emotions, thoughts, or attributes. We might first deny what we see. Then, we might display its opposite attribute. For example, a person who is overly thrifty or miserly may be trying to manage their fear of excessive spending. They also may be trying to conceal a fear of being too generous. A person who is modest to a fault or who is excessively humble may be trying to conceal their fear of being arrogant or superior. When a person's behavior is excessively aligned with one end of a polarity it is often because they feel the need to avoid its opposite polarity. This type of avoidance usually stems from feelings of guilt, fear, or shame. When this occurs a person displays too little flexibility. They have trouble adapting to situations that may call for the enactment of the feared polarity. They become rigidly stuck at one end of a polarity. This imbalance can be quite draining and maladaptive. Being excessively and rigidly thrifty diminishes appreciating the importance of being generous.

The Cosmic Mirror on the World Stage ...

A graphic example of the polarization process occurred when American televangelist and PTL Club host Jim Bakker was caught in a sexual scandal. The scandal involved a hidden romance with his former secretary, Jessica Hahn. Bakker was caught up in his own piety and could not control his fascination with the sinful side of sex. Reverend Jimmy Swaggart, another well-known televangelist, was harshly critical of Bakker on the Larry King Show. He accused Bakker of being immoral. But Swaggart himself was later caught on film with a prostitute. After that, Swaggart was arrested by the California Highway Patrol. The charge? Driving (with another prostitute) down the wrong side of the road. In an act of defensive defiance and embarrassed to own up to his own shadow side, Swaggart told his flock, "The Lord told me it's flat none of your business." Bakker and Swaggart denied their apparent shameful qualities. They also tried to lead others to think the opposite. They wanted others to see them in their public personas—as men who were holy and devoid of sin.

The resignation of New York governor Eliot Spitzer is another example of what can happen when we get stuck in one end of a polarity. Without our awareness, one end becomes exaggerated. The other becomes denied. Before his resignation, Spitzer was viewed as a "White Knight," "The Sheriff of Wall Street," and "Mr. Clean." He was a fierce defender of ethics. Then, the FBI exposed his hidden side. It was reported in affidavits that he frequently used the services of high-priced call-girls. When the FBI's evidence was publicly released, his image was fatally tarnished. Ironically, Spitzer's illicit behavior was not unlike the crimes of those he prosecuted when he was the New York State Attorney General.

From the perspective of the cosmic mirror, Spitzer was caught up in an overly inflated image of himself. This was his persona. He failed to give sufficient voice to the darkness within him. He also denied the likelihood of being caught and the real consequences to his life should others find out about his behavior. It seems that he may have been able to see only the polarity of darkness in those he prosecuted—not in himself. He blinded himself to his own self-destructiveness. And as often happens, he ended up acting out the darker and denied polarity.

Polarities operate much like Newton's Third Law of Motion. Newton's Law states that for every action, there is an equal and opposite reaction. Regarding our own perceptions, we often are aware only of the polarity associated with an action. We are often unaware of the equal and opposite polarity pushing to react back. Our perceptions become restricted. We allow ourselves to see or experience only one side of the polarity—we discount its opposite.

Here's an experiment to illustrate this. Shown below is a picture. Concentrate for about thirty seconds on the four dots in the middle of it. Then, take a look at a white wall and start blinking your eyes. You should see a darker circle of light. Continue looking at that circle. What do you see within it? Try this before reading on.

Most people will see the recognizable image of Jesus Christ. We cannot clearly see him until the afterimage is revealed. But his image is there all along. Every object and every image has a hidden polarity waiting to be revealed.

Here's another example. In the figure below, look at the space in between the dark segments. What do you see? Does an illusion of circles appear? Do the circles appear brighter than the background? In fact, they are not! This is the dynamics of opposition at work and our own inner reaction to what we are seeing in our outer world.

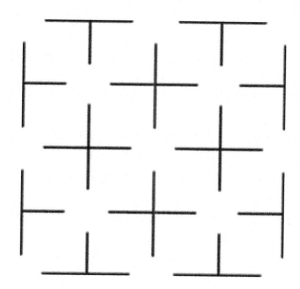

These are examples where our perception of reality becomes reversed. Reversals like these take place with our emotions as well. Although we don't intend it, we often get stuck in one end of an emotional polarity. The other end is hidden in our shadow or our aura—it is calling out for acknowledgment.

Polarities operate in our lives in many ways. They have been discussed throughout history. And they are part of the philosophy behind the well-known Chinese Yin/Yang symbol (also known as the Japanese Tai Chi symbol). The symbol represents two primal opposing but complementary cosmic forces. Together, they create a *unity of opposites*. As we have been discussing, this unity of opposites can be found in all objects and processes throughout the universe. As these two energies interact, they cause events to unfold in a manner similar to Newton's Third Law of Motion. The white polarity (Yang) is viewed as active and bright like the sun. The black polarity (Yin) is viewed as passive and dark like the night surrounding the moon. As can be seen in the symbol, each polarity also contains an element or seed of the other. This is meant to suggest that each element cannot exist without the other. Similarly, our emotional polarities are each a part of us. And yet, they are separate and distinct. Together, they define our constantly evolving whole self.

Discovering Our Polarities

It is possible for us to expand what we know about our own emotional polarities. We can learn to identify new possibilities to ourselves. When we first experience a new emotional polarity, it is often hard to maintain our awareness of it. For a time, we may keep it in mind and the impact it has on us, but then we lose sight of it. We shift back to old ways of thinking. New ideas do not always settle in quickly. New vistas are often quite difficult to revisit. It takes practice and repetition to maintain the flexibility that is needed to return to newly learned or unfamiliar places. Here's what we mean by this:

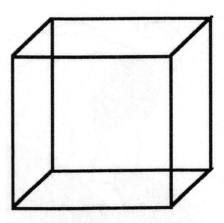

The drawing shown here is called a Necker cube. Try staring at it. What do you see? At first, you might imagine looking up at the bottom-right face of the cube. Then you might see that same face appearing as if it was on the inside of the cube. The back becomes the front; what formerly appeared on the outside becomes what seems to be on the inside. Try

The Necker Cube

focusing on different parts of the drawing and see if you can force your perceptions to shift.[1]

In the world of philosophy, common-sense *realism* states that we see the world exactly the way *it exists*. From this point of view, we see reality as objective, tangible, factual, and actual. On the other hand, the philosophy of *dualism* states that the external world cannot be viewed objectively or directly but can only be *interpreted* though ideas or through our sensations. Reality, like beauty, is in the eye of the beholder, subject to our own potentially unique interpretations. The Necker cube refutes common-sense realism. That's because, at first, we might develop one interpretation of what we are seeing, and later, we might change our mind and see something entirely different. Another way of saying this is that reality is often ambiguous— subject to interpretation. This is why eyewitness testimony is often unreliable. Two people may "see" an event in entirely different and often contradictory ways. In fact, in the Necker line drawing, there really is no "cube" at all, but just a flat drawing on a piece of paper.

Another Illustration of Perceptual Choice

Most of us are pretty flexible when it comes to shifting our point of view of the Necker cube. We can readily see it from more than one vantage point. Consider now this widely publicized drawing of a woman's profile. What do you see? Do you see an old woman with a prominent nose and chin or do you see a young woman with small features and a choker around her neck who is looking away? Once we see one of these women, most of us have some difficulty shifting our perceptions to see something else. In fact, many of us need someone else's help to prompt us to see what, at first, we cannot. When we finally realize that we *can* see what was right in front of us all along, we might have an "Ah, ha!" experience. We are amazed at discovering our own blind spot and gratified in reaching a more expansive way of looking at what we formerly thought we understood.

The principles related to polarities that apply to the Necker cube and the old/young woman also apply to newly discovered emotional polarities. They are present when we form our view of other people. And they apply to us as we shape our opinion of ourselves. What we first believe may be true we may later learn is false or needs amending. This is what led sociologist W. I. Thomas to state,

> If men define situations as real, they are real in their consequences.[2]

This statement became the basis for the idea of the *self-fulfilling prophecy*. A self-fulfilling prophecy occurs when an expectation causes an event to become true. Sometimes, the assumptions and perceptions behind our expectations are true. Sometimes they are false. Sometimes they are rigidly held. Sometimes they are flexible. A series of studies on classroom achievement is frequently cited as an example of this. It was found that when students are falsely perceived by their teacher to be "intellectually dull" they perform poorer than students who are falsely perceived to be "intellectually bright"[3] We, too, often unwittingly become what we inflexibly perceive ourselves to be. The way we are labeled has its consequences.

Quite often with the help of a guide, what we may have denied or placed into other people or objects can become "visible" to us for the first time. To vividly realize how we create our own perceptions can be quite startling. But to reach this insight can also evoke one of the most powerful forces in the universe—the profound awareness that we truly have a choice in how we see all things and all people—including ourselves.

There are many ways to explore the variety of dimensions within us. Robert, one of our workshop participants, did so in the following way. He was a quiet an unassuming man. But he reported feeling paralyzed in his marriage to a dominating woman. In a structured learning event from one of our workshops, he was asked to focus his awareness on an object of his choice in his immediate surroundings. He was then asked to talk about himself "as if" he were that object. He looked around the room and began by saying,

> I am a rug. People walk all over me. Some people spill things on me or wipe their feet on me. Others burn me with their smokes. Dogs piss on me.

He labeled this part of himself "The Doormat"— something he felt like at home and with other people in his life. Next, he was asked to focus his attention internally to consider what he believed the opposite of a doormat was. He was asked to identify it and to give a voice to whatever it was. He stated,

> I am my penis. I'm sometimes soft while sometimes I become erect. When I am erect I become hard and firm. That makes me feel cocky.

Robert was able to acknowledge this "hard" and "cocky" part of himself, but it was a part of himself he rarely experienced. He labeled this part of himself "The Prick." In his labels—"The Doormat" and "The Prick,"—he was able to identify an important polarity within himself. And as he more fully experienced each end of this polarity, he was able to make an essential shift in his view of himself. He began to see how he could constructively integrate the assertiveness in his "Prick" self with the openness and receptivity of his "Doormat" self. He labeled this newly discovered synthesis of formerly opposing polarities—his "Assertive Self."

In the classic PBS film documentary, *Faces of the Enemy*, philosopher, and social psychologist Sam Keen talks with mythologist Joseph Campbell.[4] Together, they watch a clip from *Star Wars: The Empire Strikes Back*. In the film, the hero, Luke Skywalker, enters a dark cave where he confronts

A Battle of the Light and Dark Sides

evil in the form of Darth Vader. After slaying evil with his light-sword, Luke discovers that the face behind Darth Vader's mask was Luke's *own* face. Campbell interprets the scene by saying that it is the mythological hero unmasking the inner monster. By doing so, Luke uncovers the opposite polarity—the force of goodness and light that is in Darth Vader. Luke shocks himself by realizing that Vader's humanity was part of his own humanity. He also realizes that the evil within Vader could also be a reflection of his own shadow side.

Campbell asserts that Skywalker had a vision of the light and dark elements both within himself and within Darth Vader. Campbell states that Luke's vision,

> ... came from a transcendent realization that you and that other *are* the same life—you *are* the same consciousness—and the separation is simply an effect of time and space.[4]

The light and dark sides of us are polarities. Taken together, they make up *the force*. One side cannot exist without the other.

Personal Mirror Reflection

Here's an interesting polarity experiment you can try for yourself. First, write down what you consider to be a positive attribute of your personality. Next, write down what you think the opposite of that attribute would be. Next, write down a negative attribute you believe you possess. Now, write down what the opposite of that attribute would be. Once you've done this, ask yourself, "Do I possess any part of these opposite attributes?"

How did you answer? How do you feel about how you responded? What did you discover? Now read the following passage and see what one of our workshop participants discovered.

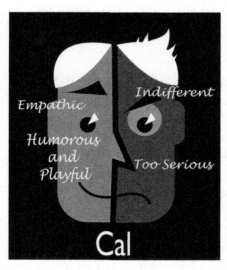

The experience of one of our clients, named Cal, provides a good illustration of the process of identifying and integrating polarities. Cal was a human relations consultant. He came across as doleful and lifeless, and he found himself getting bored and impatient with his clients. He came to one of our workshops to better understand what he was experiencing, and he completed the polarity activity described above. He stated that one of his positive attributes was being "empathetic." And he said that the opposite of that quality was being "indifferent." He also told us that a negative attribute he possessed was being "too serious" and said that the opposite of being too serious was being "humorous and playful."

Cal was then asked to "give a voice to" each listed attribute. What this means is to act as if each attribute had a mind of its own and could speak. We then invited him to have his attributes "dialogue" with one another. Here's an excerpt:

> Empathetic Cal: All kinds of people come to me to discuss their problems. I have an open ear and listen to them in a supportive way. I think they find me understanding and caring. I feel I am compassionate and can identify with the struggles that others are having.
>
> Indifferent Cal (To Empathetic Cal): You are really quite arrogant in presenting yourself as if you are a Messiah. Many of the people who come to you with their struggles you find to be a 'pain in the ass.' You want to say 'Listen, you think you got problems, who doesn't!' Your arrogance is not being able to let them know that you, yourself, are caught up in your own struggles. You are not as available to listen to them as you act. You think you can help others but you won't let others help you. Arrogantly, you think you are the only one who can help you. Yet you believe that others need you to help them because they can't help themselves.

At this point, Cal realized that Empathetic Cal was his social persona—the mask he wears with others to manipulate the impression he makes on them. Cal discovered that Indifferent Cal was his shadow that he feared would break through. As Cal spoke for Indifferent Cal, he felt the energy in this polarity—and paradoxically, the honesty. Contained in Indifferent Cal was the neglectful way he took care of himself. Cal was then invited to see what Empathetic Cal and Indifferent Cal wanted from each other. Here's another excerpt:

> Empathetic Cal (To Indifferent Cal): What I want from you is for you to assert what you need and not neglect yourself. I also need you to stop running away from your own needs and struggles. I also need your assertiveness to help me overcome my self-inflicted arrogance and let others help me with my struggles.

> Indifferent Cal (To Empathetic Cal): What I want from you is your caring—your willingness to listen closely to my feelings and needs. You listen to others. Now I need you to start really listening to me.

By having this dialogue, Cal reached a synthesis between his formerly opposing polarities. He succeeded in making contact with each end of it. As a result, he felt more capable of asserting himself when it was necessary. He felt more whole. Later, Cal followed the same procedure with his so-called negative polarities: "Serious Cal" and "Humorous and Playful Cal."

> Serious Cal: I have to be serious. There are so many problems that need to be addressed in the world. I feel overwhelmed with all the work that needs to be done. That's why I am always working on something. I want

help resolving all these problems. It's serious business.

Playful Cal: Relax. You can't do everything. You must take time to reenergize yourself. Laughter is truly the best medicine. I want to help you. I can help you. I can help you become more creative and feel closer and warmer with other people.

Cal was worried about his lifelessness. He was concerned that he may have permanently lost his ability to be playful and humorous like when he was a child. We asked if he could give himself permission to be playful with others in the workshop. At first, it felt awkward. But he found that he still knew how to be quite playful with others. Everyone, including himself, found that he actually had an engaging sense of humor. Later in the workshop, Cal became known for the fullness of his laughter and the twinkle in his eyes.

Acknowledging the polarities within us requires looking at our life from both sides. To be whole, it takes looking at our life from opposing points of view. The lines from Ecclesiastes 3: 1-8 ("... a time to be born, a time to die ... a time to love and a time to hate ...") make a clear statement how life involves continuous shifts between polarities. It is our belief that there is a time and place for everything, including looking into the cosmic mirror.

We have been discussing the cosmic mirror in terms of a constellation of opposing polarities—including its most fundamental components: the shadow and the aura. How, though, can the cosmic mirror reveal to us these hidden elements? How is this process activated? What drives it? When it makes its presence known how can we identify it? The cosmic mirror is revealed though the process of *projection*, and this is the topic of our next chapter.

"To everything there is a season,
  and a time for every purpose under heaven.
A time to be born, and a time to die;
A time to plant and a time to reap;
A time to kill, and a time to heal;
A time to break down, and a time to build up;
A time to weep, and a time to laugh;
A time to mourn, and a time to dance;
A time to cast away stones,
  and a time to gather stones together;

A time to embrace,
  and a time to refrain from embracing;
A time to get, and a time to lose;
A time to keep, and a time to cast away;
A time to rend, and a time to sew;
A time to keep silence, and a time to speak;
A time to love, and a time to hate;
A time of war, and a time of peace."

-- Ecclesiastes 3: 1-8

5

Projection and the Cosmic Mirror

"Projection changes the world
into the replica of one's own unknown face."

—*Carl Jung*

Projection is a type of psychological defense mecha-
nism—a mental process we use to emotionally protect
ourselves from uncomfortable thoughts and feelings—and
it plays a central role in the operation of the cosmic mirror. It refers to a process where we unknowingly place our
inner thoughts, feelings, and conflicts into people, objects,
and symbols in our outer world.[1] Because we are not often
aware of this process, we fail to recognize when and how
we are immersed it. Through projection, we place aspects
of our hidden face onto others. In doing so, we experience
our unknown face reflecting back at us. But we do not
see it as our own. This is the fundamental process of the
cosmic mirror—what we attribute and perceive going on in
others is reflective of what can be ongoing inside of us.

Here is a very rudimentary example of projection—the denial of responsibility and the assignment of blame. Henry bet Todd $25 on a baseball game and Henry lost. One month later, Todd asked for his $25, and Henry said he paid him, but Todd said he didn't. The reality was that Henry had paid Todd. Henry had it right, but Todd couldn't remember that Henry had paid him. Around and around they went—emotions flaring—Todd rigidly believing he knew the truth but being unable to consider himself mistaken. Todd was mistaken, however, and it was Todd's infallibility that was buried in his own shadow. It was too uncomfortable for Todd to consider that he was wrong. So he projected the idea he was mistaken onto Henry. For Todd, it was Henry who was wrong, not him. Todd could not take ownership for what was his role in the mishap. Instead, he projected responsibility and blame onto Henry.

This process can be seen all around us. We often perceive that our view is "objective" and "rational" while others' views are "biased" and "irrational." More generally, we become upset, angry, and judgmental toward others who openly display characteristics, points of view, or unsettling feelings that reflect what we may resist acknowledging in ourselves.

"Even our enemy is useful to us because in order to practice compassion, we need to practice forgiveness, and patience—the antidotes to anger." —Dalai Lama

From our everyday perceptions, we "know" that things exist out in the world because we "see" them. We "hear" them. We "touch" them. More accurately, though, the things that we see, hear, or touch in the world actually stimulate processes within us. And it is these processes that we *label as* objects or events. Similarly, when we "sense" that someone is "angry," the perception seems like it's coming from the other person. But in actuality, we are placing a label—"angry"—on them. The label is based on our internal processes of sight, hearing, what we may feel inside about them, and especially what we interpret about them. This is the basis for empathy.

Empathy is our ability to sense someone else's feelings. But empathy is actually made up of two distinct actions, not just one. First, we identify the feeling within us—for example, a sense of anger. Next, we mentally place that internal feeling into the other

> *"We see the world as 'we' are, not as 'it' is; because it is the 'I' behind the 'eye' that does the seeing."*
> *—Anais Nin*

person— that is, we label the other person as "angry." In other words, empathy is what we *imagine* the other person is feeling. At its core, empathy is an imaginative projection. We believe that we are a mirror to the other person. Then we act on our belief by projecting that reflection into them. When we are accurate we call it empathy; when we aren't, it's simply our own projection. A rose is beautiful not strictly because of an objective quality inherent in it. A rose is beautiful because we mirror its beauty.[2]

What we often see in others is a product of our imagination. We do not actually see the anger in others. We don't actually see the hurt in others. These are merely abstract labels. These labels come from our *interpretation* of the behavior of others. These interpretations are our best guesses about what may be going on with the other person. But they are always based on limited knowledge of them. Words like anger and hurt have literal meaning. But they also have figurative or symbolic meaning. The figurative or symbolic meaning that we attach to words is the product of what we project into those words. We use words like hero, leader, jerk, nice guy, brute, sexy, and so on. When we place meaning into words like these, we may or may not have specific people or objects in mind. But the meaning we assign to those words comes from what we have absorbed from our own cultural matrix. Thus, the word-labels we use as adults also are mirrors into which we often project the disowned parts of ourselves. This is especially true for the labels to which we attach strong emotion.

Busting Stereotypes

Stereotypes are a good example of this. Stereotypes are usually negative and over-simplistic labels that we give to people from a particular group. They are exaggerated labels. They are often inaccurate. And they seldom are based on personal experience. For example, men tend to be stereotyped in our culture as breadwinners. They are seen as initiators and aggressors. And they are pushed to conceal their softer emotions and weak spots. Women, on the other hand, are stereotyped as warmer than men. They are seen as more expressive of their emotions. And they are believed to be less competitive and less decisive than men.

What is important about stereotypes is that they are fertile ground for projecting unwanted parts of the self.

They are often based on the teachings from within the culture. And they are based on the collective projections of others. Stereotypes are powerful examples of how a label can become a container for our projected shadow and aura attributes. The more emotionally charged the label, the more we are drawn toward it; and the greater our unwanted emotions are projected into it. Think about the following labels: neo-Nazi, mentally ill, right-winger, criminal, mentally retarded, Fascist, Goth, corporate suit, Communist, Satanist, and gang-banger. All of these labels have a strong negative emotion attached to them. As a result, they all can become a kind of "garbage can" into which we dump unwanted parts of ourselves. While there may be some truth to a stereotype, in essence, a stereotype is often a kind of receptacle for our own buried waste. This is especially true for the parts of us that generate self-loathing and shame.

The Cosmic Mirror on the World Stage ...

   In times of trouble, groups with negative stereotypes can be fertile ground for scapegoating. In a crisis, stereotyped groups are often blamed. This is done in an attempt to simplify what actually are quite complex social issues. It also helps us contain what may be massive feelings of helplessness and rage that are triggered by the crisis. In World War II, the stereotype of a Japanese man and woman evoked horrific images of heartlessness and cruelty. In government propaganda films, the Japanese were portrayed as "vermin." Americans believed that all men and women of Japanese heritage were out to annihilate us. It was this stereotype that led our government to intern 120,000 innocent Japanese and Japanese-American citizens. In essence, the label for an ethnic group became the target for much of the projected rage and fear of a nation.

Any ethnic group can become a container for our projections. Today, some of us might be inclined to react in an overly negative way toward Islamic or Middle-Eastern Americans. We might suspiciously believe that all of them are involved in terrorism. Or we might believe that they might all be somehow responsible for subjecting us to the terrorism of others. Here's another example. In 1995, the trial of O. J. Simpson polarized a nation. It led many of us to judge the innocence or guilt of a man based on his African-American ethnicity. It also led many of us to judge the dishonesty of a city justice system based on the racist remarks and perjured testimony of one of its police officers.

Projection was first described by psychoanalyst Sigmund Freud. He used the term to explain why people who were paranoid feel that the world was so hostile. The paranoid person fears annihilation—believing they are fragile and helplessly dependent on others. What the paranoid denies is their anger and rage over having been made to feel so fearful and powerless. Freud proposed that the paranoid person projects their denied rage out into the world. They take what is an internal feeling—rage—and translate it into what they believe is a real characteristic of their outer world. This is projection in action. In essence, the paranoid's logic is, "If I *feel* fragile and powerless, then the world *must be* cruel and dangerous." Originally, Freud believed that projection was part of the normal perceptual process. He felt that our mind was filled with so many sensations, thoughts, and feelings to manage that we needed a way to cope with them. He thought that projection naturally occurred as we search for an outside reference point for what was actually an experience occurring within us.[3] Freud believed that only in its extreme form did projection manifest in mental problems. Later, he limited his use of the word projection to mean an unintentional way of reducing or avoiding anxiety. And this is how it is commonly used today. In terms of the cosmic mirror, we are using the term projection in its original, broader, and more inclusive sense—as a part of the normal perceptual process.

Even the Exalted Have Feet of Clay

Projection plays a key role in our development as healthy human beings. The psychoanalyst Melanie Klein helped us understand this. She understood that a baby adapts to their outer world by forming a representation of it inside them. But babies believe that their own inner thoughts are indistinguishable from what is happening in their outside world. This is because their thinking processes have not yet developed. They cannot yet distinguish between what is inside of them from what is outside of them. Because of this, a baby uses projection to adapt to totally new experiences. For example, by getting fed, the baby feels nurtured. The love and gratitude they feel in being fed is then projected out into their mother. The mother becomes "someone who is nurturing." Once projected out into their mother, the baby takes those feelings back inside as if they came from her. They feel loved. Eventually, they feel lovable.[4]

Projection is not simply something that young children do. It is widespread throughout our lifespan. In order to function, we must selectively attend to our senses. We are bombarded by information in our daily lives. Therefore, we must have a way of limiting what we allow in from what is coming from outside of us. We also must limit what comes from inside of us. If we didn't, we would constantly be overwhelmed with irrelevant and extraneous thoughts and feelings. Rather than actively paying attention to every specific fact or perception from our world, we develop an overriding summary or interpretation of the information and project that summary outward onto the situation—we use our summary as a organizing label. This is what allows us to sort through the information that we cannot possibly take in. Selective attention is part of how we naturally function as human beings. And projection is an important aspect of it. Projection can help us cope on a daily basis with our environment and our inner world. But, it also can undermine accurate interpretation of what we see and hear. Projection is neither right nor wrong; good nor evil. It is not pathological. Nor is it indicative of a person's need for psychotherapy. It is happening to us every minute of every day. It is our attempt to make sense of the daily world in which we are immersed.

With projection, we place on to others our own inner struggles. In the PBS documentary *Faces of the Enemy,* psychologist Sam Keen examines the process of enemy-making.[5] In doing so, he provides many vivid examples of projective processes. One of Keen's interviews is with Vietnam Veteran William Broyles. Broyles's describes one of his most harrowing wartime experiences. He tells us that in war, soldiers are trained to see the enemy as an abstraction, as simply a pronoun—"*He.*" For a soldier, this pronoun is uniquely defined as "someone who is trying to kill me." Yet, there were moments in his Vietnam experience when Broyles could step out of his role as a soldier, see through the abstractions he was trained to perceive, and identify the common humanness in himself and in his enemy. As he describes it,

> We were out on patrol out in the mountains, and we found a tunnel. And what you had to do when you found a tunnel was blow it up, so it wouldn't be used against you for your supplies or communication. And I turned to my best tunnel man and said, "Let's go," and he said, "No. I'm not going to do it!" And going down into a tunnel is not something you can really order someone to do, just by custom, at least where I was, and I turned to my other guy who was good at tunnels, and he shook his head. So, that meant I had to go *myself.* It was something you couldn't make anybody do unless they volunteered for it.
>
> So, I went down in the tunnel with just a "45", and it was very tight and dark. And I had a flashlight, but I didn't want to use it, because it would announce my coming. And I crawled down in this tunnel, and it sort of went down and went flat, and it opened up

into this room. And as I lay there, I had this horrible realization that someone else was in that tunnel, and I could feel that someone else was there.

It was like I could feel his breath; I could hear his heart beating; and I could hear his eyelashes blinking. And so, I crawled back out as fast as I could and went down, and they gave me a charge to blow up the tunnel, which is what I had to do after I checked it out. So I went back down, put the explosive on the wall of the tunnel, and before I crawled out, I said, "Di di ... Di di," which means "Get out; go away." And ... you're not supposed to do that.

This was my enemy, and I should have just tried to kill him. But, there was something about meeting a person like that in a tunnel ... not seeing them. It was just impossible to have that kind of abstraction, 'cause we were alone, and we were separated from our other soldiers and our armies and our countries and all those things that sent us there. It was like two people in a hole.

I crawled back out and set the charge, but *it didn't go off*; it was a dud. So, I had to crawl back in for a third time, and I didn't know whether I'd be shot or speared or all these things. I was very scared! It was incredibly frightening!

I got back to this opening, and this presence ... I still felt it. So, I whispered again, "Get out

... di di ... go away," and I backed up out of the tunnel. And just as I got out, the charge went off—"pop!"

Sometimes, I wonder if there was ever anybody there ... whether it was just sort of the embodiment of my own fears.

Broyles is discussing a pure instance of the projective process and the ownership of that process. His story describes him casting out into an abyss what were his own thoughts, fears, and fantasies. He also considers that the reality he believed was "out there" could have been merely a reflection of what was inside of him.

Projections contain the seeds for creating great emotional closeness *with* others. But they also can create great emotional distance *from* others. As we become more conscious of what we are projecting, we can become more awake to what may be our hidden emotional agendas. Becoming aware of the ways we project ourselves out into the world adds clarity to who we are. It makes us more complete. And it helps us become more centered. Being able to see our reflection in the cosmic mirror helps us identify and acknowledge our emerging aura and shadow. It facilitates us in unfolding our greater capabilities. And it heals the divisions within our self. We then have a choice that formerly we did not have. We can work at becoming more aware of our emerging hidden parts or remain blind to them. Nevertheless, our submerged self will influence our lives *precisely because* it is out of our awareness. For example, if we are really angry with someone and we do not realize it because it is buried deep within us we *will* act it out or express it somehow. We may become irritable toward them for no apparent reason. Or we may "forget" something important we said we would do for them. We may feel "fearful" or "depressed" when we are around them. Or we may get headaches, stiff necks, ulcers, or an "irritable bowel." We may try retreating from our anger. But that will not extinguish it.

We not only project our attributes and feelings into the people and objects around us—we also project our own wants and needs. For example, someone may say to a friend, "You look like you need a hug." Where does this perception come from? While it may be true that the other person may actually feel as if they needed a hug, the *perception* that they needed a hug can only come from our *identification* with the need for a hug—that is, it must come from within us. Although it may be delivered in a disguised form, our perception of the other person often reveals something about us—that we wanted the hug or wanted to hug our friend rather than our friend actually looking like they needed the hug. Similarly, what we wish for other people can likely be what we wish for ourselves. Another form of this occurs when we make suggestions or give advice to another person—for example, when someone says, "Take good care of yourself." While it is a wish for a friend to be kind to themselves the expression may also say something about what we may need to do for ourselves.

Personal Mirror Reflection

Imagine that you (and a romantic partner) just had a beautiful new baby. Imagine the future you would like for your new baby. What would you want for your new baby? What would you hope for your new child?

Imagine that you have a chance to communicate your thoughts to your new baby. Take a minute and consider what you would like to say to this precious new child and fill in the following sentence-completion stems with your responses. Use the space (____) in the beginning of the sentence as if to place the name of the baby, although there is no need to name him/her.

____, I wish for you _____.
____, you deserve _____.
____, to feel safe and secure, I hope you will _____.
____, one way that I can show you that I love you
today is _____.

Complete the above portion of the *Personal Mirror Reflection* before moving on.[6]

Once you have completed the sentence completion stems for you new baby, what we would like you to do is place your own name in the blank at the beginning of each sentence. Now read each of the new sentences to yourself; then say them out loud. When you are done reading them aloud to yourself, give your stems to a trusted friend, and ask them to read them to you. Really listen to your friend read the new sentences to you.

What did you experience when you first took ownership for your wishes and read them to yourself with your own name included? What did you experience when you heard your friend read your wishes out loud to you? How might this experience relate to the concept of the projection?

Finally, we want you to translate each of the completed sentence stems into "I"-statements that you to affirm to yourself. For example, change the stem that begins,

"_____, I wish for you _____" to read
"I wish for *myself* _____"

and change the stem that begins,

"_____, you deserve _____" to read
"*I* deserve _____."

After you have changed the sentence stems, read them aloud to yourself. What does this feel like to affirm these wishes?

**The Guardian Angel
We Wish For**

Casandra was one of our workshop participants, and she completed the previous *Personal Mirror Reflection* by filling in the sentence stems in the following way:

"I wish for you ... *a loving future and respect for yourself.*"

"You deserve ... *loving kindness from everyone in your family.*"

"To feel safe and secure, I hope you will ... *protect and insulate yourself from negativity that might surround you.*"

"One way that I can show you that I love you today is ... *to gently rock you and hold you close in my arms.*"

Casandra was then asked to give her stems to her partner who filled in Casandra's name in front of each sentence. Casandra did the same for her partner's stems. Then, sitting face-to-face while maintaining eye contact, one at a time, each person was asked to read back to them their partner's completed stems. The receiver was asked to "relax, breathe, and take in what you are about to hear." The receiver then heard what wishes they had crafted for the baby, now addressed to themselves. Casandra heard her partner read to her the things that Casandra wrote,

> "Casandra, I wish for you ... *a loving future and respect for yourself.*"

> "Casandra, you deserve ... *loving kindness from everyone in your family.*"

> "Casandra, to feel safe and secure, I hope you will ... *protect and insulate yourself from negativity that might surround you.*"

> "Casandra, one way that I can show you that I love you today is ... *to gently rock you and hold you close in my arms.*"

Casandra wept with gratitude hearing her wishes mirrored back to her. At the same time, she became aware of how she could take in and give back to herself the encouraging, nurturing, and loving wishes she had made for the baby. As with the *Personal Mirror Reflection above, the* words and thoughts participants created themselves and then heard from their partners were then translated into "I"-statements that the person then affirmed to themselves. For example, Casandra then reframed her sentences as self-affirmations:

"I wish for myself a loving future and respect for myself."

"I deserve loving kindness from everyone in my family."

"To feel safe and secure, I will protect and insulate myself from negativity that might surround me."

"One way that I can show myself that I love myself today is to gently rock myself and hold myself close in my arms."

Once workshop participants complete such an activity, they begin to better understand how the wishes they have for others may be a projected indication of the things they may need for themselves. They recognize how they may unknowingly cast off their own nurturing, spiritual, and loving qualities and make them less available to support themselves. And with this new insight, workshop participants begin to look after themselves the way they have wished and waited for someone else to do for them.

To remain unaware of our projections carries a heavy cost. It jeopardizes our sense of coherence and wholeness. The denial diminishes our vitality. The avoidance cuts short our honesty with others and with ourselves. It leads us to hold ourselves emotional prisoners. And if we are to sustain, affirm, and transform ourselves it keeps us from the intimacy with others that we need. It takes considerable energy to keep the unacknowledged parts of ourselves under lock and key. But the more we deny our disowned parts, the more they push within us to be acknowledged. Either in a healthy or an unhealthy way, these disowned aspects of ourselves will inevitably get expressed. Keeping them outside of our awareness can lead to feeling tired, fragmented, incomplete, empty, helpless, and hopeless.

It is difficult to look squarely at ourselves in the mirror. But, paradoxically, it makes life more difficult to *avoid* looking at our reflection. The avoidance itself can lead to a deep sense of isolation, loneliness, and feeling out of place or distant from others. Ironically, we may unnecessarily disconnect ourselves from others, never really discovering the humanness we share in common with them. What seems most private in us is often what we have most in common with other people.

Serena struggled with a degenerative illness, and it was making it difficult for her to walk. She became afflicted at an early age and began to feel as if she didn't deserve any better. She felt embarrassed about her disability—as if others were ridiculing her— but also began to wonder

Learning to Take Back Projections

why she was so hard on herself for it. She maintained a persona of independence but actually feared asking for help. In therapy, she recalled early childhood memories of frequent nightmares that someone was under her bed waiting to hurt her. She remembered pleading with her parents to sleep in their bed only to hear them angrily tell her, "Go back to sleep!"

After talking with her therapist about these long-forgotten memories, Serena became more aware how much she anticipated being admonished by others— especially if she were to ask for help—and how much she felt others would see her as undeserving of it. She also began to understand how angry she was at the way her parents had responded to her. One of Serena's projections was that others were deserving, not her. Serena had projected her deservedness onto others in her outer world, leaving little for herself. She also projected her admonishing feelings onto others—believing they would be admonishing of her—and failing to take ownership for just how admonishing she felt toward her parents for how she was treated as a child.

"Even loss and betrayal can bring us awakening." Carrying false beliefs about ourselves and others is quite common —perhaps, ubiquitous. But can we ever really see who we are in the eyes of others? Can we ever learn to embrace ourselves despite what others may misperceive? Discovering who we are at a core level is widely considered to be the path to spiritual growth and enlightenment. Often due to our own shadow or aura, every time we distort what we see in others, we create something similar to a *delusion*—or a pervasive false belief—about them. This also happens when we glorify others by denying our own talents or when we vilify others by blaming them for our shortcomings. And every time we distort something about ourselves we maintain a delusion about us.

Delusions are created within us. They can also be shared with others. The psychotic condition *folie à deux* is a powerful example of this. It literally means, "a madness shared by two." It occurs when one person holds a rigid but false belief and then projects it to another person. This psychotic condition is also known as Shared Delusional Disorder. In a television episode of the *X-Files*, Fox Mulder investigates a telemarketing employee's allegation that his manager is turning the employees into zombies. Mulder is always open to the idea of paranormal events. But he also strongly suspects that the employee is suffering from a paranoid psychosis. As the episode unfolds, Mulder is taken hostage. Under the stress, he begins to believe the employee's story. He begins to share the employee's paranoid delusion.

Shared Delusional Disorder is rare. But from the perspective of the cosmic mirror, shared delusional projections are understandable and quite common in their derivative forms. Here's what we mean by this. Cult leaders like Jim Jones of the Peoples Temple and David Koresh of the Branch Davidians are examples of those who have induced paranoid beliefs in their followers. Their followers suffered from *folie a plusieurs* or "madness of the many."[7] During the witch-hunts of the sixteenth century, millions of young women worldwide were tortured and killed by being burned at the stake. This took place because of a widespread paranoid delusion that they were "evil witches."

Adolf Hitler, Benito Mussolini, Osama Bin Laden, and the people who have supported them are other examples of those who have participated in a shared delusion. All of them viewed themselves as part of a "master race." What is most frightening about these cases is not the senseless and deranged hostility of the historical figures themselves. What is most frightening is the tendency of the people who, on a mass scale, subscribed to their delusions. Provoked by the tensions of the cold war, Wisconsin Senator Joe McCarthy and those who followed him also give witness to a shared delusion. They shared a common fear. They believed that certain Americans were conspiring with the Communists to infiltrate the Army and other institutions.

In 1954, the senate finally censured McCarthy for his deluded actions.

In terms of the cosmic mirror, shared delusions also occur in our everyday life. Take the behavior of racial bigots. If they are parents, they may try to induce in their children the delusion that they are ethnically superior. Here's another example. An abusive, alcoholic, or rage-o-holic parent is more likely to induce a delusion of inferiority in their children. At an even finer level, some parents are afflicted with severe depressive or anxiety disorders. When they are, their child might develop a sense that the world is a dangerous or meaningless place. Their child may begin to mistakenly believe that they must save their parent from their depression and from a world they mistrust. They might try to parent their parent. The opposite reaction is also possible. The child might come to believe that the only thing that they can do is to share their parent's overly dependent, avoidant, or helpless view of themselves.

We have been discussing how the denied negativity of our shadow often can create delusions that can be projected into other people, groups, or institutions. The same is true of our aura. Many of us have learned—only too well—that people from so-called professional groups can have feet of clay. Like all of us, medical doctors, professors, and priests have their limitations. They have their flaws. And they have their faults. Despite some awareness of their limitations, we often idealize them. Professionals from these groups can often become containers for our projected aura. Here's an example.

We want and need to hold priests in the highest regard. We have wanted this so much that when hearing that some of them were accused of sexual abuse we believed that these were isolated incidents. We said, "This could never be true." The John Jay Report showed otherwise. Commissioned in 2002 by the U.S. Conference of Catholic Bishops, the report found that accusations of sexual abuse were much more widespread than initially believed. In fact, the report showed that 4,392 American priests had been accused of sexual abuse—nearly 4 percent of all American priests. When we idealize our view of the priest we create a kind of lightening rod onto which we project our own notions of morality. We also project onto priests our own ideas about integrity and decency. The morality often becomes outside of us, not inside of us. Not something we live every day, as we imagine a priest might. Likewise, we do the same with other professional groups. They, too, can become containers for a projected and exaggerated sense of competence, intelligence, reliability, or other admirable quality. We rarely see the people we hold in excessive regard as containers for our distorted projections.

In 1971, Philip Zimbardo of Stanford University conducted a now-famous "Mock Prison" experiment. The study illustrates the power of projection, labels, and stereotypical social roles.[8] The college experiment was designed to simulate the psychological state of imprisonment. In it, twenty-one Stanford students were randomly assigned to one of two role labels: "guard" or "prisoner." They were provided few instructions on how to enact their assigned roles. It was in the vacuum of these vague instructions that the stage was

The Zimbardo Prison Experiment

set. The student-subjects were primed to project their own cultural stereotypes into these role labels.

Within very little time, the guards were behaving cruelly toward their prisoners. Some even exhibited great hostility and degradation. They were cold and caustic. They debased their prisoners. They threatened them. And they used nightsticks and fire extinguishers in physically aggressive ways—all to keep the prisoners in line. As might be expected from this kind of treatment, the prisoners felt intensely powerless. They felt dependent and depressed. They felt frustrated and hopeless. They felt dehumanized, and emasculated. Because of the mental decline of the prisoners, the planned two-week experiment was shut down after six days.

A "Bad" Prisoner

The cosmic mirror helps us better understand what happened here. Each group acted out and reflected a role stereotype that was comprised of the attributes that were disowned in the other group. Let's look at this in a little more detail. First, let's use the terms *dominance* and *submissiveness* to label these disowned qualities. In playing out their roles, the guards were caught in the exaggerated role of dominance. Good guards are generally seen as stereotypically dominant. They are tough and maintain control over their captives. Good guards are not submissive. The student-guards denied their own potential for submissiveness and projected it into their prisoners. The guards believed they were pure, entitled, and righteous. They saw their prisoners as impure, undeserving, wrong, and weak. In turn, for their part, the student-prisoners were trapped in an exaggerated role of submissiveness. Good prisoners do what they are told. They don't make trouble. They are not dominant. The student-prisoners denied their own dominance and potential to speak up. As a result, they projected these qualities into their guards.

When the student-guards sensed the frailty and submissiveness emerging in their prisoners they could not identify it. It was a quality that they kept hidden from themselves in their shadow. As a result, they could not be empathetic or sensitive to their own viciousness. Instead, they became more aggressive and cruel. They did this in an attempt to shut down the emergence of these shadow feelings expressed by their prisoners and from deep within themselves.

On the other hand, good prisoners are those who follow orders and are seen and not heard. The student-prisoners could only see themselves in this way. They denied their anger. They denied their own aggressiveness. They denied their own competence. And they projected these traits onto their guards. By doing so, they deprived themselves of their personal resources. They kept hidden what could have helped them manage their difficult situation. Like an abused child, the prisoners were trapped in the midst of their own imagined and inflexible role. They assumed that if they were small, compliant, and obsequious enough that they could survive their ordeal. They naively believed that they could "control" their situation by allowing the guards to treat them unfairly.

Personal Mirror Reflection

In the following *Personal Mirror Reflection* you will again have a chance to explore and better understand a hidden aspect of yourself. In completing it, we want you to freely find your own voice. Try not to censor yourself. Working with whatever comes to mind will allow you to see more clearly how you are framing your everyday world and how perceptual habits may have been imprinted in you. If you do not censor your words, you can become more aware of the templates and schemas you are using to make sense of yourself and the things around you. *A word of caution*: some people mistakenly believe that if they complete a learning event such as this just once and demonstrate to themselves how they frame, project, or deny some aspect of their world that they have learned all they can learn about it. Nothing could be further from the truth. There is no end to our projecting and no end to our learning.

The way we perceive the world is conditioned by our history, by our cultural programming, and by our own projective processes. We do not see the world around us with pristine eyes. With this in mind, try doing the following exercise. It might help you discover how you frame the daily reality of the world around you. Finish the following sentence-completion stem with *the first thing that comes to your mind*. You may make several completions if you wish.

People are basically _____,
as shown by _____.

Once you have completed the exercise, rewrite the sentence substituting the words "I am" for the words

"People are." Also, personalize the second half of the sentence by using the words "my" or "I" after "as shown by." For example, if you said,

> "People are basically *good* as shown by *all the kindness that is expressed in the world.*"

change it to ...

> "*I am* basically good as shown by all the kindness *I* express in the world."

If you said,

> "People are basically *fearful* as shown by *their reluctance to openly express their feelings especially when they are negative.*"

change it to ...

> "*I am* basically fearful as shown by *my* reluctance to openly express *my* feelings especially when they are negative."

What happened as you did the exercise? Did you discover anything about yourself? What qualities of *yours* might *you* be projecting into the world?

In this chapter, we have discussed the idea of projection and its central role in the cosmic mirror. We saw how projection is a way of handling deep within ourselves all of our feared, undesirable, or uncomfortable feelings and qualities. We often place into others and into the world what we may have difficulty looking at in ourselves. Our final chapter on the *Foundation of the Cosmic Mirror* comes next. In it, we discuss one last but crucial element in understanding the cosmic mirror. This element is called *magical thinking*.

6

Magical Thinking and the Cosmic Mirror

"We are all prisoners of our own device."

—*Anonymous*

In building our theoretical foundation for the cosmic mirror, the final concept we would like to discuss is *magical thinking*. Magical thinking takes place when false or fabricated causes are assigned to explain things that we see and feel. For example, if we wear a special jacket during a game and end up winning the game we might think that wearing the jacket *caused* the win. Or as a kid, we might have believed, "Walking under a ladder will bring bad luck." Normal and healthy children, from ages two to seven are especially prone to think in magical ways. They will falsely link their own thoughts and feelings to things happening in their outside world. Children tend to magically transform their outer world into their worst fears and their own projected ideal. For example, they might say, "It's sunny outside, because I am happy" or "Daddy left for work early, because I was angry at him" or "I am afraid, because there's a monster in the closet who's going to get me." Even though the logic makes sense to the child, these are all instances of faulty reasoning.[1]

Pediatrician and psychoanalyst Donald Winnicott described how very young children create magical objects as they begin to distinguish what is "me" from what is "not me." They locate these objects in what he called the "transitional space". This is the imaginary space between what is inside of the child and what is outside of the child.[2] For example, early on in their development, a child begins to realize that their mother is a person who is separate from them. When this happens, the child's imagined oneness with their mother is shattered. The child then tries to fill the anxiety and sadness of this loss with something that represents their mother. Winnicott called this separate representation of the mother the "transitional object." It can take several forms, such as a special blanket, a teddy bear, or an imaginary friend.

The transitional object is an illusion in the sense that it is not really their mother. But, it is something that represents their mother. It provides comfort when they need it. And it reconnects them with the safety and bond of their first love experience. In other words, a child projects their image of their mother out into this object. By doing so, they create something outside them that they believe is a source of consolation and support. At some point in healthy development, a child builds a sufficient sense of themselves and needs to depend on their caretakers much less. They learn that they can thrive independently enough on their own. And eventually, a child will outgrow their need for the transitional object.[3] But if this natural growth process is blocked a child may develop anxiety about the separation. Either as friendly or hostile, the child sees their outer world as if it was mirroring what is going on in their inner world.

New Line Cinema's *Drop Dead Fred* is a film that nicely depicts the idea of magical thinking. This comedic yet incredibly insightful film presents the story of twenty-five-year-old Elizabeth Cronin. After a failed marriage, Elizabeth moves back into the home of her mother. Once again, she is faced with her mother's abusive insensitivity and demanding need for control. As a result, she uncontrollably regresses back to her submissive and helpless childhood role. All of her suppressed wishes, fears, rage, and denied spirit reemerge, and she finds herself again needing a way to contain them.

The Regressive Pull Back into Childhood

As the only way she knew to cope, she reawakens a long forgotten memory of her childhood imaginary friend, Drop Dead Fred. He will surely help! As the story unfolds, though, Elizabeth gains insight into the side of herself she has kept hidden. She gets in touch with all her fears, wishes, and rage at her mother—things that she has denied for many years—and she decides not to suppress them any longer. By the end of the film, when she is now ready to look more penetratingly into herself, Drop

Dead Fred helps her travel deep into her unconscious. In doing so, she frees her banished childhood spirit that for many years had been kept shackled. She understands that Drop Dead Fred was a part of her suppressed self that was emanating from her shadow and aura. She becomes aware how, as a child, she had magically created an imaginary friend to help her cope with what, as an adult, she now was ready to confront head-on. In doing so, she moves beyond her cosmic mirror to a place of renewal—finally becoming prepared to let go of her need for her imaginary friend and begin to be the mother to herself she has always wanted.

The cosmic mirror takes on a special role for children living in households where there is abuse. Abused children try everything they can to make sense of their confusion. And they struggle to regain a sense of power and control over the abusive actions of their caretakers. One of the things that children who are living in family chaos often try to do is blame themselves for being victimized. When a parent makes a child feel that the child is "good" then the child uses that outside opinion of themselves as a template for seeing themselves as "good." Likewise, though, when a parent makes a child feel as if the child is "bad" then the child uses that outside opinion of themselves as a template for seeing themselves as "bad." Being "bad" explains the abuse they are seeing in their outer world. If they are "bad" then they mistakenly believe they deserve to be punished. Despite it being crippling to their self-esteem, it explains in a simple way why the abuse is occurring. It also simultaneously creates the magical illusion for the child that they may have control over how their parents treat them.

Children often show strong loyalties to a parent who has been abusive to them. Why is this? Psychoanalyst Ronald Fairbairn explains how this might come about. Fairbairn states that the abused child believes that,

> It is better to be a sinner in a world ruled by God than to live in a world ruled by the Devil.[4]

What Fairbairn means by this is that the abused child unknowingly believes that they are safer and stand a better chance to survive by believing that they are "wrong" and that their abusive parent is "right." While it is torturous to the child's sense of themselves, the

Am I a "Bad" Child?

truth of the matter is that accommodating to an abusive parent may very well keep them safer. Most abused children have little sense of their own worth, how the world works, or their place in it. Because of this, the fear of living in a world they *do not* know is more powerful than their fear of the parent that they *do* know. In essence, the child unknowingly develops the belief, sometimes accurately, that it is safer for them to buy into the parent's justification for the abuse than to fight back. This is magical thinking and the cosmic mirror in action.

Magical Thinking in Adulthood

Old habits learned in childhood often stay with us— some of these habits are for the better and some are not. In the movie *A Civil Action*, John Travolta and Robert Duvall play prominent and successful attorneys. Travolta sees Duval carrying an old and worn-out briefcase and advises him to get a new one. Duvall shakes his head and says, "You don't change socks in the middle of the world series." He's being superstitious. He is referring to the magical and superstitious belief that socks worn *while* winning cause winning. St. John's basketball coach Lou Carnesecca wore his "magic sweater" after he beat the University of Pittsburgh with a last-second buzzer-beater. Poker legend Doyle Brunson carried "Casper, the friendly ghost," his lucky card protector. These are all examples of harmless superstitions based on magical thinking.

But, adults can maintain magical thinking that can cripple as well. For example, one of our workshop participants persisted in maintaining the magical belief that if only she were good enough her abusive husband might stop mistreating her. She minimized his abuse, and she myopically overemphasized her magical hope that things might get better. She believed that if she wished for it hard enough, her wish might come true. She magically believed that her husband would change.

Kokopelli:
A Magical Charm

Magical thinking is pervasive in adulthood. The worldwide use of amulets, good-luck charms, crystals, evil-eye charms, and other such objects attests to it. Many adults believe that these charms ward off harmful spiritual beings. They believe that charms can protect them from unseen forces. On the darker side, though, voodoo dolls, curses, and spells are other forms of magical thinking. They are based on the notion that if objects are associated in time, in space, or in thought that they can influence each other. For example, in many primitive cultures, warriors believed that eating the heart of an enemy would magically fill them with courage. Today, some still believe that stabbing a photo of someone could actually harm them.

Another form of magical thinking occurs when a word or an abstract thought is falsely treated as if it were a concrete object or real event—it is the belief that something is real when it is not. For example, many people believe that just because there are words like "demon" or "angel" that they must exist in reality. This type of word magic can take many

**Dark Magic:
The Voodoo Doll**

forms. Some leaders believe that if you simply label a group a "team" it will result in improved teamwork. Some believe that if you hang a "teamwork" poster on the wall it will have a similar effect. This belief is held even though the group may not have developed any of the skills necessary to improve their teamwork.

The popular film *The Secret* revives an old idea for a new generation. It presents the metaphysical idea that our own thoughts can attract real-world events. It states that our thoughts—in and of themselves—have the power to bring what we want into our physical, emotional, and professional lives. Its ideas stem from what has been called *The Law of Attraction.*[5] The concept behind the Law of Attraction has been around for millennia. But it was so-named by the Rosicrucians in the seventeenth century.

Since its release, there has been a kind of pop-culture fascination with *The Secret*. This led minister and *Touched by an Angel* star Della Reese Lett to say,

> Child, *The Secret* hasn't been a secret since the times of Moses, if not before. But every generation needs a new way to look at things that have been around awhile. I suppose right now *The Secret* is it.[6]

The ideas behind the film can be useful. For some people, though, the Law of Attraction can turn into a form of magical thinking. The Law of Attraction is a belief that by intentionally projecting our own wishes out into the world, we can get what we want. There is some truth in this. The world reflects back to us what is in our own hearts. And this idea captures some of what we are saying in the cosmic mirror. But, in other ways, the cosmic mirror is quite different.

It is useful for us to intentionally put our wants and needs out there into the world. By consciously planning, organizing and directing our actions, we are able to control many of the things in our lives. Deliberately thinking the best of ourselves can help us make a positive impression on others. It can also aid in making our hopes a reality. But, projecting the negativity that we keep hidden from ourselves can leave others with unwanted impressions. If our negativity is hidden in either our shadow or our aura we cannot control it—we cannot control what we are not aware of. We then can unknowingly project this negativity into the world. And if we are not aware of the negativity we are projecting, it will undermine many of our best intentions.

To draw closer to ourselves the things that we want in our life, it can be important to visualize and vividly imagine them. It helps us see the creative possibilities for a more meaningful life. But shear force of thought is not sufficient to bring what we want into our physical world. "Positive thinking"—in and of itself—is not sufficient to change the physical universe. We must also take constructive action. Otherwise, our thoughts become magical and grandiose. For some of us, though, "thinking positively" can become an obsessional way of living—where we "don't allow" ourselves to have uncomfortable thoughts. Unknowingly, many of us begin to justify the need to hide from ourselves our own fears or our own legitimate anger or our shame. We "try not to think about it." We distract ourselves with other things. We "keep busy." In the language of the cosmic mirror, too much focus on positive thinking can become a way of avoiding important personal shadow and aura issues that need to be worked through.

As the Law of Attraction suggests, we might say to ourselves, "The things that I want are coming to me with ease and without effort." Or we might say, "I am attracting into my life the 2010 Jaguar X100 I want." Positive affirmations like these can be useful to us in attaining our goals. But in order to be effective, they must authentically relate to what is actually unfolding in our lives. Simply ignoring our negativity undermines our efforts and turns self-affirmations like these into hypnotic forms of deluded and rose-colored self-talk. *By themselves*, self-affirmations are akin to the use of a magical mantra aimed at wish fulfillment. And they can lead to an unhealthy avoidance of real unhappiness and genuine despair. All of us face negative events on our journey. Leaning how to understand

and use them to help us get what we want is a lifelong process.

Occurring on a daily basis, probably one the greatest areas of magical thinking takes place when we believe that other people cause our feelings. Although it is completely false that others are responsible for what we internally are feeling, many people have learned at a young age that this may be true. There is no invisible umbilical cord that connects us with others. When we believe that others have caused our feelings it is an accusatory form of scapegoating. "You" make me angry or "You" hurt me are examples of such thinking. This is purely illusory. While the actions of someone else may trigger within us the feeling of anger or hurt, these feelings are inside of us and not something that anyone else has access to. It is truly an illusion that others actually cause or control our feelings.

Taking ownership for our inner experience takes the form of stating or expressing that "I" am angry or "I" am hurt. Our feelings can be related to another person's behavior, and this can be accurately expressed in such statements as, "I felt angry when you _____" (describing the other person's behavior) or "I felt hurt when you _____." What is essential in these statements is that we are claiming the anger and hurt as our own. Focusing on the emotion itself rather than the event that triggered the emotion unleashes our capability to break out of the habit of assigning someone else responsibility for our feelings—and the magical thinking associated with it.

It is indispensible to understand the dynamics of our feelings—when they occur, how they occur, what triggers them—but thoroughly analyzing our feelings is something that can only be successful with time and reflection. In the moment, however, what is most important is to take ownership for our feelings rather than attributing them to someone else. It is crucial for us to guard against believing that the other person "did something" to us. What we can do instead is to allow ourselves to deeply experience the feeling—"I hate", or "I am angry", or "I am so hurt." To better manage our feelings requires first acknowledging, experiencing, and owning the feelings inside us.

Personal Mirror Reflection

Again, choose a partner that you know and trust that you can work with in this *Personal Mirror Reflection*. Imagine an experience you recently had in one of your relationships. Choose a scenario that elicited a strong negative emotion for you. Recall the strong emotion you felt. Now, imagine that your exercise partner is the other person. Say to your exercise partner something that implies that they are causing your feelings. For example, if you felt anger in the scenario, say to your exercise partner, *"You are making me angry!"* Try to say it in a forceful way like you really mean it. In the scenario you are recalling, if you felt sad or hurt, for example, say to your partner, *"You are making me sad,"* or *"You hurt me,"* etc.

As you say your statements, say them in an accusatory way. As you do, point at the other person as you accuse *them* of causing *your* feelings. Once you are finished, let the other person take a turn. After you have done this, take turns owning the feeling you formerly attributed to the other person. For example, if you felt anger, say *"I am angry,"* or if you felt sad, say, *"I am sad,"* etc. Finally, discuss with your partner your experience with each of the scenarios you used. Compare the feelings you experienced when you used the accusatory "You"-statements with the experience you had when you took ownership for the feelings. What did you discover?

In this chapter, we have discussed the fifth and final element of the cosmic mirror—magical thinking. We have also discussed the concepts of the shadow, the aura, polarities, and projection. These are the central structures and processes that comprise the cosmic mirror. Now, we invite you to see how these concepts can be applied to the everyday problems we all face. This is the focus of the next section—*Everyday Illustrations of the Cosmic Mirror.*

Everyday Illustrations of the Cosmic Mirror

7

Mothers and Fathers as Mirrors to Their Children

"A torn jacket is soon mended;
but hard words bruise the heart of a child."

—*Henry Wadsword Longfellow*

Some children grow up having their spirits nourished. Others don't. Psychiatrist Heinz Kohut had a great deal to say about this. As Kohut used the term, a parent "mirrors" their child when the parent is empathetic and when they admire their child's achievements. When parents do enough mirroring the child's view of themselves grows and matures in emotionally healthy ways. A parent mirrors a

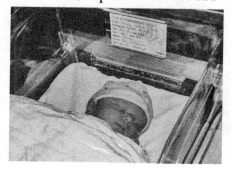

The Newest Mirror

child by encouraging them to discover their own radiant reflection in the sparkle of their parent's eye. In a similar vein, psychoanalyst Donald Winnicott has also discussed what he called the "mirror-role" played by our primary caretakers. The long, steady, and loving gaze by a mother or a father is a mirror that reflects their caring perceptions of their baby. As Winnicott writes,

> In individual emotional development, the precursor of the mirror is the mother's face. What does the baby see when he or she looks at the mother's face? I am suggesting that, ordinarily, what the baby sees is himself or herself.[1]

A mother's face or a father's face is a window to their child's soul. Imprinted in the child, their face is a window to what the child comes to believe they should expect from the world. It is a prelude to how the child imagines that others will see them. And it is a cue to how a child sees themselves. The impression we form of ourselves is based on how the influential people in our lives have seen and treated us. We form much of our impression of ourselves based on the powerful experiences we have had with them.

The Mirror-Role

In time, with the loving approval of parents, the child develops healthy feelings of self-worth. The child uses the parent's own reflection as a mirror in developing their own sense of self-worth. Here's an example. When out of frustration a two-year-old throws their toy, a parent might mirror their child's anger and scold them. This teaches the child that they are "bad" for being frustrated. But the parent might mirror an understanding of their child's frustration by empathizing with what the child was thwarted in accomplishing. In either scenario, the child uses the parent as a mirror and a model. The child takes in the parent's behavior, which becomes part of them. They come away from the interaction with a more developed image of who they are—either good or bad. To express it another way,

> If children live with criticism they learn to condemn; if children live with acceptance they learn to love.[2]

Personal Mirror Reflection

In many ways, we are products of our experiences with parents. They act as powerful mirrors for us—particularly in our early years. In order to see the effects of our early experience within the cosmic mirror, try the following exercise. Write out descriptions for each of the sentence stems that are shown below. After you do this, we will help you discover what your responses might reveal.

What I liked most about my mother _____.

What I disliked most about my mother _____.

What I liked most about my father _____.

What I disliked most about my father _____.

Matthew came to one of our workshops telling others that he felt "blah." There were no crises in his life, but his excitement for life was gone. He felt adrift. He felt as if he had little to look forward to. The relationships in his life had lost their passion, their spark. After considering the sentence stems, Matthew responded this way:

> What I liked most about my mother ... *was her gentle and calm intelligence. She did not need to brag. But she quietly radiated a sense that she knew what she knew. When you realized what knowledge she possessed, you were grateful being near her. It was as if being around someone so wise protected me from all the confusion and chaos outside.*

> What I disliked most about my mother ... *was that when it came to standing up to my father, particularly in defending me, she was a spineless jellyfish. It's as if she became frozen in fear. But she came across as if she had no conflicts about her passivity. A week after my father died, she privately told my uncle that she was relieved. After I discovered I had feelings I could actually identify and discuss, I asked her how she felt about her life, but she typically responded, "Why are you always asking me how I feel?!" I hated how her cool intellectualism prevented her from sharing with me the softer and more vulnerable side of herself.*

> What I liked most about my father ... *was his sense of responsibility. He worked hard every day at his job, Monday through Friday—he left on time, he came back on time, week after week after*

month after year. He'd tend to the yard; he'd go grocery shopping on Saturday mornings; he'd get up early on Sundays and make pancakes or waffles for us. There always seemed to be enough money, and he was dutiful in bringing his two sisters' families into our lives. There was an order to our lives, and he preserved it.

What I disliked most about my father ... *was that he was a rigid and dispassionate family tyrant. He was a baby who acted like he was a king. When he disagreed, no one else was ever right, and nothing from anyone else was ever good enough. Every few years, I heard my mother say how my father, with pride, told someone else about some accomplishment of mine. But I never heard it from him. He never formed an openly loving relationship with me. I used to hate him for it; then it disappointed me that I never got what I longed for; now, I still wish he were different, but I have forgiven him for how he treated me.*

Thinking About Our Parents in New Ways

We then asked Matthew to substitute his own name for those of his father's and mother's. His completion stems revealed insights into himself he had been reluctant to consider. He wrote,

What I like most about *myself ... is my gentle and calm intelligence. I do not need to brag. But I quietly project a sense that I know what I know. When others realize what knowledge I possess, they feel grateful being near me. It's as if being around someone so wise protects them from the all the confusion and chaos outside.*

What I like most about *myself ... is my sense of responsibility. I work hard every day, Monday through Friday—I leave on time, I come back on time, week after week after month after year. I tend to the yard; I go grocery shopping; I get up early and make breakfast. There always seems to be enough money, and I am dutiful in bringing my sisters' families into my life. There is an order to my life, and I preserve it.*

What I dislike most about *myself ... is that when it comes to standing up to my wife, particularly in defending the kids, I can be a spineless jellyfish. It's as if I become frozen in fear. But I come across as if I have no conflicts about my passivity. Thinking about my wife's eventual passing makes me privately feel relieved. Sometimes I get tired of other people asking me how I feel. I hate my cool intellectualism and how it prevents me from sharing with others the softer and more vulnerable side of myself.*

What I dislike most about *myself ... is that I can be a rigid and dispassionate family tyrant. I can be a baby who acts like he's a king. When I disagree, no one else is ever right, and nothing from others is ever good enough. Every few years, I tell someone else about some accomplishment of my kids, but I never tell the kids. I have never formed an openly loving relationship with my children. They might hate me for it or they might be disappointed in what they longed for from me but never got. I hope they can forgive me.*

When Matthew read out loud his completed sentence stems about what he liked about himself he did it with a solid assurance. He recognized that what he liked about his parents were qualities he had not fully acknowledged liking about himself. He revealed more of his aura to himself. He acknowledged in himself more of the qualities that he ascribed to his parents. Up to that point, he hadn't really taken in just how much he could appreciate his own quiet wisdom. He became more aware of how protective it

Revived Luminescence

might feel to others to be around him. He began to better recognize his own diligent sense of responsibility and his steadfast devotion to his work. He also got in touch with how affirming he could be to himself for having created an order to his life. He could see how that order now gratefully and spiritually connected him to his father.

Matthew also soberly considered his own disavowed shadow-side. He could see how he withdrew from his wife by keeping his most intimate feelings from her. He recognized how he denied a part of himself that wanted to run away from her. But after thinking about this, he realized just how much he loved her. He reflected on how his own cool intellectualism kept him from sharing with others the softer and more loving side of himself. He became more aware of how his self-centeredness kept him from the closeness he could share with them. He also realized how sad he felt with his failure to convey to his wife and children just how proud he was of them as well as how grateful he was that they were in his life. Although initially quite humbling to him, as the workshop proceeded, Matthew became enlivened with what he could now say to his family about who he was and how he felt about them. He began to feel less "blah," and more impassioned about his life than he had in a long time.

Personal Mirror Reflection (Revisited)

If you are done writing the descriptions of your parents, now rewrite them like Matthew did. Replace the parent name with the word "I," "my," or "myself." Once you have done this, read your descriptions over to yourself. Did anything new come to mind? How did it impact you?

One of our workshop participants responded to this exercise with amazement, saying, "Mirror, mirror on the wall, I'm like my mother after all." There may be some truth in the aphorism: "The apple doesn't fall far from the tree." Having said this, though, we do not wish to imply that we are helpless in making constructive changes in our lives. With enhanced awareness we can transform our patterns of thought, feeling, and action to forge a new and healthier path for ourselves. Using the cosmic mirror, as we become more aware of how we maintain the impression we have of ourselves, we give ourselves another choice. We can alter the process. We can change our opinion of ourselves and move out of old patterns of thinking.

Identifying or recognizing attributes in our parents or children does not necessarily imply that the attribute is an unacknowledged aspect of our self. Our perceptions of the other person may be quite accurate. Other family members may readily agree with our assessment of the parent or child. When, then, do our observations of others say something about ourselves? The attribute we assign (whether it is accurate or not) says something about us when to see it in another evokes an excessively strong emotional reaction within ourselves. When this occurs—when our "buttons are pressed" if we were to witness the attribute— then it is not likely that we are fully taking ownership of that attribute within ourselves (or our *potential* to exhibit that attribute). For example, if we make too big a deal out of someone showing emotional support—if it "sickens" us to see how overindulging, enabling, or overly permissive it might be—then we may be overlooking how we, ourselves, may have been overindulging or enabling of someone else or may have had difficulty acknowledging how we, ourselves, may have been overindulged or enabled. The fact that we can see the characteristic in someone else tells us that we have personal knowledge of the characteristic. And if we overreact when we see another person exhibiting the characteristic—if we intensely loathe that person for it or if it "makes our blood boil"—then we may be denying or minimizing acknowledging that we, ourselves, could be capable of exhibiting that same attribute. It seems clear that when we have either a strongly charged negative or positive emotional reaction to the attributes of someone else we are most likely also projecting our own mirrored attribute.

Conrad was fifty-three when he entered therapy. Initially, he wanted help with his depression and with his difficulty managing his romantic relationship. His partner was verbally abusive to him, and in our sessions together, he raged incessantly about her. He also had a great deal of unresolved anger toward his parents. He carried on long diatribes about his mother and his father. From how he described them and the fights they continued to nitpick with him, it seemed that there was more than a kernel of truth to his perception of them as controlling and hostile. Tears, though, were a stranger to Conrad. He could not cry. He could not acknowledge his vulnerability. Nor could he feel sadness about the losses in his life. Desperately clinging to the idea that others in his life might eventually change and become the people he hoped they would become, his rage was unrelenting. He thought it was his parents' and his partner's fault that he was unhappy. *They* were to blame. *They* were the ones who had to change.

Conrad's fury served him, though—but not in a constructive way. It served him in the sense that it helped him maintain the fantasy that he could somehow make his parents and his partner feel the pain he was experiencing. Maintaining his unhealthy fury kept his hope alive that he could make them feel his own sense of helplessness. Later in his therapy, Conrad realized that his rage was a *reenactment*. Reenactments are a common occurrence for all of us in our everyday life.

They take place when a difficult emotional situation from our early life is mirrored in our current life circumstances. Old feelings are stirred. And we react not like a mature adult but as we might have as a child. For Conrad, his rage was a reenactment of childhood feelings of powerlessness in his relationship with his dominating and controlling parents. His childhood fantasy was to become the omnipotent master of the universe. If he did, no one could dominate or control him. Coming to grips with the limits of his own power—experiencing true acceptance of who and what he was powerless to change— was an important part of his cosmic mirror.

Eventually, Conrad was able to take back his projections of helplessness and sadness and experience them firsthand. In doing so, he was able to look into his own shadow. He could then see the underpinnings of his rage, and in doing so, discover he could tolerate his sadness. It was then that his tears began to freely flow. In time, he moved past the projection that others in his life were those against whom he needed to wage a crusade. What he denied and relegated to his aura was the sense of his own power. Once he took it back, Conrad was able to then more fully choose his own battles. With a heightened awareness of himself, his depression lifted.

Christina was severely depressed. When she spoke, her facial muscles barely moved. Before she spoke, she sat expressionless for exceedingly long periods. Despite being assisted by antidepressant medications, she could not sleep or eat. Her voice was as quiet as a whisper—as if she was trying

The Reenactment of Old Wounds

to be as small as she possibly could. She entered therapy after being unfairly ousted from a long-time job that she loved. She had worked in a male-dominated profession that was riddled with women-haters, and Christina spent months feeling victimized by it. She just could not seem to escape her depression. She felt traumatized; she felt powerless; and she feared she might again be the target of the hostilities of her former bosses. To cope with her feelings and feel protected, she isolated herself.

In the course of her therapy, Christina's intense childhood fear of her father came more and more to mind. Although he had long since died, she began to see how she was reenacting the past victimhood she felt with him—now in the form of fearing her former bosses. Make no mistake; her bosses were chauvinists and discriminated against her. But her reaction to them was fear, not self-validating and empowering anger. What she denied and projected was her rage. This was her cosmic mirror. What she disavowed was her inner hostility toward her perpetrators. She wanted to hurt them for what they had done to her, but she was not able to acknowledge it. She did not grasp that when someone is hurt, they want to hurt back. Instead, she projected her anger out into them. She imagined that their hostility would be turned against her once again. Slowly, though, she began to identify, experience, and eventually harness her angry, aggressive, but disowned feelings. Taking ownership for what she had been expelling into others, Christina began to emerge from her depression with renewed excitement about her life.

Just as parents are mirrors for their children, so, too, can children be mirrors to their parents. Recently, a psychologist we know was asked by the court to evaluate a mother's fitness for parenting. In doing so, he learned about this family's tragic plight of ire and victimhood. The mother in this family was being evaluated, because it was learned she was mercilessly contemplating a murder-suicide of her three-year-old son and herself. She had told her grandfather of her plan, and he was worried about how honest and open she would be if asked about her thoughts. Fearful of what she might keep to herself, he informed the court of what she had said to him—that the child's incessant crying was intensely and intolerably exasperating to her. Her grandfather also reported that she had recently told her sister that she had placed a pillow over the child's face to shut him up. How might the cosmic mirror explain this disturbing set of events?

This mother's thoughts about killing her child and herself likely stem from her own disowned and unacceptable rage over the crying, helpless, and dependent side of herself. She saw her own undeniable but disavowed image of dependency and helplessness in her child. This was an image she both detested and felt compelled to smother. Helping this woman will take much effort over a long period of time. But it would involve helping her to see that what she is projecting into her child is her own helpless, dependent, and smothered qualities. These are the qualities that she has not yet acknowledged about herself and which she has been unwilling to accept.

At the opposite end of the emotional spectrum, Ruth was the most giving person you could ever meet. Her heart was pure gold—she was selfless to a fault. She dearly loved her daughter (now an adult) and would do anything for her. But this included indulging her when it was better to set reasonable limits. She frequently worried whether she was being a "good enough mom" to her daughter. Ruth worked as a social worker for a nonprofit agency. And truth be told, she had always aspired to be a "Mother Theresa." Tirelessly helping all those in need, she tried to do so with relentless passion. But she settled for being so underpaid that she could not afford to make ends meet. Despite her talents and her tireless efforts, she did not feel appreciated by her daughter, by her boss, and by many of her clients. With her health declining, Ruth considered leaving her job and the field in which she had become so invested.

From the vantage point of the cosmic mirror, Ruth projected her needs to be cared for onto her daughter and her clients. What she denied was the need to take good enough care of herself. Focusing on the needs of others was her way of avoiding focusing on her own needs. For Ruth, taking care of herself was something that she felt she didn't deserve. Ruth needed to give voice to the unexplored mirror that was being reflected to her in both her daughter and her clients. And in one of our workshops, she decided to dramatize it. As she described it,

> I am one of Ruth's clients. I love Ruth. I love how she loves me and wants to take care of me. But I won't tell her this, because I have learned that if I show my vulnerability to her, she will try to take even more care of me. And I want to take care of *myself.* So I silence myself. I need her so, and I am glad she is in my life. But I will never let her know how I feel, because I don't want to think about how much I need her.

Ruth began to look behind her cosmic mirror. She recalled the harsh treatment she repeatedly received from her own mother. She remembered how she had vowed never to be anything like her mother. But she also realized that by trying to avoid being like her mother, she wound up treating herself like her mother treated her—neglecting to honor her own needs.

Ruth wanted so much to be an independent woman— so much so, though, that when she would momentarily become in touch with her natural desire to rely on others, she would not honor it. What she needed was to begin taking better care for herself by letting others take care of her. In the course of the workshop, Ruth began to appreciate why her daughter rejected her help. It was not because her daughter didn't love her. It was because her daughter needed to experience for herself her own capacity to be independent. Ruth, in turn, needed to give herself permission to rely on others.

One of the most powerful ways that the cosmic mirror is formed in our lives is through our early relationship with our parents. We learn how to treat and relate to others and ourselves by the ways that we learned how others treated and related to us. The words and actions of others can bruise us.

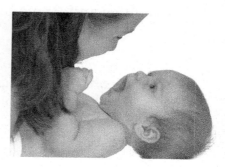

The Reflected Sparkle in a Mother's Eye

But by not understanding, by not appreciating, and by not mending how we have been bruised, we are likely to spend our adult lives bruising ourselves. Our heart tells no lies— fearlessly following it frees us to look behind the cosmic mirror.

8

The Gender and Romance Mirrors

"Here's all you have to know about men and women: women are crazy, men are stupid. And the main reason women are crazy is that men are stupid."

—*George Carlin*

A great deal of blaming goes on between the genders. No doubt, you have heard others make statements like, "He's a fag!" or "She's a dyke!" or "He's a dumb jock" or "She's an airhead" or "He's a wimp" or "She's a bitch." What's it like for you to read these statements? You might be experiencing some of the intense emotion that is implied in them. What does the cosmic mirror tell us about these gender-related slurs? What can it tell us about who we are as men and women?

In any culture, it is expected that men will behave differently than women. This is true in every culture. In primitive cultures, the distinctions were clearer. Men were the warriors and women were the homemakers. Many of us still hold some of these expectations today. Most of the role expectations surrounding gender are the product of social customs. For example, men are permitted to show their anger and expected to hide their fears. Women, on the other hand, are permitted to openly show their affection and warmth but are discouraged if they show their anger. Research also shows that women more easily identify and express their emotions than do men (especially fear and disgust). Women also appear to be more skillful in interpreting vocal intonations and facial cues used in expressing emotions.[1] While this seems consistent with the popular gender stereotype about women and emotions research has not yet clarified how much of their findings is a result of differences in socialization practices and how much may be attributed to biology.

Personal Mirror Reflection

To some degree, gender role stereotypes are embedded in all of us. How much are they embedded in you? In the list on the next page, you will find sixteen characteristics, feelings, and preferences that men and women have. Which ones do you associate with men? Which ones with women?

Which ones did you choose? How might your upbringing or your culture have influenced the image you hold of each gender?

Stereotype	Men	Women
Sexy		
Passive		
Violent		
Fearful		
Delicate		
Engineer		
In control		
Fixes cars		
Aggressive		
Never cries		
Empathetic		
Good at math		
Enjoys cooking		
Good at English		
Likes to arrange flowers		
Doesn't take "no" for an answer		

We are each imprinted with a cultural gender role. It begins when we are young. As we show "appropriate" behavior for being a boy or a girl, we are rewarded. As we show "inappropriate" behavior for being a boy or girl, we are criticized. The more often those consequences are repeated, the more clearly the pattern within us takes shape. It takes place through our family programming. It occurs through our relationships with peers. And it also takes place through our cultural conditioning. We all learn what it means to be a boy or a girl. Later, we learn what it means to be a "real man" or "real woman."

Some of us can clearly see the extreme way that gender roles play out in us and in others. Some of us can take ownership for how it takes place. Some of us recognize the utility and disutility of these gender roles. Others do not. Social and psychological well-being requires a balanced mix of these gender-associated qualities and emotions. To the extent that we have a balanced mix of these roles, it is a sign of greater emotional wholeness and self-enlightenment. If a person discounts, denies, or undermines the utility of a balanced mix of gender roles, it is often unhealthy—it is often a sign of discord in their relationships with people of either gender. Sometimes it can affect a person's relationships with both genders. It can alienate us from others. It can also be emotionally draining for us to maintain an assigned role that does not fit all the parts of our self.

What can the cosmic mirror tell us about how these gender roles are set up and come into being? To some degree, everyone is at least partially *androgynous*.[2] This means that everyone possesses at least some female and some male social attributes as they are defined by their culture. Taken together, the male and female attributes make up the attributes of a complete and whole person. Some women exhibit many of the female attributes and few of the male attributes. Other women typify the opposite mix. The same kind of diversity exists in males. *Healthy androgyny* occurs when there is a conscious acknowledgment and an attempt to integrate the gender-related parts of the self. The more a person has at least a partial awareness that gender role attributes of theirs have been split off or minimized, the more likely they will succeed at creating an internal synthesis and harmony between different and seemingly conflicting gender roles.

The denied gender role attributes are contained in distinct parts of the shadow that Carl Jung labeled the *anima* and the *animus*.[3] Men contain in their anima the female attributes that they wish to deny or bury from their own view. Women contain in their animus the male attributes that they wish to deny or bury. When our gender role is rigidly circumscribed we have difficulty in effectively adopting work or family roles that may require the strength of both genders. The gender role becomes an emotional straight-jacket. We may bring only half our talents to parenting, to leadership, or to other roles. In healthy androgyny, a man is aware of and is able to integrate his female side, which otherwise he may have a tendency to discount or minimize. Similarly, a woman is aware of and is able to integrate her discounted or minimized male side. With a balanced blend of the two gender roles, we gain vitality. In fact, Jung's concepts were derived from the Latin word *animare*, which means, "to enliven." He believed that as long as these forces could be understood, acknowledged, and utilized within us, they were living, enlivening life forces for both men and women.[4]

The Male Animus Personified

When we take on too much of one gender role we often discount the attributes that are associated with the opposite gender role. Those discounted attributes are pushed outside of immediate awareness. All around us, though, we can see imbalance in these roles. Why does this take place? Why is there such a sharp splitting of gender roles in our culture? What is the attraction that leads us to create a "Barbie Doll" persona for females and a "Rambo" persona for males? The soft-feeling attributes—like being tender, warm, open, or receptive—are contained in the Barbie Doll form of the female stereotype. All these qualities describe a woman who is vulnerable and dependent. In turn, the hard-feeling attributes—like being assertive, aggressive, competitive, or stoic—are contained in the Rambo form of the male stereotype. All of these qualities emphasize a male who is fearless, rugged, and independent.

This kind of stereotyping is found throughout our culture. It is also found across cultures. Females are seen as more nurturing, warmer, and more expressive of their feelings. Males are seen as more objective, more powerful, and more competent.[5] This is because males and females are taught at very early ages to accept these stereotypes of themselves and of each other. This splitting apart of a person's wholeness is widely viewed as desirable by popular society.

www.PoppyW.com

The Female Anima Personified

It is desirable for males to have hard attributes but undesirable for them to have soft attributes. It is desirable for females to have soft attributes but undesirable for them to have hard attributes. These attitudes are changing—Hillary Clinton was a frontrunner in the 2008 Democratic presidential primary. Ellen Johnson Sirleaf is now Liberia's (and Africa's) first female president—but the pace of change is slow. As a result of our cultural norms, we are still quite likely to see men and women project their disowned attributes into one another. But in reality, emotionally mature and healthy males exhibit so-called soft attributes, and emotionally mature and healthy females possess so-called hard attributes.

Sure, you can cry if you want to. Crying is right near the top of our 'acceptable behavior' list.

THE MEN'S MOVEMENT HOTLINE 73-6912

As the Sidney Harris cartoon illustrates, breaking a stereotype is difficult. Overcoming it sometimes takes a willingness to risk acting in a way that may be ridiculed or criticized. A direct attempt to undo gender role stereotypes took place during the 1989 Christmas holiday. At that time, a group calling itself the "Barbie Liberation Organization" conducted an experiment. They did it to reveal and correct what they considered the problem of gender-based stereotyping in children's toys. They bought three hundred talking Barbie Dolls and three hundred talking GI Joe Dolls. Next, they "operated" on the dolls, exchanging their voice boxes. After they finished, the Barbie dolls spoke with GI Joe's voice, saying things like "Dead men tell no lies," "Eat lead, Cobra," and "Vengeance is mine." The GI Joe Dolls spoke with Barbie's voice saying things like "Let's plan our dream wedding," "I love shopping," and "Will we ever have enough clothes?" Then they replaced the dolls on the store shelves. As you might imagine, this caused quite a public reaction. Each doll shattered its own stereotype. In terms of their gender, they uttered remarks that seemed to contradict their gender role stereotype. But simply exposing a stereotype is not enough to change a stereotype. It takes looking into the cosmic mirror and examining what we are doing on a daily basis that is keeping these stereotypes alive.

For women, the female stereotype leads them to submerge their male attributes. For men, the male stereotype leads them to conceal their female attributes. For all of us, one set of gender attributes is usually less available than the other. The important thing about gender roles is that they are our mental image of what it means to be a man or a woman. We use these images to judge ourselves and to judge others. Many of these images are not in our awareness. And when they are not, they are often projected onto someone of the opposite gender. In many relationships, though—and particularly in gay and lesbian relationships—the disowned attributes of each stereotype can be projected into people of the same gender.

Gender splitting in romantic couples can make for passionate attraction. Or it can make for grim aversion. Psychologist Jolande Jacobi, a colleague of Jung's, felt that each of us is actually trying to heal our divided or split-gender self. And we often unknowingly choose a mate on that basis. Being "turned on" with "love at first sight" may well have to do with the activation of repressed gender attributes. This may be the reason the emotional charge in romantic relationships can run so high.[6]

Homophobic heterosexual men often project their repressed female side onto other males—and often do so in derogatory ways. They may call another man "a queer," "a fag," "a sissy," "a girly man," or "a mama's boy." Their targets are picked by the degree to which their own denied female attribute is openly displayed or expressed by the other person. A man may say, "I don't care if he's gay; I just don't want to see it." In fact, this is likely the basis for the U.S. military's position on gays in their ranks: "Don't ask; don't tell." In terms of the cosmic mirror, the homophobe unknowingly sees his denied shadow reflected in the actions of another. When he does, he is repulsed by what he sees. This was shown no more clearly than in the 1999 Oscar-winning film *American Beauty*.

In one of the film's most powerful and climactic scenes, Marine Colonel Frank Fitts confronts his son, Ricky. To this point in the film, Fitts has formed the mistaken impression that his son is a homosexual. Disgusted, furious, and ashamed of his son, Fitts scathingly berates him for it. Fitts then banishes him from their home. Upset and flustered with what has just occurred, Fitts goes next door in search of a sympathetic ear. There, Fitts pitifully approaches his neighbor, Lester Burnham. Fitts believes— also mistakenly so—that Lester is a homosexual as well. When Lester tries to comfort his obviously upset neighbor, Fitts kisses him. Lester calmly rejects his advance. But Fitts is now utterly humiliated and bewildered. His repressed homosexual desires have now been publicly exposed— and furthermore, he has been rejected for them. Utterly humiliated, Fitts then retrieves a handgun from his home and kills Lester—magically thinking that he could kill that part of himself.

The viewer discovers that beneath his tough, macho exterior, Fitts is a closet homosexual. He has suppressed this side of himself. And he has projected it onto his son.

Distorted by his own lenses, Fitts also sees Lester in the same way. Flooded with his own feelings, Fitts risks exposing his shadow to Lester in the hope of healing it. At the same time, he unwittingly exposes it to himself. In doing so, Fitts shatters his own phony persona. He also releases at Lester the magnitude of his pent-up contempt and rage at himself. We learn that the polarity to Fitts's homophobic and macho public persona is his denied homosexuality that is hidden deep within his own shadow.

The Cosmic Mirror on the World Stage ...

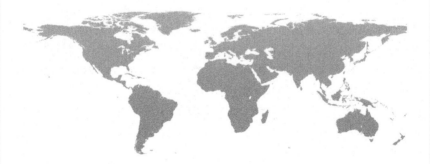

One of pop culture's most recent iconic events occurred when Miss California USA, Carrie Prejean, voiced her views on same-sex marriage. As a result, our gender role expectations became a compelling force at work in this story. Nothing could be more stereotypically female than the winner of the Miss USA pageant! Contestants are, in essence, judged on that stereotype. For many people, when Carrie Prejean voiced her strong opposition to gay marriage it crushed what many envision to be our stereotypical image of femininity—someone who is nurturing and accepting of others, someone without prejudice or intolerance. When our stereotypes are shattered, emotions can run high. Carrie Prejean left us with a strong impression of her rigidity and her absolute and unquestioning certainty in her own beliefs. Not only did this shatter our female stereotype, it also fueled the split within all of us—the desire to be a pure and protected member of an in-group and the fear we have of those who are unlike us and whose strong opinions may differ from ours.

When our denied gender roles are not fully explored, we can become trapped in a gender prison. Men often feel trapped into revealing only hard feelings or attributes. For example, when a man is angry and expresses his anger it is more in tune with his gender role than it is with the gender role of a woman. Alternatively, females often feel trapped into expressing only soft feelings and attributes. To display affection or show sadness is more in tune with a woman's gender role stereotype than it is with a man's. This is part of what has trapped women below the "glass ceiling" in the corporate world. It has been difficult for men to accept women executives who are forceful and dominant. It has also been challenging for women to adopt such a role.

When romantic partners are trapped in such a role-lock, each tends to exaggerate their own gender role. The man might express his own anger. But he also absorbs and acts out the anger placed in him that is denied and unexpressed by his female partner. Similarly, the woman might express her own dependency, hurt, or affection. But she also absorbs and acts out the dependency, hurt, and affection placed in her that is denied and unexpressed in her male partner. But two split-off halves do not make a whole person or a whole relationship. Each person in the relationship must take ownership for *all* of their attributes, especially the ones that are being projected into them.

When this occurs then the relationship is made up of two whole and healthy people.

The Romance Mirror

People often seem to fall in love with and marry their disowned parts. They do so after they unknowingly project those parts into their "soulmate."[7] The attraction begins if the other person openly reveals these wished-for attributes.

"The less you open your heart to others, the more your heart suffers."
—Deepak Chopra

Each partner then sees in the other what they themselves need. In "love at first sight," one can be relatively sure that projections are involved. Processes like these are also the basis for the popular observation that "opposites attract." John Sanford, a Jungian analyst and couples therapist, asserts that in our mate, we are looking for the undiscovered part of us. As he puts it,-

> [It is] the choice every man and woman makes of his or her partner in life—in some way, the partner represents something we need to understand in ourselves.[8]

Spouses can't avoid bumping into their partner's shadow and aura. Such disowned elements need to be made conscious and acknowledged if each spouse wants the relationship to be based on mutual wholeness. If these elements are brought into awareness, then each person can see the other in more authentic, unfiltered, and accurate ways.

There is no better example of romance and the cosmic mirror in action than what underlies flirting on the internet. Everywhere around the world, people are "logging on" for romance … and more. Computer-based romantic relationships like these blur the boundary between what is real and what is virtual reality. Quite often, though, casual contact begun in an online "chat room" or "instant message" turns into a "serious" (virtual) relationship. Despite not having met or spoken to one another, online partners go through phases in a relationship similar to the phases involved in "face-to-face" relationships. Virtual computer partners can experience an "amazing connection" or go through "rough periods" where their "big love" has "dumped" or "burned" them.[9] As one virtual partner wrote after two weeks of intense emailing, "I love you more than anyone I have ever met in my whole life."

The Online Relationship

In the absence of face-to-face contact, how are these intense online romantic relationships forged? We suggest that it is the cosmic mirror at work. In the beginning stages of sexual attraction and in the absence of a more complete picture of the other person, we are prone to project our idealized image of our hoped-for soulmate.[10] What is in a person's awareness is the match between what they might really know about the other person and what they consciously and clearly know they like about them. There is, though, an unreal aspect to the experience. What each partner does not know about the other person creates a void in their relationship. And online partners often project into that void the qualities they need from the other person. They "see" in their partner what they feel they need in themselves. They imagine that their wish is being fulfilled. Here's an example.

Diane was recently divorced and very lonely. She left the marriage feeling devastated and rejected. She felt her "time had passed" when she could lure men with her flirtatious ways. She felt unattractive and undesirable. At a friend's suggestion, she joined an online dating service and posted a picture of herself and a short profile of her interests. One her first email responses was from a man on the other side of the country who to Diane "seemed unusually kind." It touched her when he began placing "XOXOXOX" on his email sign-offs. She believed she could feel his passion for her. For the first time in many years, Diane felt sexually appealing, and her feelings for him seemed to grow stronger with every email exchange. At her workplace, she felt distracted and found herself longing for him. She couldn't wait to return home to see if he had responded to her last message. It was an exhilarating experience. She felt like a schoolgirl and could not seem to control her passions. She felt she had never met a man like him before.

After only a few days, she daydreamed about living with him. But when he didn't write her for several days she was crushed. She couldn't sleep or eat, and in his absence, she felt devastated. Diane had never met this man, never spoken to him on the phone, but felt a profound connection to him. For Diane, it was like something magical had happened to her. She was transformed and felt she had found the man she had always dreamed of. But Diane was caught in her own cosmic mirror. Although her online companion may have actually possessed some of the qualities she imagined in him, Diane had projected into him the qualities she so longed for and desperately wished he possessed. What impassioned her were her own projections. Because she was not able to acknowledge how much the loneliness from within her own shadow was clouding her perceptions, she could not appreciate how she was perceiving her online romance with distorted and amplified lenses.

Mirror Enchantment

What goes on in a virtual relationship online is a kind of *mirror enchantment*. This is a term coined by psychoanalyst Jacques Lacan. He used it to describe the experience infants have when seeing their own image in a mirror.[11] Seeing themselves in the mirror shapes the infant's mental structure of themselves. This is the beginning of their relationship with their own inner being. It becomes the foundation of their self-image. Lacan witnessed how much pure delight infants experience when they become aware of themselves. They are enchanted to first see themselves. When this milestone of self-awareness is accompanied by playful banter from their mother or father the enchantment is further enhanced. In a similar way, internet users are often blinded by love at first keystroke. Using Lacan's model, online partners are enchanted with the image of themselves they believe they are seeing mirrored in the other person. But much of what they are seeing is a fantasy. The enchantment of the other person is in the (imagined) eye of the beholder.

Some of the people who are looking for "love" on the internet are sexually promiscuous. These are the people who are searching for instant romance and sexual intrigue. This pattern of behavior—where someone is intentionally seeking sex or confusing love and sex—is an obsessive and recurring hunt for the denied aura. It is our pursuit of someone or something outside of our self that is driven by the mistaken belief that finding that "special someone" will fill up our inner sense of emptiness. They are looking outside themselves for love that they cannot feel about themselves. They are literally "looking for love in all the wrong places." We are not saying that "true love" is a myth that cannot be experienced. We are saying that love from someone else can never substitute for the love we must be able to give ourselves.

The cosmic mirror occurs in face-to-face romances as well. What we have just discussed is not distinct from the process of falling in love in real life. When the actual qualities of the other person match our desires, we feel attracted to them. We might be physically attracted. We might share meaningful interests. Or we might share common attitudes or values. There is an aspect to the romance where the couple is consciously aware of their mutual attraction. But either partner can become compellingly attracted to something about the other person without being able to explain the power of the attraction. What is often experienced as a vague and indefinable feeling can feel strangely familiar to them. Often heard when this takes place are comments like, "I feel I have known this person *all* my life" or "I can talk to this person about *anything*!" This sense of déjà vu stems from a momentary awakening of disowned shadow and aura attributes.

Our parents are the original source of our felt love and support. A parent can build their child's sense of self-esteem or they can emotionally wound them. Attached to each experience is an image and an emotion. All the images, qualities, attributes, and emotions that are attached to our parents or other powerful and influential people in our lives blend to create a composite image or "blueprint" of intimate experiences. This blueprint becomes translated into our wished-for and feared images of a close relationship. More than that, though, we also unknowingly hope that our partner can help us mend our old wounds and complete unfinished business from earlier in our lives. To the extent that we are not aware of it, many of us are compelled to seek out a mate whose qualities match that internal blueprint. We may set out to seek positive relationships with others who we imagine possess the positive qualities of our wished-for caretakers, our real caretakers, or others in our lives. But if we are unable to see the entire blueprint we can become blinded to the negative characteristics in the other person. We may say, "There is something about them that is familiar." But our wishes cloud our view of the negative qualities in them.[12] We miss what our friends or family may see as obvious in our partner. We may look back and say, "How in the world did I not see it?" Or we might say, "Wow. It's happened to me *again!*" Here's an example.

Jake was hauntingly attracted to Jackie. She was quite beautiful and mysteriously seductive with a quietly flirtatious allure. At first, he couldn't keep his eyes off her. She was the "prized beauty" in the room. Everybody wanted her, including Jake. And as their relationship grew, Jackie became *totally* devoted to Jake. Later, in their relationship, though, Jake began to feel jealous of others. He began to blame Jackie when he saw her innocently or playfully displaying with others the same traits that first attracted him to her. Jackie was initially attracted to Jake's steadfast stability and quiet manner. Up to that point, she had experienced a great deal of chaos in her life. And she loved how predictable he was. It was calming for her. She saw in Jake his inner strength and his ability to commit to something and see it through. But later in their relationship his steadfast and predictable qualities became to her a "boring routine." For her, his behavior became dull and monotonous. And she began to resent him for it. He seemed stubborn and overly conservative. Jackie felt Jake was unwilling to spontaneously let himself have fun and try new things.

In almost every romance, the honeymoon period ends and the partners' infatuation toward each other declines. At this point, some kind of conflict often emerges. The qualities that one partner has denied in the other become painfully apparent. These qualities begin to annoy us. They gnaw at us. And we often see them in an overstated or exaggerated way. When this happens, projection and the cosmic mirror are almost always involved. But how each partner handles this tension is central to how the relationship unfolds. It is then up to each partner to take back their own projected qualities. They must re-own what they mistakenly see belonging only to the other person. Each partner must look at their own shadow and aura. They must examine how their own denied qualities may be getting placed into the other person.

Let's again take a look at Jake and Jackie. For their relationship to flourish, Jake must learn to accept his own denied zest for life. He must discover what bothers him about *his* own innocent and playful flirtatiousness. He must learn what it is *in him* that fosters his jealousy and prevents him from seeing just how devoted Jackie is to him. He also must become more aware of the meaning he holds about Jackie's silence. He equated it with mystery. But, to be sure, it has other meanings as well. Seeing her own denied reflection in the cosmic mirror, Jackie must learn to better examine her disowned need for excessive exhilaration and drama. She must discover the unrealized tranquility of just being with herself in quiet solitude. And she must learn more about her inner chaos and how it may prevent her from creating a routine and predictability in her life that can enhance it.

True love means falling in love with the whole person. It is falling in love with our partner's flaws as well as their best qualities. To accurately see and accept another person in their wholeness entails honoring all the parts of our self, and it requires forgiving and loving our own flaws. Before we can accept the limitations in our partner, we must be able to acknowledge and honor our own limitations. This takes an open heart. It also takes the courage to look deeply into our reflection in the cosmic mirror.[13]

In this chapter, we have examined the split that takes place in the roles we attach to each gender. This often occurs as we disown attributes, feelings, and actions that we associate with the other gender and project them into the opposite gender. Looking into our cosmic mirror enables us to see this. Seeing this is the first step toward reversing the process and taking back those projected attributes. Only then can we become more whole and complete. We have also explained how the process of gender role projection affects our romantic choices and the behavior we exhibit in romantic relationships. It often happens in such a way that each partner only brings to the relationship a constricted part of themselves.

Not surprisingly, the splitting that takes place around gender roles can be a fertile ground for scapegoating our partners—blaming them for *our own* unhappiness. In the next chapter, we explore the process of scapegoating and the role that scapegoating plays in our own cosmic mirror.

9

Scapegoats as Mirrors: The Dynamics of Blaming

"Our worst fault is our preoccupation with the faults of others."

—*Kahlil Gibran*

The social role of scapegoating is timeless. They abound in our lives. They are present in our two-person relationships—like romantic relationships, friendships, sibling and parental relationships. They flourish in the family system of relationships. They are common to our work groups, and they occur between sects and other larger groups within societies. Scapegoats are created to magically rid us of responsibility for our own failings and shortcomings, and they are powerful mirrors of our own shadow. In lieu of acknowledging and taking responsibility for our own flaws, we blame others.

The origin of the word dates back to early tribal culture. There, a magic ritual was performed to rid the tribe of its sins. The ritual involved symbolically placing the sins of the tribe onto a goat. The goat was then killed or driven off into the wilderness. Performing this ritual generated a sense of purification and renewal for the tribe. As written in Exodus, Numbers, and Isaiah, the sacrificial lamb later became for the Jewish people what earlier the goat was for the tribe.

For millennia, we have blamed others for our failings while denying similar failings in ourselves.[1] Jesus Christ cautioned us about this. He said we focus too much on the small speck of dirt in another's eye while discounting the large clump of dirt in our own. Christ also rebuked a group who planned to stone to death a woman who they believed had committed adultery. To them, he said, "Let he who is without sin cast the first stone."

Scapegoats can be found in almost any work setting. When a crisis is brewing, the active search for them begins. We see "witch hunts" and departmental warfare. Employees often place blame onto those in authority. We might hear them say, "Those idiots at the top don't know what the hell they are doing." CEOs are often singled out for declining performance or moral breeches in the company. In turn, leaders aim their sights on lower-ranking workers. Or they target "whistle-blowers" for the role. Like Adolf Hitler used the Jews, authoritarian leaders have manipulatively used scapegoats to direct attention away from their own evil.[2]

Scapegoats are especially prevalent in family systems. Often, it is one of the children who are asked to take on this role. When a child is having problems in school or with other family members, the family often identifies that child as "the one with the problem." Parents play a prominent role in this process. Sometimes, siblings can unknowingly collude with parents in the scapegoating. This scenario is so common in family therapy that the therapist usually labels this child as the "identified patient"—meaning that the therapist recognizes that while the family might assign the role of "patient" to one of its members, it is usually the family-as-a-whole that must make any necessary changes. This "identified" child is typically the family scapegoat. How does this occur? What factors are operating here? From the perspective of the cosmic mirror, this is the shadow in action. Shadow issues are usually present when the rest of the family has difficulty seeing how their own behavior is playing a role in the crisis. Let's look at an example.

Joey was in the fourth grade when he began to have problems in school. He was not focused and often daydreamed in class. His parents felt he was "misbehaving." They tried to put a stop to it by "grounding" him until he "straightened up." His school counselor thought he might have Attention Deficit Disorder. This is a psychiatric label that is given to a child (or adult) who may be easily distracted, may be careless, may have difficulty concentrating, may not listen well, may be forgetful, or may have trouble organizing things. At home, Joey was becoming more reclusive. So his parents decided to get him professional help. He then began seeing a child therapist.

In the course of her interviews with Joey and the family, though, it became clear that a very important family issue was being avoided. Because of her age and health condition, Joey's grandmother had recently begun living with them. Her medical problems were serious. And mom and dad were understandably concerned about her. This was a topic, though, that was not openly discussed with Joey. In fact, when Joey's grandmother needed help mom and dad would come to her aid, but they did so with pained and worried looks on their faces. Joey was very close to his grandmother. And her condition made him worry about her death, his own death, and the death of his parents.

Mom and dad felt that Joey was the problem. But with the help of the therapist, they began to see their own role in the crisis. By keeping their fears silent, mom and dad inadvertently placed their worries into Joey. Joey was not aware of his fears. He didn't know how to access them. So, Joey became distracted and emotionally overwhelmed. Initially, the school counselor and his parents attributed the problem to Joey. After the therapist helped the family openly talk about their fears, though, Joey's school problems began to decline and eventually disappeared. Unintentionally, Joey had become the scapegoat for the undiscussable fears of the family.

When a family creates its scapegoat—intentionally or unintentionally—the family attributes to the scapegoat the larger interpersonal issues from within the larger family system. This allows the rest of the family to maintain its façade that the problem is not theirs. Unknowingly, the family scapegoat absorbs the unwanted projections of others. Once the scapegoat begins to do this, they usually act out or openly display what others wish to rid themselves of. In doing so, the scapegoat makes themselves distinctive and an obvious target for further unwanted projections. But the emotional stresses and strains are not simply the scapegoat's. They belong to the family-as-a-whole.

It's usually not the family's conscious intention to avoid examining the prominent emotional issues taking place within the family system. They simply do not know what else they can do but assign the blame to one

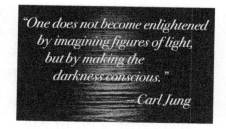

"One does not become enlightened by imagining figures of light, but by making the darkness conscious."
—Carl Jung

person. It is a well-established principle within psychology that when there is conflict within a group its members are inclined to assign responsibility to one of its members and not to the group's processes. In essence, the family creates their own myth: if only the "problem member" could be "fixed" then the family would function "smoothly." This, of course, is an illusion—it's magical thinking. In actuality, for the family to function more effectively, every member of the family system must make changes—not just the scapegoat. Every member of the family needs to learn how they contribute to the problem. Then they must change their own behavior accordingly.

There is a widespread primitive belief that a single person is the "cause" of others' feelings or actions. When a group performs well the leader gets the credit. When a group does poorly a scapegoat gets the blame. Why does this occur? It stems from a deeply embedded fear about the uncertainty we feel in social situations. Because social events are often complicated and ambiguous, they can feel chaotic and filled with danger. As such, they are fertile ground for projective processes. In reality, there is no simple explanation for how group efforts turn out. Any explanation must include how group members manage their relationships with each other. It also must include the need that group members have to adhere to their cultural norms and customs. The terror of facing a wall of uncertainty and ambiguity can lead us to conclude that one person is the cause of the things we are afraid of.[3] Blaming someone else for our misfortunes also creates the illusion that we have control over our world.

At the start, few of us are aware that we are creating a scapegoat. This makes it almost impossible to understand how we are using the scapegoat to meet our own and others' unconscious wishes and needs. We choose scapegoats because they tend to be more visible in openly revealing what is denied or discounted by us and others. In Joey's case, his school problems absorbed much of his family's attention. Although doing so in a disguised way, Joey revealed the denied emotions, thoughts, and attributes lurking in the shadow of the family system. Joey's reclusiveness was the behavioral equivalent of what mom and dad were doing emotionally—that is, avoiding looking at or talking about their concern for grandmother's health issues. Joey became the target for the family's denied projections. For their part, his mom and dad "identified" with the issues revealed by Joey's behavior. But they denied them—and they did not give voice to them. As a result, the family pushed their own undiscussable fears of (grandmother's) death into Joey. And unwittingly, Joey was the container for these feelings.

Here's another illustration of scapegoating in action— scapegoating in the workplace. Tony wasn't new to his work group. But all the other guys in the group had more seniority than he did. When the production line on his shift started going down, the supervisors began to get concerned. It was very expensive for the line to go down. And when it did, the plant manager growled at the shift supervisors about it. Tony's group was using several pieces of older equipment. But the plant manager, under pressure from the vice president, did not set aside enough of his budget for training and maintenance. Before it was approved, the budget was presented to the supervisors. While the supervisors didn't like the budget allowances they didn't want to make waves for themselves. They simply nodded their agreement to it.

This was OK with Tony's group. They thought more training was "boring" and "a total waste of time." Training reminded them of being in school. When the supervisors finally confronted Tony's group about the line breakdowns, they shrugged their shoulders in bewilderment on why they were occurring. Tony's group wasn't deliberately hiding it. They really didn't know why the line was breaking down. Even if they did know, though, they knew not to take any responsibility for the stoppages. If they did, they feared that they might be transferred or let go. That was the tradition in this company—the "troublemakers" were weeded out. So they kept quiet. Tony, on the other hand, wanted to help. So he began speaking up about his responsibility in the breakdowns. He told others that he didn't have enough training to effectively run the equipment. When asked, the other group members denied that this was a problem for them. The result? People felt Tony wasn't a "team player," and so he was transferred to an area of the plant they called the "graveyard."

Tony was scapegoated. He made himself a visible target by disclosing thoughts and feelings that others suppressed or denied. He brought up the subject of inadequate training. And no one was willing to face this. His coworkers could not speak to it, because it touched a sore spot in them about being in school. His supervisors could not speak to it, because it exposed their agreement to a training and maintenance budget that was inadequate. Tony, on the other hand, was quite transparent in voicing his opinion about the matter. Because of that, he became the target of the plant manager's and supervisors' own projected shortcomings. To them it was Tony's fault—not theirs.

Aggressive people are often picked as scapegoats. They express their dissatisfaction, but they do it in an abrasive and hostile manner. They are often disliked and seen as "loose cannons." But they also may speak to a legitimate dissatisfaction from within their group. Despite voicing what may be a piece of truth for the group, the red flag is raised on the way they express it. Their valid frustration is dismissed as mere babblings of discontent. This is a clear sign that the person is touching on issues from within the group's shadow.

In scapegoating, the shadow is often guarded by rules that prevent its contents from becoming conscious. "Don't make waves." "Never get angry." These are examples of gate-keeping rules. They inhibit us. They keep us from expressing criticism or frustration with what we see going on in the group. To keep the shadow from being exposed, we commonly use denial to hide it. When someone begins to directly reveal the shadow's contents, others commonly use denial and projection to keep it at bay. The undiscussable frustration with how the group is operating that is denied by others is projected onto the scapegoat. Two things then happen. First, others feel relief. By projecting their frustrations and aggressive urges onto someone else, they emotionally distance themselves from those urges. It also is a source of satisfaction for them. They see their projected feelings being acted out by the scapegoat. This keeps them safe from what they fear will be the consequences of expressing the taboo thought. It also allows them to vicariously experience the feelings behind the thought—safely, though, through the scapegoat. Scapegoating is reinforcing for the group, because other group members are paradoxically drawn to someone expressing what they dare not express.

When a scapegoat speaks or engages in some action, they don't simply do it for themselves. They unknowingly do it to act out and express hidden forces at work within the group.[4] Those forces cannot be permanently suppressed. They will eventually surface. For instance, it is almost never the case that only one group member feels dissatisfaction with the group. When one member is seen as being the only one with a certain feeling, thought, or wish, it is a clue that the scapegoating process is taking shape. Symbolically, the scapegoat serves as a container for projections that others have trouble accepting in themselves. This makes it extremely difficult for scapegoats. They not only have to deal with sorting through their own emotions. They also must cope with the emotions being "pushed" into them by others.

The group shadow often contains the need for dependency and the need for approval. When someone openly expresses the need for the leader's approval, that person often becomes "the teacher's pet," "the suck up," or "the brown-nose." It's understandable that we would want the leader to like us. But it's embarrassing for many of us to admit it. When someone does, though, others are often threatened by it. The threat is looking into the cosmic mirror and seeing what we don't wish to see. Expressing the shadow in words is not required. Nonverbal cues are also meaningful to others and can trigger shadow issues as well. From the perspective of the cosmic mirror, what we dislike in the scapegoat

"What we dislike in a scapegoat is often what we dislike and cannot accept in our self."

is often what we dislike but have trouble acknowledging in ourselves—that is, we may have trouble accepting our own need to depend on others. It's difficult to admit our need for approval.

> *"Whatever your heart clings to and confides in, that is really your God."*
> *—Martin Luther*

We delude ourselves to think that the behavior of any one person in a group is the sole product of their personality. It is not. As a culture, we value rugged independence and devalue the useful aspects of dependency. We'd like to believe that we are free of social influences—we are not. When we are in a group, we don't easily grasp the boundary between ourselves and the group. We tend to err in believing that the group or social system itself does not significantly affect our behavior. We often mistakenly assume that we are alone in having a particular thought or feeling. This is usually inaccurate.[5] This is the cosmic mirror in action. Here's another example of this.

In one of our cosmic mirror workshop, other workshop participants saw Crystal as a "basket-case." She was being singled out and subtly attacked by others. She cried openly and often in the group. And others considered her to be quite fragile. During breaks, some of the members of her small group gossiped about her holding them back. Crystal was a scapegoat for them. She didn't know it, though. You could not deny that she was fragile and tearful. But you could also see that others in the group were being insensitive, even verbally cruel to her and toward one another. It was this insensitivity that the group was denying about itself.

Other group members pumped up those qualities in Crystal by projecting into her what they denied in themselves. They feared their own fragility and their need to be fixed up. It triggered their own denied dependency needs and their fears of being ridiculed by others for having normal human fears. Crystal was a reluctant but unknowingly cooperative screen for these projections. She felt alone in her fragility. In turn, others in the group acted as if she was the only one who was being affected by their insensitivity. She was under the illusion that it was her own individual problem and not a more widely shared problem from within her group.

Slowly and with some facilitation, Crystal's small group started to discuss some of its denied qualities. As they did, they began to take back some of their projections. They did this by acknowledging the hurt that was being inflicted within the group. For the first time, they began to show their sadness much more openly in the group. Crystal became a mirror through which others began to see more clearly their own disowned reflections. As a result, they were able to look behind the cosmic mirror and grow past what had formerly stifled them.

Scapegoats are usually reluctant victims. They don't like their role. But often, they have found themselves in that role before. A scapegoat usually has had a history of guilt with "not fitting in." Not surprisingly, when pushed into that role they tend to blame themselves and not those around them. They may say to themselves, "Everything bad is usually my fault." When they do this, the dysfunctional and destructive aspects of the larger social system—in which they are a part and that has created their role—goes unexamined.

As long as the scapegoat can be blamed, the behavior of others never changes. Getting rid of the scapegoat is a common ploy but puts people in another bind. The systemic problems contributing to the creation of the scapegoat resurface. People are then confronted to look at what they may be trying to keep hidden. It stirs up their own unwanted emotions and attributes that they are trying to use the scapegoat to contain. Getting rid of the scapegoat doesn't really work, because when we do someone else is quickly "pulled" into that role. With the expulsion of the scapegoat, the emotions being projected into them once again begin to surface. To put a lid on these disturbing emotions our search for a new scapegoat begins.

Scapegoating: How to See It Coming

How can we tell when scapegoating might be in the making? Here are some clues to look for:

1. One person is verbally attacked.

2. No one else defends that person.

3. The accusers use "you"-statements and negative interpretations, like "You are manipulative." "You are seductive." "You are defensive." "You are passive-aggressive." "You are too dependent." "You will never be a leader."

4. The logic of the attacks is circular. "You aren't a team player. Therefore, I can attack you." Scapegoats are accused of many things, including complaining, talking about their flaws, assigning responsibility to others, taking responsibility for what they group may

collectively deny, showing dissent, and expressing risky or unusual ideas.

5. Others insist on maintaining an emotionally safe and superficial way of working with one another. For example, a group will inhibit or prevent itself from discussing its uncomfortable feelings.

6. The scapegoat is believed to be the only person that is guilty of the accusations. In other words, others believe that it is only the scapegoat who is the cause of the problem. Ironically, this belief ascribes a considerable amount of power to the scapegoat. It also absolves others of any personal responsibility for their role in what is taking place.

7. The scapegoat infrequently responds with anger and rarely counterattacks or interrupts the attacks.

8. The scapegoat defends against the *content* of the accusations. They don't discuss the *process* of being accused. They rarely express their right to do just what they are doing without providing anyone with any explanation or justification.

9. The scapegoat seems trapped in the role of victim.[6]

We see scapegoats in all kinds of groups. But we also see them in two-person relationships. If one person expresses a vulnerability that the other person might pick up on and exploit, there's a good bet that disowned projections within the cosmic mirror are involved. Bullying is a good example.

> *"Do not blindly believe what others say, even the Buddha. See for yourself what brings contentment, clarity, and peace."*
> *—Jack Kornfield*

Remember when you were on the playground and a bully badgered or beat up on you or one of your schoolmates? Maybe you have a young son or daughter or know someone who has gone through something like this. You may have observed that this pattern usually persists until the victim stands up for themselves and fights back. When this happens, the bullying usually stops. Why though? What can the cosmic mirror tell us about this? The actions of a bully are usually explained with the notion that the bully is overcompensating for an inner sense of inadequacy. The victim is understood to feel meek and terrified of the bully. But, when the victim overcomes his fears and confronts the bully, the bully's façade of dominance seems to change. From the perspective of the cosmic mirror, though, we believe that there is much more going on here.

Bully Psychology

Kids who are routinely victimized by bullies are undoubtedly fearful of them. But they also are children who often deny their own strength and power. They feel small, unworthy, and with little authority. These are the characteristics that the victim contains in his aura. Often, the victim feels helpless or inept in other arenas as well. Sometimes, these patterns of behavior and ways of relating to the world carry over into adulthood. Furthermore, children who are victims often deny their own power and their healthy capacity for dominance. They place these qualities out into the world—others are powerful, not them. To them, their outer world and others in it can seem harsh, cruel, hostile, or unfair. One place that the child unknowingly directs his own denied capacity for dominance and power is toward the bully. They pick the bully toward whom to direct these denied qualities, because the bully seems to openly exhibit these qualities. In turn, the victim's expressions of fear reinforce the bully's exaggerated self-perceptions of dominance—as the victim cringes, the bully feels powerful.

Make no mistake. The bully also has his own shadow and aura issues. The bully's shadow contains his own painful vulnerabilities and inner victimhood. The bully keeps their shadow a secret from others and from themselves. They do so in two ways: by denying it and by placing its contents into their victims. What is also denied in the bully is their capacity for empathy and compassion. These positive qualities are contained in the bully's aura.

After the victim stands up for themselves, the bully often befriends their former victim. Why does this occur? From the perspective of the cosmic mirror, the victim stops their bully's projection of weakness into them by standing up for themselves. The victim is no longer willing to play the scapegoat role. The bully then sees those new characteristics in their victim. The bully then identifies those reflections as their own. They see their dominance and power in the mirror of their victim and like what they see. Furthermore, in the act of liking the victim, the bully sees for the first time their own hidden compassion. The victim recognizes the compassion in the bully—their own softer qualities being reflected in the mirror of their former bully. The victim then likes what they see.

Here is another example of how scapegoating is played out in two-person relationships. Jim was a bully to his wife, Jean. Not so much in the physical sense, but in the psychological sense. He controlled the finances and the decision making for the two of them. He was also domineering, overbearing, and critical of her thoughts and suggestions. The ironic thing was that Jean was creative. Her judgment was sound and practical. And she had vision and a valid point-of-view. But as the years of their marriage wore on, predictably, Jean withdrew. Emotionally she tried to make herself very small and invisible. She dwelled in the world of her fears. And to evade Jim's criticisms, she became lethargic.

Jim was caught in his own projective processes as well. Paradoxically, Jim responded to Jean's smallness with more condemnations. He regarded her passivity and avoidance as "laziness." Jim was faced with his own intolerable feelings of "smallness" eating at him from the inside out. So, he tried to eradicate them by pushing them into Jean. Ironically, as Jim did this, Jean began more and more to take on the very qualities Jim loathed.

Antoine/Consuelo de Saint-Exupery

Looking Not With the Eyes But With the Heart

After his wife finally left him, Jim was miserable. He was forced to examine the mask of his own intolerance and arrogance. In doing so, he clearly saw his harried plight to build wealth. He became aware of his fears of failure that he might not do so. He uncovered his doubts that he would ever be enough. It was these aspects of himself that he could not face. He was like the Businessman in Antoine de Saint-Exupéry's *The Little Prince* who constantly counted the stars he thought he owned so that he could use them to buy more stars.[7] Even as a child, Jim prided himself on not being afraid and "not taking any crap from anybody." He denied the humanity of his own fears. But he saw them in the cosmic mirror of the fears of his wife. He could not avoid the reminders of them. They made him angry. And he took it out on Jean. Only later did Jim learn an essential lesson from Saint-Exupéry's insightful book: "The essential things in life are seen not with the eyes, but with the heart."

Of her own doing, Jean took on Jim's rage. She justified his rage at her "flaws." After leaving him, though, she was able to examine her own cosmic mirror. She saw how she took on Jim's rage as a way of reinforcing and justifying her own self-loathing—in essence, Jean believed she should be punished. And she saw how it led her to remain with a man who treated her so poorly. Once she began to examine her cosmic mirror Jean was able to shed her scapegoat role and enter the most life-affirming and constructive phase of her life.

Personal Mirror Reflection

Why is it that many of us are fascinated by the exploits of figures like Tiger Woods, Mark Sanford, Eliot Spitzer, or Britney Spears? Could they be scapegoats for us? If they are, what are we denying in ourselves and attributing to them? Aside from their apparent self-destructiveness, is it possible that they may trigger within us our fears of being exposed for something we have done but may be denying? Is it possible that we identify with their shame and embarrassment? Could this give us a vicarious but safe way to connect with similar feelings inside us? Many of us have been in friendships, work relationships, or romantic relationships that ended in conflict—each person blaming the other.

Many of us have had the experience of being a scapegoat or have been involved in scapegoating another person. Take a minute now to recall when you may have been scapegoated. What was your experience when you were a scapegoat? Looking at the experience now, what do you believe was being scapegoated into you by another? What were they trying to push into you? Can you recall a time when you may have scapegoated someone else? What was your experience in this situation? Reflecting on it now, what might you have been denying in yourself and pushing into them?

The cosmic mirror helps us understand how scapegoats are created. Attributing this kind of power to one person helps us focus our terror in one place. It gives us the illusion that what we are seeing might be within our control. It helps us avoid the complexity involved in applying the concept of a process that is diffused throughout a seemingly chaotic and uncertain group, society, culture, or organizational universe—especially when assigning the blame to a single person is so much simpler. Scapegoats are the product of this avoidance. A similar process unfolds in the creation of leaders and icons. This is the focus of our next chapter.

10

Icons and Leaders as Mirrors

> *"If you are looking for a hero, look again;*
> *you are diminishing some part of yourself."*

> —*Sheldon Kopp*

We are often blind to our own talents. This is the aura at work. And it appears alive and well in our projections onto icons and leaders. Stated a little differently, people who we label as leaders or see as heroes or icons often serve as targets for containing the projections of our own aura. What is projected is our denied ability to create a vision for ourselves or to inspire ourselves. We often place in others our own discounted inner power to guide ourselves toward a meaningful life. In pop culture, celebrities often become containers for those projections. It is quite common for us to fill celebrities with positive qualities we only imagine they possess—qualities that we often feel that we ourselves do not posses. In turn, celebrities often buy into these projected attributes—taking on an exaggerated persona and living it out.

The Cosmic Mirror on the World Stage ...

Britney Spears is a good example of someone who absorbed our collective aura projections. Spears had tried to live out the public image of the ultimate "All-American girl." Teenagers enshrined her as a pop superstar. But, she fell from their grace when her drug, legal, and parenting problems were eventually revealed. It appeared she became caught up in the idea of her own super-human stardom. This was an illusion. As a result, she seemed to become trapped in a role of the "All-American girl"—a role that could not work for her. She was overcome by her self-destructiveness exploding out from within her shadow.

Leaders in many different settings are often seen as icons too. There is no doubt it's a valuable quality to know when to follow someone else's vision for the future. It is the basis for cooperation, constructive interdependency, and effective teamwork. But, when we look to others for vision and direction we often diminish constructive and creative parts of ourselves. In looking to a hero or leader to provide a vision *for us*, we often avoid developing our own capabilities for creating a vision *of our own*. In doing so, we also often avoid joining with others to create a shared vision.

When a group first forms, the "push" to assign or elect a leader is quite strong. But there is no scientific support in the management, psychological, or social science literature for the idea that a group with a single leader

> *"Through our senses the world appears. Through our reactions we create delusions. Without reactions the world becomes clear."* —*Jack Kornfield*

is any more effective than when a group organizes itself and makes decisions by using group consensus. In fact, there is data supporting the idea that groups who reach consensus are *more* creative and satisfied with their group than are those groups who are run by a single leader.[1] Nevertheless, members of a group usually feel compelled to assign a leader—an idea for which there is a great deal of supporting research.[2] A group whose focus is to study its own ways of operating inevitably discovers that the pull to assign a leader stems from their own panic and anxiety.

But from where does this anxiety and panic arise? It comes from the members of the group not knowing enough about one another. It comes from group members' fears of how power and authority will be managed in the group. It comes from fears of being left out of the inner circle of the group. It comes from group members' feelings of inadequacy—that they may not be able to contribute something meaningful to the group. It also comes from the anxiety and panic over what it means to be responsible for the group's outcome. Because of these fears, the leader role is often avoided. At the same time, it is also projected into the one member of the group who chooses to hold the illusion that they have the power to manage all the group's fears and aspirations about its fate. Group members often create a stereotypical perception that a leader is a kind of god-like figure who takes on excessive responsibility for the group's product or outcome. Of course, it is an illusion that a single cause or person (a leader) is somehow more responsible for the group's outcome than the cumulative contributions made by the group's members. It's magical thinking, but it feels safer to maintain this belief than to confront their own fears about contributing to the leadership role. In actuality, all group members, by their action or inaction, contribute to the group product.

Have you noticed how quickly a newly formed group moves to establish someone as a leader? Many group members sense that such an action will reduce their anxiety. But, there is rarely, if any, open discussion of why they really need a single leader—it's rarely discussed. No one seems to question what a solitary leader might really do for the group that the group could not otherwise do for itself.

When groups are created without an assigned leader they are rapidly drawn to a more familiar social form. It is like a learned social instinct or a deeply embedded or culturally induced program that is put in motion. The creation of a leader as a requirement in a group's inception is, for the most part, a learned social defense. Over time, the need to maintain the defense has become socially wired-in. Eventually, the idea of entertaining the question— "Why is a leader necessary?"—was removed from our social consciousness. Subsequently, the leader becomes assigned as a reflexive reaction—its position is self-justifying. The notion that the group actually has a choice about it never really gets fully thought through.

The ritualistic-like creation of a leader role provides a group with a social illusion. Group members can mask the feelings of being overwhelmed, falling apart, or feeling unsure. They can create a familiar structural form within the group so that they can feel as if they have control over the powerful forces within the group and within themselves. Like the scapegoat, the leader role allows the group to focus its uncertainty and terror into a singular identifiable place. Otherwise, it would be diffused throughout what is feared to be a murky and ambiguous social environment—one that is potentially harmful and without order. Appointing a leader is seen as a solution. It helps the group attain an illusory sense of control. Group members feel, "The leader will take care of any conflict and protect us." Or they believe, "Assuming that kind of power and responsibility is way too risky."

The leader is falsely perceived as the "cause" of success or failure in the group. When a leader is assigned, the rest of the group often moves away from taking ownership for leadership. By placing excessive levels of responsibility for leadership into a single leader, the group becomes entrapped by their own fears. They de-skill themselves from acts of leadership. These avoided leadership qualities are contained in the group's aura, and they are placed into anyone who acknowledges these qualities in themselves.

Psychotherapist Sheldon Kopp wrote extensively about our denied talents. One of his most influential books addresses the pilgrimage of clients in psychotherapy. He provocatively entitles it, *If You Meet Buddha on the Road, Kill Him.*[3] The idea implied by his title is this: stop looking outside yourself for the meaning in life. Ultimately, no one

Buddha's Wish

can provide that for you or lead you to it. To find your own leadership qualities requires looking within to your higher self. Buddha advised, "Be a lamp unto your self." Sometimes, this process means confronting uncertainty head-on. To look into ourselves often requires an ability to tolerate feeling awkward. It requires exploring and experimenting with new ways to authentically express ourselves in the world we create. Others can inspire us, but we do not necessarily need to look to someone else for this. We can learn to inspire ourselves. We can break the cycle of denying and projecting our own potential for leadership. Here's what it takes:

1. Asking ourselves what specifically it is that we want a leader to do,
2. Then risking doing it ourselves, or
3. Discovering what prevents us from taking the initiative, and
4. Struggling on our own to find the meaningfulness in the endeavor.

As the Harris cartoon parities, many of us look outside of ourselves for the answers.

"MY ASTROLOGER SAYS ONE THING, MY GURU SAYS ANOTHER, MY PSYCHIATRIST SAYS SOMETHING ELSE — I DON'T KNOW <u>WHO</u> TO TURN TO ANYMORE."

Although we might wish otherwise the courage to grow stems from the awareness that as adults, we must take care *of ourselves.* As the airlines advise, we must put on our own "air mask" before we try to help others. We must find ways to make our own lives meaningful. No one can be there to look after us any better than we can for ourselves. Ultimately, no one else can take responsibility for us creating a meaningful life. With the courage to grow, we can take better charge of our life and live it with fewer illusions. But the pull is strong to distill our view of ourselves and the world into simpler but more extreme elements. We are often tempted to polarize and oversimplify the world and our place in it. As Kopp writes,

> Believing that things usually turn out bad is
> as naïve as believing that this is the best of all
> possible worlds. An overly optimistic Pollyan-
> na attitude is simply a more obvious form of

pseudo-innocence than a cynically paranoid outlook. Both postures deny nature's indifference to the human situation. One person may imagine that there is someone out there watching over us. Another believes dark forces rule. Either extreme is an oversimplified view of life's ambiguities, an illusion of a unified coherent universe in which human beings hold a special central position. Beyond the limitation of that shared romantic assumption, each of these polar attitudes has its own advantages and disadvantages.[4]

The Mirror of Authority

The mirror of authority is a special case of how we collude with others to be our heroes or leaders. We place a great deal of power in the hands of those in authority. Many times, we do it because we have imbued them with an inflated sense of strength, ability, righteousness, or control. Sometimes this has been earned—sometimes not. In making sense of human relationships, power and authority are always key issues. The cosmic mirror helps us reinterpret and better understand these often puzzling aspects of interpersonal life. And we can learn a great deal about power and authority from several classic studies from the field of social psychology.

The first set of studies were led by psychologist Solomon Asch. He showed groups of people a set of lines that were not clearly drawn. He then asked them in a group forum to individually report what they saw. Over time, they unknowingly began to align their judgments with one another.[5] The results from these studies are usually explained by stating that the experimental subjects were unknowingly conforming to each other or that they were deliberately trying to avoid conflict with one another. But neuropsychologist Gregory Berns and his colleagues found something entirely different else going on. They put subjects through an Asch-style experiment. But they also scanned their brains using an MRI (Magnetic Resonance Image). Berns's experimental subjects "conformed" to one another just like the Asch subjects did. But their MRIs showed real changes in areas of the brain devoted to vision and spatial perception. The subjects were actually seeing the drawings differently.[6] What caused their perceptions to change?

The results from the Berns experiment shows that if we disagree with others we can actually begin to visualize things in a distorted way. Similarly, the cosmic mirror says that when we conform to others' points of view we may be de-authorizing a part of ourselves. We fool ourselves into believing that our divergent view of the world may be invalid. We distort our own perceptions. We disbelieve ourselves. We alter (physiologically and psychologically) our own view of reality.

The second set of studies also deals with how much we authorize our own perceptions and beliefs. These studies— led by psychologist Stanley Milgram—were designed to learn more about the atrocities that took place in Nazi Germany. They plainly show how blindly obedient to those in authority all of us can be. The studies were begun in 1961, shortly after Adolf Eichmann was placed on trial for war crimes. In these experiments, ordinary people cast off their sense of personal conscience in order to obey someone they believed was in authority. Although no one was ever in real danger, everyday people administered what they believed were deadly levels of electric shock. Why did this take place? Milgram explains,

> The essence of obedience consists in the fact that a person comes to view himself as the instrument for carrying out another person's wishes, and he, therefore, no longer sees himself as responsible for his actions. Once this critical shift of viewpoint has occurred in the person, all of the essential features of obedience follow.[7]

We want to see our heroes and our leaders without flaws. We do not want to see in our therapists or our gurus any of the failings that we might see in ourselves. This, of course, is a fantasy. To some extent, everyone is flawed. The rationality of this logic, though, becomes lost in the shadowy depths of the cosmic mirror. We often over-idealize our authority figures. When we do this we discount the seats of our own strengths and project them outward. We deify our authority figures. This is shown no more clearly than in the magnificence some clinicians attribute to Sigmund Freud. Like all therapists, though, Freud had feet of clay. And this is no more apparent than in the following frequently overlooked quote of his.

> I have found little that is "good" about human beings on the whole. In my experience most of them are trash, no matter whether they publicly subscribe to this or that ethical doctrine or none at all ... If we are to talk of ethics, I subscribe to a high ideal from which most of the human beings I have come across depart most lamentably.[8]

A leader's flaws are always eventually revealed. Mahatma Gandhi captures this no better than when he said,

> When I despair, I remember that all through history the way of truth and love has always won. There have been tyrants and murderers and for a time they seem invincible, but in the end, they always fall ... think of it, always.[9]

When we see someone in authority there is a pull to discount the authority within us. We can be "drawn into" inflating their personal power and role. At the same time, we often devalue our own. But this process can spiral to extremes. We project onto others our capacity to lead while we bury our own potential deep within our aura. But as we will describe in the final chapters of the book, the escalation stops when we are able to take back our projections. We grow as we begin to trust, have faith in, and follow our own heart. As this takes place, we are able to reasonably question the authority of others. We are also better able to honor our own admirable and evolving qualities of leadership.

Personal Mirror Reflection

How much do you see yourself as a leader? Do you often take a leadership role when the situation may call for one? What might inhibit you?

List three qualities or attributes that you look for in a leader, and write them below:

_____   _____   _____

Now take ownership for each of the qualities you have listed by completing the following sentence stem:

> "I have _____ (one at a time, insert each quality you listed above).

After you have inserted the quality, repeat the sentence stem three times before going on to the next quality. Amplify your voice each time you repeat the sentence.

What did you experience? How did you feel about taking ownership for each of the leadership qualities? What might this say about what you may have difficulty acknowledging in your self that may be contained in your aura?

Here are three other sentence stems that may help you connect with denied, dismissed, or discounted aspects of your own leadership qualities:

> In a group without a leader, I usually _____
> _____.
>
> When I take a leadership role I am afraid to _____
> _____.
>
> What a leader does for a group that I cannot do is
> _____.

In this chapter, we have looked at how we project the qualities of our aura into those we view as icons and leaders. These projections diminish our own talents and detract us from realizing our own leadership potential. When we downplay the attributes in our aura we deplete our vital and creative powers. Looking into the cosmic mirror allows us to see these projections more clearly. In doing so, we take the first step to reclaim the constructive qualities within us. We have seen how examining our cosmic mirror helps us better understand our relational life with friends, with family, with romantic partners, and with our own leadership potential. But the cosmic mirror also can help us better understand the way work groups behave. This is the subject of the next chapter. In it, we explore how the aura, shadow, and other cosmic mirror concepts operate in our work lives and in our professional careers.

11

The Cosmic Mirror in America's Work Groups

"Conformity is the jailer of freedom and the enemy of growth."

—*John F. Kennedy*

For a few years, we were consulting with a bank on their decision-making processes and on issues of staff development. Early on, we encountered a hostile conflict between the retail side of the bank and the commercial side. They were located in different buildings that were connected by a common corridor. In the connecting corridor, the retail side had established what they called "The Wall of Fame." It was here that photos were proudly placed of retail personnel whose service to customers was considered extraordinary. There was considerable antagonism between the departments, though. As corporate consultants, this was part of what we were being asked to address. The personnel from the commercial side referred to these wall photos as "The Wall of *Shame*." What message do you think this was indirectly expressing to the other work group?

Later in our work with the bank, we helped them start a program called the "WAVE." The bank executives named the program, because they liked the word and its image. The program was designed to help the bank change its own culture. One of the changes they wanted to make was to reduce interdepartmental conflict. Everyone wanted a way to deal with conflict more openly and constructively. In the first session, the employees were asked to use the word "WAVE" as an acronym to describe what they thought about the social climate in the bank. The retail side came up with, "Win by Achieving Visions of Excellence." The commercial side came up with "Why Antagonize Valuable Employees." As this acronym implies, feelings in any organization can go underground and then surface in indirect and distorted ways.

We have consulted with many schools, local governments, and corporations. And we have found that applying the cosmic mirror to the operation of their work groups has been quite helpful to them. It has enhanced their performance in powerful and pragmatic ways. As we discussed in the last chapter, the cosmic mirror is present in two-person relationships and within groups. It also occurs between groups. What one group sees in another group quite often is *itself*. To uncover these group-level projections within and between work groups, we use a simple mirroring technique. It consists of three questions:

1. "How do we see the other group?"

2. "How do we imagine the other group sees our group?"

3. "How do we see our own group?"

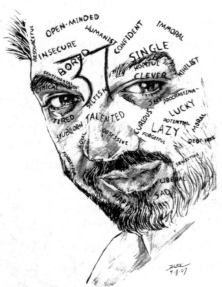

Derek Chatwood

What We See in Others Is Our Self

Without concern for artistic skill, each work group is instructed to respond to each question using both words and pictures. Each group is provided with their own space in which to work. And they are given large sheets of paper on which to record their responses—what we call their *group mirrors*. In creating their mirrors, each group is asked to avoid censoring or editing their responses in any way. When the groups are finished they are brought together to discuss what they have created.

The sheets of paper with their responses to each of the three questions resemble a canvas on which the group reveals its inner world. Each of the group's mirrors is then examined for symbols and themes used to describe their group and the other group. As each group presents their mirrors, they discuss what their words and pictures mean to them. This provides additional data to explore and clarify any themes and symbols contained in their verbal summary of their mirrors. These descriptions are crucial for uncovering their underlying meaning. That's because the meaning of the mirrors are not just in the drawings themselves. They also are in the personal meaning that the drawings have for the group members that created them. The group also is encouraged to explore how their mirrors of the other group(s) may actually reflect denied and projected issues of their own.

Figure 11a illustrates a set of group mirrors developed by one work group who named itself the "Red Hot Group." The workshop in which these mirrors were created was comprised of human resource managers and engineering managers. Each group had ten members.

In the first of the three mirrors—"How we see the Tea Party Group"—the Red Hot Group described the Tea Party Group. As you can see from figure 11a, they put only negative themes into their mirror. They use terms like "boring," "polite," "anxious," "restrained," and "intimidated." Initially, they did not want to admit the possibility that some of the issues that were represented in their image of the Tea Party Group could also be issues that may have been present in their own group. With further discussion, though, the Red Hot Group realized that boredom was also a significant issue in their own group. Because it was difficult for the Red Hot Group to see these issues inside their own group, they projected them into the other group. By placing these negative characteristics outside their group, it helped them avoid facing them. As long as their boredom was projected onto the Tea Party Group, the Red Hot Group would likely perceive the other group as boring—they would not be able to come to grips with their own boredom.

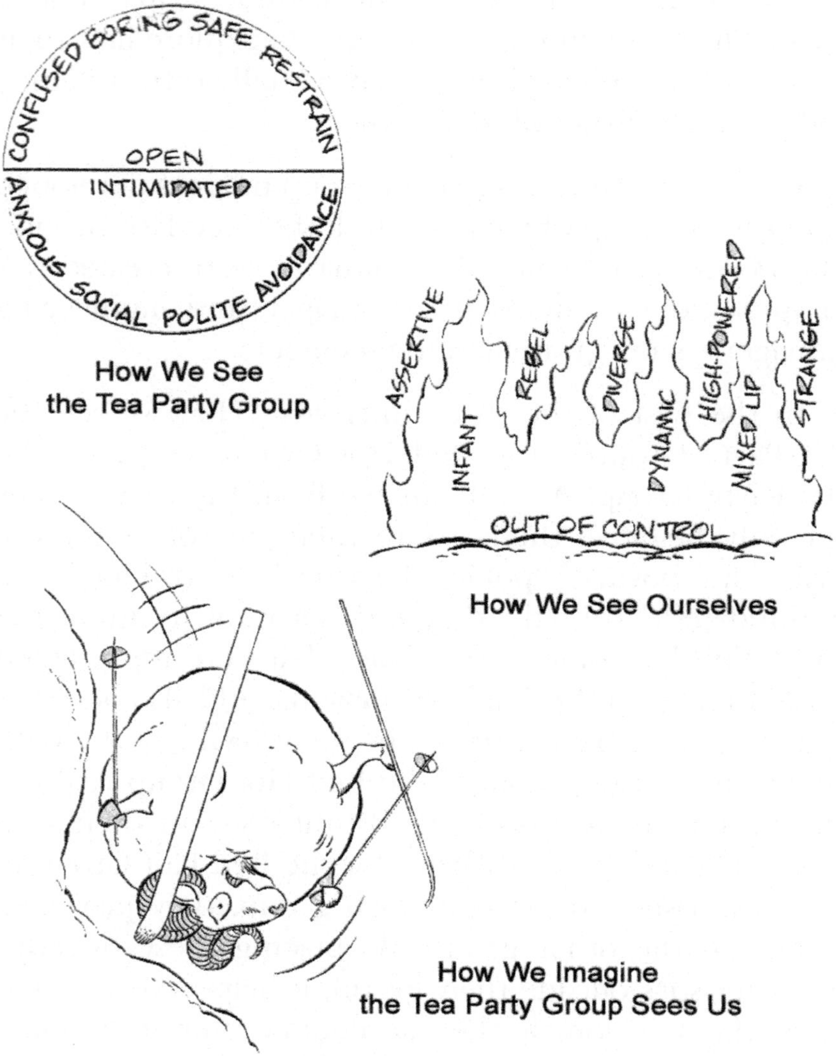

How We See
the Tea Party Group

How We See Ourselves

How We Imagine
the Tea Party Group Sees Us

Bob McLeod

Figure 11a: Mirrors from the "Red Hot Group"

Figure 11a also shows an image that contains words cast among flames. This is the Red Hot Group's portrayal of how they saw themselves. They described themselves as "vital," "passionate," and "without simple boundaries." They described themselves as "assertive." They viewed themselves as "high-powered." And they believed they were a "dynamic," "diverse," and "rebellious" group. When they presented this mirror, they were proud of themselves. They saw all the words they used to frame the experience of being in their own group to be characteristics of a progressive and well-developed group. Euphemistically, they boasted that they were "out of control," because they saw themselves as spontaneous and willing to take risks. Unlike the other group, they perceived themselves to be progressive and out of the "box".

The final panel of figure 11a shows how the Red Hot Group "imagined" the Tea Party Group would see them. The responses to this question are almost always loaded with projections that are hidden within the group's shadow. The Red Hot Group wanted to see itself as "energetic" and "vital." But later, they were able to reveal that they also feared being consumed by misdirected energy. They used the image of a fire to describe their energy and vitality. But when they thought about how the Tea Party Group perceived them, they imagined an icy snowball that was "out of control." They described the snowball careening down a hillside and overtaking skiers in its path. They later realized that the drawing signified their own fear of being out of control and being run over by members of their own group.

Group mirrors can be quite useful to identify strong emotional issues and bring them to the surface. This is especially true when a group is not able to acknowledge or express these issues in more direct ways. Unraveling the underlying meaning of group mirrors is a three-step process. It involves,

1. Drawing out the emotions and thoughts that group members associate with each image or word or phrase in the mirror,

2. Formulating possible interpretations of the emerging shadow and aura issues, and

3. Exploring further—after the mirrors are initially presented—any additional reactions of group members.

It is very important to recognize that the words and symbols do not have any meaning in and of themselves. They only hold meaning for the particular members of the group that created them. The mirror is a self-portrait designed by the group itself. It is a blank canvas on which the group members paint their own inner world. They project onto the canvas their heartfelt concerns. They project their shifting anxieties. And they project their felt faults and strengths. Their mirror is not something to be *externally* interpreted by others—it may not have universal meaning. When working with groups like these, the job of a consultant is to facilitate the group's own process of self-examination. It is not to impose an interpretation or process on them. Pulling a flower does not make it grow.

With that being said, we have found that there are recurring words, pictures, and symbols that do emerge across groups. And they can reveal the common struggles we all may share. These images are called *archetypes*. An archetype is a meaningful image that is common across groups, cultures, and even civilizations. An archetype is a kind of universal symbol. Sometimes we are aware of its meaning; sometimes not. Examples of archetypal images can be found throughout art, literature, and cinema. They include characters like *the wise-old man* (Obi Wan Kenobi and later, Yoda from *Star Wars*); *the shadow* (Darth Vader); *the trickster* (Bugs Bunny, Bart Simpson, or The Joker and The Riddler from *Bat Man*); and *the hero* (Indiana Jones or Spiderman).

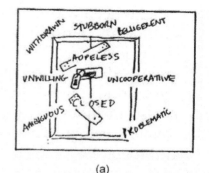

(a)

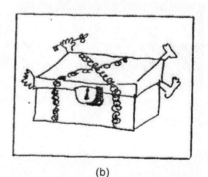

(b)

Bob McLeod

Archetypal Images

Objects can be archetypes as well. For example, a national flag, a mountaintop, a deep hole all stir up commonly held thoughts and feelings We have noted that common images have appeared in many of the mirrors we have seen drawn by work groups. For example, the "bolted door" and "being locked in a box" are images we have seen many times. To their artists, they often symbolize their own flaws and vulnerabilities that they may have difficulty acknowledging. Other archetypes we have seen are a fortress with no exit, a partly closed door, a dark cave, and rooms with no windows or doors.

The negativity cast into the shadow of the group is a shifting and murky pool. It takes on many forms. And like other polarities from within a group, it shows itself in the mirrors drawn by the group. To name a few possibilities, the shadow contains feelings of boredom, envy, and anger. It also includes feelings of hostility and despair. And it contains feelings of helplessness, confusion, competitiveness, and ineptness.

Sarah Pants

Loaded Perceptions

In the life of every group, there unfolds a never-ending sequence of polarities. These group polarities take on many forms, but they almost always can be seen in their group mirrors. A group may be able to acknowledge only one attribute of itself. But the presence of its antithesis or polar opposite attribute often lurks in the emerging group shadow. The group shadow is like a warehouse for polarities that are threatening. Members of a group may be aware of and prefer to see themselves as supportive. At the same time, though, they may block out the hostilities that exist among them. With these hostilities submerged in their shadow, two things then can take place: (1) they can be projected onto other groups or (2) the group can self-implode and find scapegoats within it. But with awareness of these hidden polarities, a group is less likely to act out their hidden shadow. In safeguarding against what will otherwise be inevitably and destructively acted out, the group can enhance its effectiveness and its sense of self-satisfaction.

The Harmony Illusion in Work Groups

Ethnic groups are often a fertile breeding ground for feelings of superiority. Whites may see themselves as better than blacks—and vice-versa. Americans are down-to-earth—Europeans are stuffy. The same is true in corporate work groups. The divide between "Union" and "Management" is a good example. A work group or a department may judge itself to be better than the rest. The Accounting Department may see itself as more important or more competent than the Human Resources Department—or vice versa. They may also judge others harshly by comparison. It's called an "in-group bias".[1] "We" are "good." "They" are "bad." But why does this take place?

From the perspective of the cosmic mirror, a group thinks of itself positively and other groups negatively in order to relieve itself of some of its own pain, discomfort, and fears of internal conflict. They do so by displacing these in-group tensions outside the outer boundary of the group. When they do this, the capacity for open dissension within the group seems like it's lessened. The group acts as if it has no real conflicts. It presents itself as if it is cohesiveness when it is not. The stronger the polarities in the group, the less the group is able to see its own negative attributes. And the stronger the polarities, the more likely the process of external projection becomes. Members of a group easily see the negativity in other groups—but not so easily in themselves. Similarly, group members easily see their own positivity. But they block themselves from seeing it in others, and their shadow is displaced. We call this the *harmony illusion*, and it is present when,

1. The group presents itself in exclusively or predominantly positive terms.

2. Other groups are portrayed in exclusively or primarily negative terms.

3. The group imagines that other groups see their group primarily in negative terms.

The harmony illusion can be seen in the group mirrors shown in figure 11b. These mirrors were drawn in one of our corporate workshops by a group who called itself the "Breaking Egg Group."

Let's first look at the egg drawn in the first panel of figure 11b. It was drawn in response to the question, "How do we see our group?" The Breaking Egg Group was asked what it meant, and they said it was a "positive image" of an "outstretched hand" emerging from an "egg shell." They were eager to admit that the emerging hand "symbolized" that they had "not learned everything" there was to know about their group—they were "still developing and growing." They did so, however, in a snobbish and haughty tone that they later revealed was an attempt to beat their critics to the punch by admitting they were not perfect. At first, the Breaking Egg Group saw themselves in strictly a positive light. A harmony illusion had developed.

After we worked with the group to process what they drew, they became aware of their cosmic mirror. Later, the group suggested that the human hand was not simply a positive symbol but was "caught" and reaching out of a "fragile" eggshell. They later said that the drawing also suggested feelings of vulnerability that they had previously denied. Some of the members admitted they were afraid

How We See Our Group

How We See the Moving Hand Group

How We See the Presidios Group

How We Imagine the Other Groups See Us

Figure 11b: Mirrors from the "Breaking Egg Group"

of "cracking up" or emotionally injuring other members who they viewed as fragile. After working through some of these feelings, The Breaking Egg Group also speculated that they were communicating something about their "fear of walking on eggshells" around each other. Later, in fact, a few group members took the risk telling others more details about these fears. When they did, they became aware that they had been concealing it not only from others but from themselves. The group then relabeled itself "The Assertive Group."

Now let's look at the cannons that are shown in the second row of figure 11b. They were drawn by the Breaking Egg Group in response to the question, "How do we see the Presidios Group?"—another group in the workshop. The Breaking Egg Group was asked what came to mind when they thought of cannons. When the mirror was first presented, they said that the cannons represented "battle lines" caused by "strong personalities." They described strong "male-female clashes," "aggressive and hostile humor," and "anger." Perhaps needless to add, they did not consider these descriptions to be flattering. The Breaking Egg Group believed that they had seen these negative qualities expressed in the Presidios Group. As you can see, no positive attributes were attached to the Presidios Group. This is another distortion inherent in the harmony illusion. As our discussion with the Breaking Egg Group progressed, though, they began to feel safer in talking about more deeply held feelings. As they did, they were able to acknowledge their fears about their own aggressiveness toward one another. They were able to see their own shadow and how they placed it in the other group.

You can also see how the Breaking Egg Group was hostile to another group in the workshop, the Moving Hand Group. This is shown in the second row of figure 11b as well. There, they negatively portray the Moving Hand Group as "teddy bears." They sarcastically name them "Snuggles & Cuddles." The

Massimo Merlini

The Budding Awareness of Our Mask

Breaking Egg Group described the teddy bears to mean that the so-called harmony specifically expressed by the Moving Hand Group was "too good to be true." When the Breaking Egg Group presented their drawing of the teddy bears, they accused the Moving Hand Group of presenting itself as if they were without conflict or without any problems. They saw them as "a bunch of wimps." The Breaking Egg Group was seeing in the Moving Hand Group what they could not yet see in themselves. They felt as if its members tried to come across as totally selfless and without conflicting opinions. In fact, the Breaking Egg Group accurately saw a great deal of underlying conflict in the Moving Hand Group. They stated that the Moving Hand Group was like "a pressure cooker ready to explode."

A strong polarity was clearly revealed. Initially, the Breaking Egg Group openly and pointedly labeled the two others groups as "their opposite." The Breaking Egg Group labeled the Presidios Group as the "Rambo Group." And they labeled the Moving Hand Group as the "Wimp Group." Once again, before they had a chance to fully process the splitting and the presence of the cosmic mirror, no positive attributes were associated with either of the other two groups.

The final row of figure 11b shows the Breaking Egg Group's response to the question, "How do the other groups see us?" It illustrates that they expected to be seen negatively by the other groups. As the Breaking Egg Group explained, a Joker is making an obscene gesture in response to attacks by the other two groups. They described the Joker as "impenetrable" and "uncaring." They also said that it was "unaffected" and "laughing." As the Breaking Egg Group was only later able to acknowledge, this represented some of the fears within their own group. Their fear was that their own members did not really care about each other. They also wondered if they had anything constructive to offer each other.

After working with them, the Breaking Egg Group began to disclose some of the contents from within their cosmic mirror. They saw that beneath their illusion of harmony was the fear of being mocked and ridiculed. They feared that they would be seen as "touchy-feely." For much of the workshop, members of the Breaking Egg Group found it very difficult to deal directly with either their conflicts or their tenderness. In the early stages of the workshop, the group used hostile humor. As we later learned, their hostility was unknowingly designed to distance themselves from painful feelings and conflicts that were stirred up within their group. We also later learned that several of its members had recently suffered serious personal losses. These were still painful and unresolved for them. As a result, the Breaking Egg Group had a difficult time dealing with their own and others' emotions.

They were mourning and felt fearful that they may be on the verge of tears.

In their mirror, the Joker holds a can of "Lite Beer." The Breaking Egg Group spoke of their initial desire to maintain a level of interaction with each other that was at a surface level. They wanted to relate to others in a way that was "not too heavy" or "not too serious." They needed to talk to each other in a way that was "not intimate" and "not threatening." The harmony illusion and the splitting of "good" and "bad" attributes in the Breaking Egg Group were clear. They initially perceived themselves only positively. They perceived the other groups negatively. And they imagined the other groups perceived their group negatively.

The Breaking Egg Group was readily able to see the conflict and the avoidance in the other two groups. But, eventually they became aware that the images they drew in their mirrors also described their own internal struggle. They feared that conflicts would arise in their own group. They also feared how close to one another they might become. They feared being too close; too intimate; and too caring toward one another. Their drawings highlighted the difficulties they were only later able to acknowledge. The Breaking Egg Group managed these challenging emotional issues by externalizing them onto the other groups. The hard (cannon) and soft (teddy bear) attributes in the Breaking Egg Group's mirror of the Presidios Group and the Moving Hand Group represented dynamics that were coming from within their own group. Once able to see and talk about this, they felt more bonded and became more productive than ever before.

Personal Mirror Reflection

If the opportunity is available to you, you can use the group mirror technique in your own work life. All it takes is two interacting work groups. For example, you could use it to explore similarities and differences in perceptions between an Accounting Department and a Marketing Department or a Research & Development Department and a Sales Department—any two organizational groups who interact with each other. The use of group mirrors can also be extended to explore similarities and differences in perceptions between any two or more groups that are categorically differentiated—men vs. women, Republicans vs. Democrats, or Americans vs. Arabs. Such applications are limited only by your imagination and ability to find people who are willing to participate in the exploration of similarities and differences.

The steps in implementing the group mirror technique are actually quite straightforward. Each of the groups works simultaneously to provide answers to the three group mirror questions: (1) How do we see the other group? (2) How do we imagine the other group sees our group? and (3) How do we see our own group? Each group is encouraged to avoid censoring their answers and encouraged to use symbols or drawings if they wish. Once each group has completed its set of group mirrors, the two groups meets and each group presents its mirror to the other group. Each group discusses its reaction to the other group's mirrors and to the mirror experience. Facilitators, consultants, or outside managers can be used to assist in the process and in the interpretation of the mirrors.

The Dynamics of Enemy-Making

"The Cold Within" is a poem written by James Patrick Kinney in the 1960s.[2] We found it taped to the wall of a classroom at Auburn State Prison. It reads as follows:

Six humans trapped by happenstance
In dark and bitter cold
Each one possessed a stick of wood,
Or so the story's told.

Their dying fire in need of logs,
The first woman held hers back,
For on the faces around the fire,
She noticed one was black.

The next man looking cross the way,
Saw not one of his church
And could not bring himself to give
The fire his stick of birch.

The third one sat in tattered rags,
He gave his coat a hitch,
Why should his log be put to use
To warm the idle rich?

The rich man just sat back and thought
Of the wealth he had in store,
And how to keep what he'd earned
From the lazy, shiftless poor.

The black man's face bespoke revenge
As the fire passed from sight,
For all he saw in his stick of wood
Was a chance to spite the white.

The last man of this forlorn group
Did naught except for gain
Giving only to those who gave
Was how he played the game.

The logs held tight in death's still hands
Was proof of human's sin,
They didn't die from the cold without,
They died from –THE COLD WITHIN!

The poem graphically describes the kind of social destructiveness that can occur when people are unwilling to look into the cosmic mirror. Each of the six characters sits around a dying campfire. Each of them is unwilling to look at themselves much less examine what it is that they are projecting into others. Aside from the cold outside of them that was overtaking the warmth of their burning fire, they died from the emotional coldness that was inside of them. The cold within them kept them from cooperating with others to keep the fire going. They died from their inability to see, understand, and use the reflections of themselves that were contained in one another. In essence, it was a group suicide.

As we discussed in Chapter 5, projection is an integral part of enemy-making. Furthermore, enemy-making occurs if there are fears, competitiveness, hostility, or other important issues and concerns that have not been fully discussed or worked through. Whatever might be going on, it is not uncommon for a group to find an enemy— either inside or outside of its ranks. The group does this as a way of avoiding and burying the concerns that are coming from within itself.

"Whatever we fight about in the outside world is also a battle in our inner selves."
—Carl Jung

An outside enemy serves as an emotional release for a group. It reduces the tension that is coming from within the group. It also functions as a means of avoiding conflict that may be present in the group. The enemy is a bull's eye (a mirror). Creating an enemy group is not healthy. But it makes it possible for the group—in the only way it knows—to manage its own internally generated and emotionally laden tensions.[3] When a group is caught in enemy-making, it polarizes itself from others. It sees itself as "good" and sees others as "bad." The group develops an "Us" versus "Them" or "We" versus "They" mentality. This form of splitting provides a container for their denied polarities. With this sharp polarization, the positive attributes become the social persona or mask of the group. At the same time, the negative attributes are buried in the group's shadow and projected outward.

A group selects and sustains an enemy group to maintain a positive view of itself. It also does so to protect itself from what it might fear. It also may choose more than one enemy with which to fight. It may fight with its enemy in an active way. Or it may fight in a quiet or passive way. In either case, within the enemy-making group lies a need to split and externalize the unacceptable parts of itself. That is to say, a critical mass of people from within the group has a need to cast their unwanted qualities outward. Groups often seem to need an enemy group to manage their internal ambivalence and contradictions. When a group looks at the "face" of its enemy, it also is looking at a reflection of its own shadow. As has been so graphically stated,

> So long as the enemy is seen as wearing the mask, which we have superimposed onto it, we inevitably must see a face we despise when we look upon the enemy. The enemy, in essence, wears our disavowed features: that is the psychic function of the enemy.[4]

In a similar vein, psychologist Sam Keen asserts,

> Since this process of unconscious projection of the shadow is universal, enemies "need" each other to dispose of their accumulated disowned, psychological toxins. We form an adversarial symbiosis of integrated systems that guarantees that neither of us will be faced with our own shadow.[5]

Over time, a group can become quite trapped in its own overly flattering mask or social persona. It might silhouette its own shadow onto an enemy group. The group's mask has two functions: (1) it helps maintain the group's idealized image of itself; and (2) it prevents the group's dark shadow from seeping into its awareness. By hardening its mask, the group keeps their disowned shadow attributes at what they believe is a safe distance—it implants them into the enemy group. But as humanistic psychologist Carl Rogers points out, this inevitably comes with a significant cost:

> In my relationship with persons, I have found that it does not help, in the long run, to act as though I were something that I am not. It does not help to act calm and pleasant when actually I am angry and critical. It does not help to act as if I had the answer when I do not. It does not help to act as though I were a loving person if actually I am hostile. It does not help to act as though I were full of assurance if actually I am frightened and unsure."[6]

When we are unable to see our own reflection in the cosmic mirror we *create* our enemies. In doing so, we become our own worst enemy. This is a primary reason that so-called mental health issues arise. Our negativity becomes trapped inside of us. We do not understand it. And we feel powerless to exorcize it. But even worse, we are sometimes told that our problems and internal conflicts are just "chemical imbalances," and we are persuaded to search outside of ourselves for the answer. This is a masquerade. And this is the subject of the last chapter on *Everyday Illustrations of the Cosmic Mirror*: "The Crazy Mirror."

12

The Crazy Mirror

"The sane are madder than we think; the mad are saner."

—Anthony Storrs

Many of us become quite frightened around someone who is paranoid. People who are paranoid are terrified that something or someone is out to harm them. Their fear is unmanageable. But why does someone who is paranoid alarm us? Although we might be cautious around someone who seems strange or different from us, we also might feel quite fearful of that person or with to remain distant from them. The cosmic mirror suggests that we may see in the paranoid the parts of ourselves that we fear. We may see the parts of ourselves that we do not know how to manage. We may see the parts of ourselves that we can't tolerate or that might frustrate us. And we may see the parts of ourselves that we feel might need "fixing up." We may also imagine seeing in the paranoid the secret parts that we fear others could find out about *us*. This is an example of what we call *the crazy mirror*—the assignment of emotional problems to others and the denial of emotional problems in ourselves.

Others who we label "mentally ill" are isolated—often physically—from main society. We don't often think about them. Consider many people's attitude about the homeless. Why is it that we try to put out of our minds the needs of those who are different from us? The crazy mirror suggests that in many ways, we are trying to lock away the parts of ourselves about which we feel fearful or ashamed— the parts of ourselves that we feel need "locking up" or need "incarcerating". When we see others struggling with emotional issues what we are most likely seeing is neither a "disease" nor an "illness" but a reflection of submerged parts of our self.

In the fourth century, Greek and Roman physicians believed that mental illness was an imbalance in the four basic substances or "humors" in the body. Blood-letting was a common treatment. During the Middle Ages, many thought mental illness was the work of the devil. Paracelsus, a sixteenth century physician, thought that it was caused by the cycles of the moon—he called it *lunacy*. In the eighteenth century, it was not unheard of for husbands to lawfully place their defiant but sane wives in lunatic asylums. In the nineteenth century, the first medical categories of mental problems were introduced. Slavery was justified by the notion that slaves suffered from mental diseases. In fact, in 1851, a psychiatric diagnosis was actually given to slaves who desired to flee from their bondage—it was called *Drapetomania*. In his now infamous article on the subject, Samuel A. Cartwright, a Louisiana physician, implausibly states,

[With] proper medical advice, strictly followed,
this troublesome practice that many Negroes
have of running away can be almost entirely
prevented.[1]

For much of the twentieth century, mental illness treatment
was dominated by theories that formed much of the
basis for the cosmic mirror. In the 1950s, though, the
use of medications, shock treatment, and other medical
interventions became more prominent in treating mental
distress. In fact, for the last thirty years, the American
Psychiatric Association has adopted the position that
"mental disorders are a subset of medical disorders."[2]
Is mental distress a medical illness? Certainly, mental
problems can be quite severe. And there is no doubt that
some categories of mental distress—like schizophrenia
or bipolar disorder—have a physiological component.
But, emotional stress makes the symptoms of all so-called
psychiatric illnesses worse. This idea is well accepted across
the medical community.[3]

Joan makes our point. Not too long ago, Joan's mother
died, and her normal period of bereavement did not resolve
her grief. Eventually, her emotional distress developed
into a serious depression. For years, Joan had dutifully
followed her mother's suggestions about important life
choices. She also had difficulty confronting her mother
when Joan disagreed with her. One day, Joan attended a
work meeting that was to focus on important issues in her
department. Her boss and her boss's boss were there—and
both forcefully stated their opinions. But Joan silently
disagreed with them. Joan wished that she could have
voiced her dissenting opinion. But, she was very aware
of the unspoken rule in her work culture: "Don't make
waves." So she kept quiet in the meeting.

She left the meeting more depressed than when she arrived. Her heightened depressive feelings were not caused by a medical condition. They were triggered by the feelings induced by the prospect of confronting someone in authority with whom she disagreed. Clinical depression is commonly viewed as a medical condition, but what Joan felt was not the result of a medical condition, an illness, or a disease. To say that Joan had an illness is like saying that the anxiety someone experiences after being assaulted is due to a medical cause. How can we better understand Joan's reaction to what happened in the meeting? What does the crazy mirror have to say about it?

Contained in what we are calling the *crazy mirror* are all the buried reflections of the self, acted out in ways that resemble symptoms of so-called mental illnesses. People hospitalized with psychiatric problems often display such symptoms. Some are admitted to drug and alcohol treatment programs. Many others are incarcerated in prisons. Do they have serious problems that need to be addressed? Yes, they do! Could medicines be helpful in their treatment? Yes, they could! Are they afflicted with mental *diseases*? We suggest that many, if not most, are not.

We believe that the word *disease* is an inappropriate metaphor for mental distress. A good example of the misuse of this term is the way that Alcoholics Anonymous uses it. They consider alcoholism a disease. AA's use of the term is helpful to their mission. It underscores the seriousness of the condition. But, they do not advocate for the use of psychiatric medicines in an alcoholic's recovery. They recognize that it is the fellowship of AA—the relationship with other members—that cures. It is here that AA's disease metaphor breaks down. In AA, it is universally recognized that it is the people who are involved in AA's activities—not medicines or physicians—who are crucial to an alcoholic's recovery.

If it isn't a disease then how does mental distress become so severe? Much of it stems from the impact that others have on us. One example of this is what family therapist Virginia Satir has called "family crazymaking". This occurs when a person buys into the idea that the impossible and contradictory demands of family members *must* be met. Consider a mother who constantly criticizes her young son for not showing displays of affection. Once he shows his affection toward her, though, she is distant or rejecting of him. This is a double-bind—no matter what he does, she will not be satisfied. Many boys in his position might begin to show early signs of depression, anxiety, or other mood problems. Is this boy suffering from a disease or medical illness? We think not.

"WHICH IS IT— DO PEOPLE HATE US BECAUSE WE DRESS THIS WAY, OR DO WE DRESS THIS WAY BECAUSE PEOPLE HATE US?"

In opposition to the medicalization of mental problems stands the *antipsychiatry* movement. Psychiatrist Thomas Szasz has been one of its leaders. Szasz argues that it is a myth to think of mental distress as an illness or a disease. For Szasz, "mental illness" is merely a pseudo-medical term that fosters a myth created by the medical community to label what he called the "problems of everyday interpersonal living."[4] For many years, though, among the mainstream psychiatric community, Szasz's views have been in disrepute.

"If you do not have compassion for yourself ... wholeness will escape you."

One of Szasz's harshest critics was Karl Menninger. Menninger was one of the most influential psychiatrists in America. He was founder of the Menninger Clinic, which is the largest psychiatric training facility in the world. During his time, Menninger spoke with the support and backing of almost the entire psychiatric community. In 1988, though, near the end of his life and looking back on his many experiences with psychiatric patients, Menninger wrote a historic letter to Szasz. In it, he renounced his own criticisms of Szasz's approach to psychiatry—criticisms Menninger, for years, had so forcefully and publicly expressed. With tenderness and regret, he proclaimed to Szasz,

> Long ago I noticed that some of our very sick patients surprised us by getting well even without much of our "treatment." We were very glad, of course, but frequently, some of them did something else even more surprising. They kept improving, got "weller than well" as I put it, better behaved and more comfortable or reasonable than they were before they got

into that "sick" condition. We didn't know why. But it seemed to some of us that kind of the "sickness" that we had seen was a kind of conversion experience, like trimming a fruit tree, for example. Well, enough of those recollections of early days. You tried to get us to talk together and take another look at our material. I am sorry you and I have gotten apparently so far apart all these years. We might have enjoyed discussing our observations together. You tried; you wanted me to come there, I remember. I demurred. Mea culpa.

The letter, in its entirety, and Szasz's response can be found in the Appendix.

Psychiatrist R. D. Laing has convincingly argued that the concept of "normal" can actually be pathological. He pointedly states,

What we call "normal" is a product of repression, denial, splitting, projection, introjection, and other forms of destructive action or experience. The condition of alienation, of being asleep, of being unconscious, of being out of one's mind, is the condition of the normal man.[5]

In a similar vein, sociologist and psychoanalyst Eric Fromm argued that there is a "pathology of normalcy." What he means by this is that sometimes entire cultures can be considered insane. Nazi Germany and Al-Qaeda might be examples. To try to adjust to an insane society would be pathological. Consider, how you might advise a woman living in Iran who comes to you for help to manage her desire to have a career. What would you say to her if she wanted to better handle her longing to be more open and freely speak to others? Her culture is certainly one that levies a heavy price on such desires. It considers them abnormal and even pathological. But would you judge her to have a mental illness to want such things? Philosopher and historian Michael Foucault has argued that the concepts of "sanity" and "insanity" are not medical terms. They are social constructs. They are not measurable patterns of human behavior. They are indicative of the power levied by the "sane" over the "insane."[6]

Mental problems are not medical illnesses. In 1973, psychologist David Rosenhan led two well-known field studies demonstrating this.[7] Eight sane assistants of Rosenhan's gained admission to twelve hospitals in five states complaining that they were hearing voices. Once they were admitted, they all stopped simulating symptoms of any kind. Each was told by their hospital that they would be discharged once the staff thought they were sane. While most of their fellow patients recognized them as impostors, none of the hospital staff did. All were eventually released. But some were not discharged until as long as fifty-two days after admission.

In a second study, Rosenhan falsely told staff members from other hospitals that they might be admitting one or more patients who would be normal but faking their symptoms. In fact, no one faking their symptoms was ever sent. Of 193 patients that were admitted during the following three-month period, though, 41 of them were believed by the staff to be normal. These two studies show the blurry boundary between people who have a so-called mental illness and those who are normal.

The Cosmic Mirror on the World Stage ...

In 2009, the Oscar for best actor in a leading role went to Sean Penn for his portrayal of Harvey Milk, gay rights icon and San Francisco Supervisor. In 1978, fellow councilman Dan White murdered both Milk and Mayor George Moscone. During the trial, White's lawyers offered the court the idea that the murders coincided with White's increased consumption of high-sugar and other junk foods. White was convicted of manslaughter, not murder, and served five years of his sentence before being released. White's lawyers argued that he suffered from *diminished capacity*, and the press dubbed it the "Twinkie defense."

The irony of the label is that Twinkies never appeared in the court transcripts. Nevertheless, the public has maintained the misperception that a physical phenomenon, akin to a sugar rush, explains White's cruel and despicable acts. The "Twinkie defense" is an example of the crazy mirror in action. Over the last 30 years, we have medicalized our explanations of aberrant social behavior.

Insistently attributing medical causes to explain cruel social actions does not make them accurate or true. From the perspective of the cosmic mirror, the cruel and inhumane treatment of others stems from buried reflections of the self, acted out in ways that mirror the darkness and cruelty contained within us. The film *Milk* depicts the troubled inner world of Dan White leading to his assassination of Moscone and Milk. In the film, Milk shares with others his intuition that White was secretly closeting from himself his denied inner fears and conflicts about his own homosexuality. White kills Milk, who is merely the outer representation of White's own shadow. This is the nature of the cosmic mirror—that we often project into the world what is denied within us. In Dan White, we clearly see the destructiveness of being unaware of the depth of our shadow.

Over the last thirty years, the American Psychiatric Association has classified people into medical categories of pathology.[8] If you have enough symptoms of depression in the APA system, then you have contracted depression. For the APA, mental disorders—such as depression—are considered to be merely a subset of medical disorders.[9] APA's current diagnostic system has many flaws. Symptoms excessively overlap different diagnoses. The diagnostic boundary between normal functioning and a mental disorder is arbitrary and unstable. And people with the same diagnosis vary widely in their symptoms.[10] One of the biggest problems with the APA's diagnostic scheme, though, might be called the "Rumpelstiltskin Effect". This is the illusion that by putting a name to a mental health issue, it implies that you know something about it.[11] When it comes to the diagnosis of a so-called mental illness, nothing could be further from the truth. Psychiatrist Hanfried Helmchen is considered an expert in assessing psychiatric diagnostic systems. In judging the systems used in Europe, Japan, Africa, the United States, and elsewhere, he states,

> The ultimate purpose of diagnosis is prognostic information and successful treatment of the individual patient. However, current diagnostic systems in psychiatry are far from serving this purpose.[12]

The idea is widespread in our society that problems with mood are diseases that call for a pill to treat them. The television airwaves are filled with commercials that push for it. There, you will find the boundless promotion of antidepressants to cure depression. These ads try to persuade. One recent ad states that of those who were taking antidepressants, 70 percent reported that some of their symptoms remained. The advertiser goes on to boast that their medication effectively addresses this problem. Regarding antidepressants, the facts are that when they do work, they do less than half the job. They are designed on the assumption that depression is caused only by a chemical imbalance. As the everyday examples we have offered show, depression is influenced by many other factors.

There is a vast amount of research that indicates that medications for depression, when used on their own, are no more effective than psychotherapy.[13] There has also been a great deal of research on anxiety medications. And it shows that medications for anxiety are *less* clinically effective and *less* cost effective than psychotherapy.[14]

But the psychiatric community and the pharmaceutical manufacturers promote the notion that depression and anxiety are illnesses that only something outside of us—like a pill—can cure. We call this *the magical illusion of healing.*

The magical illusion of healing refers to the excessive and unwarranted belief that something outside ourselves can exclusively heal our emotional wounds without us needing to take the necessary actions *on our own* to assist in the healing process. Many of us adhere to an excessive—sometimes exclusive—loyalty and devotion to a form of healing that can only come only from outside of ourselves. It is based on an assumption that it is not necessary to fully search inside of us for the things that we want and for the answers that we seek. The magical illusion of healing denies our faith in the talents within us. Here is a story—perhaps familiar to you—that illustrates this point. A minister tells his parishioner,

> You know, you remind me of the man that lived by the river. He heard a radio report that the river was going to rush up and flood the town—and that all the residents should evacuate their homes. But the man said, "I'm religious. I pray. God loves me. God will save me."
>
> The waters rose up. A guy in a row boat came along and he shouted, "Hey, hey you! You in there. The town is flooding. Let me take you to safety." But the man shouted back, "I'm religious. I pray. God loves me. God will save me."

A helicopter was hovering overhead. And a guy with a megaphone shouted, "Hey you, you down there. The town is flooding. Let me drop this ladder and I'll take you to safety." But the man shouted back that he was religious, that he prayed, that God loved him and that God will take him to safety.

Well ... the man drowned.

And standing at the gates of St. Peter, he demanded an audience with God. "Lord," he said, "I'm a religious man, I pray. I thought you loved me. Why did this happen?" God said, "I sent you a radio report, a helicopter, and a guy in a rowboat. What the hell are you doing here?[15]

The magical illusion of healing is different from faith and trust. Faith and trust in someone or something outside of ourselves is often useful. In fact, in the next section of the book, we will talk about how the faith and trust we place in others helps us know and heal ourselves. We cannot narcissistically believe that we have all the answers—there is more to relationships than seeing them as mirrors. Encouragement from others is life-affirming. We learn from the inspiration that we get from others. It is important to look outside of ourselves for the things that are not revealed in the cosmic mirror. We cannot live as islands. We *do* need others. Others *can* inspire us. But what often accompanies the belief that something outside of us can heal our emotional wounds—a pill, a lover, a guru—is the belief that we cannot guide ourselves to heal those wounds—that we cannot embark on our own on a search to find the answers that lie within us.

The magical illusion of healing has been practiced by shaman, priests, witchdoctors, medicine doctors, and other healers for thousands of years. It still is. It is present when a person expects a healer to cure them purely by virtue of their special powers.[16] While not what it seems, this can result in real changes in those who are under its influence—and it can take many forms. An Evangelical parishioner with cancer asks their minister to perform a "laying on of hands." A Catholic priest performs an exorcism on someone who is believed to be possessed by the devil. A troubled Haitian visits his witchdoctor who kills a chicken to heal their soul. A patient with marital problems asks their physician for an antidepressant. A Siberian tribesman asks his local shaman to perform a ritualistic dance to heal the grief over the death of his son. When it occurs, some of this healing relates to what in modern medicine is referred to as the "placebo effect".

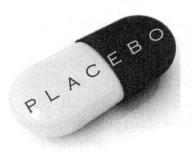

Before a drug is approved for use, it must be tested. And to show that the drug is effective, it must be tested in what's called a "placebo-controlled" study. In this type of study, the effectiveness of the drug is compared to a placebo (or sugar pill). This is done, because inevitably, the control group of people who take the sugar pill almost always improves. They get better because they *believe* they will get better. And this happens because people are very suggestive.

The documented evidence of the placebo effect is substantial. Here's an example. In a widely cited set of studies, people with bleeding peptic ulcers were given injections of distilled water. They were told it was a new drug that could cure them. Seventy percent of these patients improved. Some of the patients feared drugs, though, or did not trust doctors. These patients suffered severe nausea and diarrhea to the injections of water.[17] In a 2010 study published in the Journal of the American Medical Association, it was found that placebos were only about 3% less effective in treating depression than commonly prescribed antidepressants.[18]

Here's another example of the crazy mirror. At some point in almost every effective psychotherapy, *transference* issues must be given some attention. In the transference, the client feels compelled to act out unresolved emotional conflicts with their therapist. It's normal. And good thera-

The Unseen Transference

pists expect it. Therapists cannot always be perfectly "in tune" with their clients. At some point, the therapist will disappoint their client, if even in just a small way. At that point, the client then sees the therapist as someone who is similar to others in their past who may have disappointed them. In other words, through the process of projection the past is transferred into the present. The therapist then becomes a here-and-now mirror that reflects the client's unexamined and unresolved issues from their past.

Clients learn that working through transference issues with their therapist can be very helpful to them. To do so allows them to work through similar problems that they may have had with others in their life. Resolving issues from within the transference is a critical juncture in therapy. It is here that the client's wishes and fears about the therapist are carefully examined. These feelings are given a voice. When a therapy client gives a voice to their own thoughts and feelings it is therapeutic to them. Examining issues within the transference also helps the client better understand how their thoughts and feelings in the here-and-now relate to unresolved conflicts from their past. Most importantly, the client can learn how to better accept all of their feelings—even the ones that they may be afraid of. They do this by working through these thoughts and feelings with the therapist in the here-and-now. They learn how to constructively work through them and how not to fall prey to them.

This is a very powerful moment in the therapy, because the feelings and experiences are right there in the therapy room. They do not need to be described or retold from the client's experiences outside the session. The power of understanding the transference is huge. It comes from the client's experience that another human being really wants to know them. They realize that someone else wants to help them work through separating what is real from what is merely a projected reflection of their cosmic mirror.

Here's an illustration of this. For many years, Kathi had been a faithful and loving wife to Harold. But she was getting sick of her husband's demands. She knew she was too accommodating to Harold's insecurities. If she were more than five minutes late coming home, he began to panic. When she finally arrived, he scolded her for being late or for not calling. He expressed to her how worried he was that something bad had happened to her. She could not leave the house without informing him where she was going and when she would be back. He might call her ten times while she was out to see if she was safe. He insisted that she go to bed when he did. If she wanted to go to bed earlier he pleaded with her to stay up with him. Kathi humored him by being polite, but the truth was that Harold's behavior it was burdensome to her. She couldn't tolerate it any more. So she began to assert herself.

The more Kathi asserted herself, though, the more intensely angry and fearful Harold became. She loved her husband. But she was clear, nevertheless, that his demands were his own issues—not hers. She told him, point blank, that she could no longer live with it. To save his marriage, Harold sought professional help. He first went to his family physician for medication. The doctor felt, though, that he might be helped from psychotherapy, so he referred Harold to a therapist the doctor had worked with before. Her name was Maude.

Maude was quite experienced. She also was generally regarded as a warm and open person. Early on in his therapy, though, Harold expressed to her,

> I am thinking about dropping out of therapy with you. I am not sure I really need it. I also find you to be rather distant, remote and cold. I realize you are only in this for the money and that you really could care less about me other than as a source of income. You never call me or hug me. You also never start our sessions early, even when we both are here. I very much dislike being here with you.

Harold was in the midst of a transference relationship with Maude. He was seeing Maude like his wife—as a woman who was unwilling to accommodate to his needs. Examining it from another perspective, Harold was looking for the magical illusion of healing. He wanted something outside of himself that could defeat his insecurities. Having been coddled and pandered by Kathi for many years, he avoided owning up to his own fears. He did not take responsibility for understanding them and addressing them on his own. In her own gentle but skilled way, though, Maude suggested to Harold that what he wanted from her was similar to what he wanted from Kathi. At first, the stark comparison initially shocked him; so he dismissed it. But in time, he became aware that it had some truth to it.

As his therapy progressed, Harold began to speak about his longings and his intense wish that his wife could satisfy them. He told Maude of his longstanding fears that his wife might desert him. He also feared that Maude might not want to work with him in therapy, once she learned about the extent of his problems. He explained to her just how much his feelings of abandonment swelled out of control when he found himself alone in a room without his wife. He felt that he could not be without her, and he was ashamed it. He was ashamed of his dependency, and he looked to his wife to take care of it for him.

If Maude, like his wife, was not going to meet Harold's needs it was understandable why he might not want to continue therapy. And Maude told him that. Reflecting on his own life, Harold began to talk about a subject he had long put out of his mind. He talked about his parents' divorce when he was seven and his longstanding fears that his mother might abandon him like his father did. Harold told Maude how terrifying it was for him going to bed after the divorce. His room seemed so far away from his mother's. For Harold, this was a turning point in therapy. His fears of abandonment had now surfaced and could be dealt with more directly. Maude told him how they could use this insight to better understand his urge to drop out of therapy. His urge to reject Maude arose because he feared that she, like his mother or father, might abandon him. As Maude put it, "Why risk getting close to someone who might leave you?"

Hearing this, Harold began to weep from a depth he never did before. It was strange to him. He felt crushed, but he also felt relieved to experience these feelings. Translated into the language of the transference, Harold's earlier statement to Maude about dropping out of therapy can be rewritten to read,

> Mom (Maude), I am terrified you will leave me. I can't bear to think about how much I need you. But, I also found you so distant, remote, and cold. I always felt you disliked me. And I feared that I wasn't good enough for you to take care of me—that you only stayed with me for the money you got from child support. When I am not in your arms I worry if I can survive. I hate needing you so much. I wish I could be a big boy and take care of myself.

Harold was anxious and depressed, but he did not have a mental illness. His answer did not lie outside himself. He did not need to seek relief in a pill. To describe Harold's anxious and depressive dependency as a mental illness is to overlook its real nature. To say that Harold had a mental disease prevents us from unraveling the relevance of his relationships—both past and present—to his current struggles. From the perspective of the cosmic mirror, Harold's denied shadow and aura were being revealed. His wish that someone or something outside of himself could save him—like his wife, his mother, or a pill—was a magical illusion of healing. Until he wept with Maude, he had felt unable to sit alone with his feelings. His fears of being alone and away from his wife were thinly veiled in his fears that something bad might happen to her if she were not at home on time. His fears also represented part of the unacceptable set of feelings from within his shadow, which initially, he felt unable to share with Maude.

Discussing the feelings that are contained in the transference can bring an enormous amount of insight to a client. This cannot be understated. And the failure to openly discuss feelings from within the transference can lead to needless and unwelcome results. Coyne Campbell was former head of the Department of Psychiatry at the University of Oklahoma School of Medicine. When he was in medical school, though, as part of his own training, Campbell himself was required to be a client in therapy. His analyst was a senior staff member in the department. Campbell describes his experience in one of his sessions in the following way:

> One of the most distressing and annoying incidents in my training analysis was my detection of a horrible stench while lying on the coach. It was unbearable, but the analyst denied emitting flatus, though with quite evident embarrassment. At that stage, the transference (hypnotic) relationship was so prevailing, that I accepted his denial, in spite of the evidence of my own nose. This brought on a strong fear that I suffered an olfactory hallucination, known to me as a serious symptom of damage to a brain lobe.[19]

With too much reverence for his therapist, Campbell was fooled into mistrusting his own perceptions. It was his therapist's shame that was getting projected into Campbell. Because he believed that it wasn't discussable, it became buried in Campbell's shadow.

A client can imagine that the therapist is feeling something that the therapist is not feeling. Likewise, the therapist can vividly imagine that the client feels something that the client does not. This is called *countertransference*. While the therapist is a mirror for the client, the client is also a mirror for the therapist. Countertransference arises when a therapist emotionally overreacts to something that has happened in a session. The feelings that arise in the therapist become exaggerated and often are unmanageable

Countertransference Rage

to them. It occurs if the therapist has issues of his own. It also occurs when the feelings of the client are induced in the therapist. In this instance, the therapist begins to take on some of the client's feelings as his own. Sometimes therapists are aware of this process—sometimes not.

A humorous but clear example of countertransference is nicely portrayed in the film comedy *What About Bob?* In the film, Dr. Leo Marvin puts his patient, Bob Wiley, in the hospital, because Marvin can't handle Bob's intrusion into Marvin's vacation. The rest of Marvin's family loves

Bob and can't see what all the fuss is about. Later in the film, in an attempt to finally rid himself of Bob, Dr. Marvin straps dynamite to him. Marvin explains to Bob that it is "Death Therapy." This is an obvious example of a therapist having his own issues and over-reacting to them. But let's now consider a much more common example of countertransference.

A therapist begins seeing a client who is mildly depressed. The client begins talking about her sense of isolation. The conversation then begins to trigger feelings in the therapist about his own marriage. But these feelings are unknown to him—the therapist is overwhelmed by these feelings, but he cannot identify them as his own. He cannot see how they might relate to the distance and isolation he feels in his relationship with his own wife. When his client has car trouble on her way to her next appointment, the therapist flounders. She is late, and she has not called. Overwhelmed, he mistakenly believes she may be suicidal. Acting out on his fears, he calls her in a panic, thinking she may be in danger.

From the perspective of the cosmic mirror, this therapist has projected his own emotional issues out onto his client. He has not yet looked into his own cosmic mirror. The fears and isolation that are getting denied in him become something he believes he perceives in his client. His perceptions are distorted—the therapist is having an unmanageable set of reactions to his client that stem from his feelings about his wife. His feelings are persistent. They are intense. And they are disrupting his work life. Might the therapist be depressed? Perhaps. Does his condition constitute a mental illness or a disease? We think not.

From the perspective of the cosmic mirror, the therapist's feelings of anguish and helplessness for his client stem from his marital relationship. They are buried within his own shadow and are unavailable to him. As a result, they can't be managed in a direct or healthy way. Instead, they are projected into his client. He places his own dependency into his client in a form he perceives is her denied aura—that is, he believes she cannot take care of herself. Although it was distorted the therapist uses his client as a mirror of himself. He doesn't know it, though. He is blinded by the image within his cosmic mirror. Of course, once the therapist sees what is really going on, he can look into the mirror and discover what he is projecting. He can then access and repair more directly his own feelings of detachment and disconnection from his wife—and not act it out with his client.

Personal Mirror Reflection

Because we live in a culture where mental health symptoms are medicalized, most of us have at least some inclination to take a pill to remedy our problems. We might take vitamin pills to compensate for not regularly eating enough fruits and vegetables rich in natural vitamins and minerals. We might take an over-the-counter sleep aid because we may not show enough discipline to maintain a regular sleep schedule. We might even maintain a regimen of taking an antidepressant medication but avoid going to see a psychotherapist to address the underlying psychosocial causes.

Take a minute to consider how you might seek out your own magical illusions of healing. Are you taking medicines to address issues for which other solutions are available? How often do you find yourself doing this? What other solutions might be available to you? How much are you relying on other people or products for solutions that may be available to you by looking within yourself?

In this second section of the book, we have provided examples of many of the ways that the cosmic mirror can be seen in our everyday lives. But to see something and to do something about it are two different things. To look *into* the cosmic mirror does not tell us how to look *behind* it. But take heart. Everything starts with awareness. Now that we have looked at some of the ways that the cosmic mirror takes form, it is time to use this knowledge to make the needed and constructive changes we all want for ourselves. How do we do this? This is the subject of the last section of the book: *Reparation and Healing*.

Reparation and Healing

13

Seeing Through the Mirror Darkly

*"There is no light without shadow and no psychic wholeness
without imperfections. To round itself out, life calls
not for perfection, but for completeness."*

—Carl Jung

It takes another person or object to see our self clearly.
This is one of the most important principles of the cosmic
mirror. The fact that we can see our self in others is an
invaluable tool for reclaiming our disowned parts. In our
quest to take back the lost parts of our self, we evolve
toward an ever-greater sense of completeness. But what
does it take to become more aware of our emerging
shadow and aura? How do we accomplish this? We first
must identify the reflection of these central elements in
those who populate our interpersonal world.

To some extent, we are all in a state of bewilderment.
As the Apostle Paul said in Corinthians I 13:12, "For now

we see through a glass, darkly; but then face to face: now I know in part; but then shall I know even as also I am known." To find our shadow and aura is awkward. It's uncomfortable. It's not easy to learn a new skill. From our vantage point, though, this discomfort is a relatively small cost to pay for the benefits we can reap from developing our ability to identify, acknowledge, and express our full range of emotions. This can awaken us to ourselves in a much more complete and fulfilling way.

"You need other people in order to become yourself."
—*Heinz Kohut*

To varying degrees, we are all asleep to knowing our full self. We blind ourselves to our own awakening through our words and through our actions. For example, if you come from a family that did not openly hug one another then learning to embrace another person with a hug can initially be an awkward experience. Do I ask them if I can give them a hug? Do I just do it without asking? Where do I put my hands if she is a woman? Where do I put my hands if he is a man? How long do I hug them? How do I end the hug? With continued experience, though, these questions are answered. In time, the whole hugging process becomes spontaneous and flows smoothly without us thinking about it. But we first must risk getting started.

The illustrations shown in figures 13a, b, and c show how we come to terms with the shadowy parts of ourselves. In figure 13a and 13b, our shadow can be relatively small. But as a consequence of denial, avoidance, and neglect, it increases in size and power. Like the characters in figure 13c, we, too, can become aware of our growing shadow. We can acknowledge it in a way that increases our wholeness. Looking through the mirror darkly, we can decrease our fear of what we imagine is monstrous within us.

Figure 13a: Denial and Awareness of the Shadow

Figure 13b: Fleeing and Confronting the Shadow

Cruelty Envy
Greed Anger
Lust Hostility

Figure 13c: Recognizing and Accepting Our Shadow

To identify and acknowledge the submerged parts of us is a necessary step to experience greater unity with ourselves and others, It also allows us to begin to heal our divided self. By doing so, we develop our capacity for intimacy. We also are able to more creatively manage our internal experiences. And we can find a greater ease in expressing our thoughts and feelings. To acknowledge or to take ownership for how we are actually experiencing our world leads to the resolution of our stress of living in that world —this is called *the paradoxical theory of change.* The theory states,

> Change occurs when one becomes who he is,
> not when he tries to become what he is not.[1]

What this means is that we often vacillate between who we think we *should* be and who we *are*. Unsure of who to be, we torment ourselves with incessant vacillation. We make tradeoffs. We settle. We never fully become who we are or who we can be. We get caught up in trying to become what others want us to be—never acknowledging the fullness of our self. We try to become an image of our self rather than spontaneously being our self as it unfolds.

From the perspective of the cosmic mirror, the goal is to recognize and accept both our aura and our shadow. This, of course, is not easy. Larry Hirschhorn, an expert on the submerged culture of organizations, captures this idea well when he states,

> Although people labor to avoid anxiety by splitting their consciousness and by projecting their bad feelings onto others, they also wish to restore their own sense of wholeness. But to do so, they must take back their projections and therefore see others (and themselves) as whole or real people who are both good and bad.[2]

If we continue to do what we have always done in our lives and in our relationships, our results will be the same. There will be no change in our life. Like a music CD that is stuck on one groove, we will play the same phrase of our lives over and over. To make constructive changes in our lives, we must take the risk to explore new ways of being with ourselves and others. It's difficult. But it's the only way we can change the world we inwardly and outwardly experience.

How do we accomplish this kind of reparation and pull ourselves out of a life pattern where the avoidance of anxiety has been the primary goal? Realistically, it takes a significant amount of emotional work. It requires examining our own vulnerabilities. It takes ownership in our daily lives for living out our whole self. In reality, all of us are truly mixed blessings—we all have both a shadow and an aura.

Moving Beyond Projections

The Breakfast Club is a humorous film about adolescent maturity. It also conveys a powerful message about the fundamental process of denial, reparation, and integration of the shadow and aura parts of the self. In the movie, five students from Shermer High School attend a compulsory day of school on Saturday. They are each being punished for their bad behavior. There are five main characters in the film who are initially stereotyped as "The Brain," "The Basket Case," "The Athlete," "The Princess," and "The Criminal." In the beginning of the film, each is portrayed within their own rigid persona.

The Breakfast Club has enduring appeal because it captures a microcosm of our society. It's a mirror of our world portrayed in miniature. Each character is an archetypal image from within our culture. Each character has their own vulnerabilities and their own defensive walls around them. By the end of the film, though, each of the students becomes comfortable enough with one another and with themselves to put down their protective walls. Each of them reveals the things they feel proud of and the things that they are ashamed of. By doing so, they allow themselves to show who they really are—eventually blossoming into more complete and balanced people. They allow their classmates to see a more complete picture of themselves. But they also attain insights into their own very human characteristics— qualities that they all have in common but have felt fearful to share.

At the close of the film, the group is asked to write an essay for the detention teacher. They are to explain what they have learned about themselves during their detention day. "The Brain" volunteers to write it. In his brief summation of their experience, he explains that while the teacher will see them as he wants to see them, contained in each one of them are attributes of a brain, a basket case, an athlete, a princess, and a criminal. In the course of their Saturday detention, each character moves beyond their own limited image of themselves. They discover in themselves a more complete and whole person. In effect, they take back the projections that they had placed into one another. By doing so, they transcend and move past their own contrived personas. They move from being five individuals to become "The Breakfast Club." They replace the distant remoteness that they felt from one another with a closeness that they could not have imagined they could experience.

But old life scripts from our childhood die hard. We bury them over layers and layers of defenses. Then we unknowingly act those scripts out. Letting go of old life patterns takes time, effort, persistence, and courage. At the same time, it means allowing change to emerge on its own and in its own time. It takes doing the best we can. And it takes using others as mirrors to understand ourselves.

We must be willing to risk delving deeply into our denied polarities for they have much to tell us about ourselves. Words alone are insufficient to describe the difficulty and complexity of this task. To truly know the actual process necessitates that we experience it. There's an astonishing paradox in all this, though. Our avoidance of self-knowledge is the greatest when we most need to examine ourselves. We tend to avoid examining our feelings when we are most frustrated, most bored, most fearful, most angry, or most sad. Yet, it is precisely at these moments when our greatest insights can be revealed. These feelings are the birth pains of the unknown parts of ourselves that are entering our consciousness for the first time. Growth and reclaiming submerged parts of our self are not about feeling comfortable. They are about learning different ways of being.

Our past can no longer be managed. But often, it manages us. This is especially true when we are unaware of its influence in our current life. The following event took place in one of our personal growth workshops and illustrates this point. Steve was the Research Director at a large pharmaceutical firm. Throughout the workshop, he would become irritated when Richard (another participant) would get up and start walking around the room or go into the nearby kitchen. The next time Richard went to the kitchen, Steve became livid with him. He told the group that he disliked Richard moving around all the time and felt it was disrespectful. Steve was asked if he would like to try a brief experiment that might help him understand his anger with Richard. When Steve agreed, he was asked to close his eyes.

Following his intuition, the facilitator loudly said, "Steve, don't you dare move; sit there and don't move." Steve flashed to a memory of his grandmother punishing him. She was making him sit in a chair and look out the window at other kids playing outside. Steve then began to realize just how much this past incident—and incidents like it—were affecting him in the present moment. He then began to talk about just how much this image had stuck with him over the years. He recalled how he envied those children playing outside and how angry he was with his grandmother. He felt she had been unfair.

Steve then began to think about how, in so many ways, he was "paralyzed" in his life—how "stuck" he felt. It occurred to him how much he felt as if he were unable to move with the freedom he so envied seeing in Richard. This was a powerful moment for Steve. He became acutely aware just how much these polarities—constraint and freedom—that he had tried to push out of his mind were being triggered by his relationship with Richard. He grasped more than ever just how pervasive his reactions to these polarities really were in his daily life.

Personal Mirror Reflection

As with Steve, how we associate our current experience to past events can help us see our own darker reflections. Here's another way we can tap into it. Imagine a boss, named Chris, who is unhappy with a subordinate of theirs. Imagine that Chris feels as if their subordinate cannot do anything right. To deal with their subordinate, Chris reprimands and incessantly criticizes the person. What do you think of Chris's strategy? If you were Chris's boss, what might you have to say about it? Imagine you have scheduled a meeting with Chris. What would you tell Chris about their actions? Think about this a minute and write out what you would say before you read on.

Many groups of people have been told this same story, and they have been asked these same questions. Almost universally, they will find fault, put down, or condemn the boss. How did you respond? Those same groups of people then have been asked a key question that we now are going to ask *you*: "Are you doing to the boss what you are concerned the boss was doing to their employee?" For those who have had this scenario posed to them, this last question usually has led to an eye-opening moment. It usually highlights a disparity between how we may "*talk the talk*" and how we may "*walk the talk*."[3] This is an example of how we unknowingly find others around us into whom we project our own disowned negativity. We often do this despite our intent to do otherwise.

"I CAUSE ANXIETY? BUT I HAVE ANXIETY."

Jerry had been part of the sales force since the start-up of the company. He was a showoff. And too often, he ranted or threw tirades. But these were some of the very qualities his bosses liked. Jerry wasn't timid; he'd speak his mind; he was passionate; and he wouldn't succumb to group pressure when he felt he was right but outnumbered. When he was promoted to be the regional manager, though, the very same characteristics that served him well as an employee were troublesome to those he managed. He was autocratic when he made decisions—refusing his employees the chance to take part. Moreover, his aggressive style was grating to them. They saw him as an arrogant, rigid, and stubborn manager. With all his experience, though, Jerry knew the technical aspects of his job. This was undeniable. What he didn't know, though, was how others were his mirrors.

After some "coaching" sessions, Jerry began to disclose a fear that had been with him for some time—that he would be "walked on" by his new subordinates. He wasn't about to be bowled-over by people who could take his new job or show him up. As he put it, "I've fought too hard to get to where I am. I'm not about to lose it!" Jerry's primary fear was that his bosses would disapprove of him. And in the course of his coaching sessions, he realized how he was using others to contain this fear. He became aware that what he was doing to his workers was what he feared his bosses would do to him. He also realized how he had denied and cast off into the abyss his own gentle personal power and confidence.

Jerry worked hard and put a considerable amount of emotional effort into his coaching sessions. Because of this, he was able to take the biggest risk of his career. He was able to ask his bosses for their reassurance. He knew this was what he needed from them. Once they told him that they had faith in him, he was able to put a stop to his autocratic style. Once he realized that his bosses liked him and believed in him, he was able to reconnect with the benevolent power and confidence within him.

When we work with clients in our consultations and in our workshops we often ask them to write interpersonal feedback to others. This turns out to be a useful way for clients to look into their cosmic mirror, especially in their relationships where they are experiencing a strong negative or strong positive emotional charge. It's less important that the feedback is actually delivered. What's more important is that the person who writes it has a chance to use what is written to look more closely at themselves. We suggest that they formulate their feedback using the following four questions:

1. How do you experience the other person's behavior?

2. What issues within the other person do you believe are troubling them?

3. What do you see as strengths in the other person?

4. What would you like to encourage the other person to explore in future interactions with you?

We suggest that they write their feedback like a letter. We want them to speak from the heart. We ask them not to censor or edit in any way what they have to say about the person.

First, we ask that they write the feedback to the other person. Then, we ask them to go through it and circle or check the things they feel may also be true about themselves. Because projections are rarely on a blank screen, the chances are pretty good that the other person has the quality being attributed to them. But, the feedback written to the other person almost always says something about the person who is writing it. When we find someone's behavior difficult to handle, it often speaks to something about us that we may find difficult to acknowledge. When we examine our own feedback to others it is a useful way to look for the reflection of our inner self. This can be a very useful vehicle for reclaiming disowned attributes. And it can lead to repairing bruised or damaged parts within us.

Gary was a mentor to George. He helped him develop his skills as a group facilitator. At the three-year mark in their working relationship, Gary began to see some unusual behavior from George. And it concerned him. So he wrote the following feedback to him:

> George, you have developed many wonderful and constructive skills for facilitating groups. I am concerned, though, that in your style, you have become too much like me. Several participants have commented to me that your voice, body posture, and interventions seem to be just a copy of me. I was startled when you bought that new belt, the one with the sailboat inclinometer buckle, and I asked you where you had seen it before. You didn't realize that it is the same one I wear almost all the time. I worry that you have become too dependent on me. I also find myself a little disappointed that you have not yet developed your own style. So I think, maybe, you need to go out on your own to find it.

At the time he wrote his feedback, Gary was going through a major transition in his work life. He was about to take early retirement from a long and successful career at a university. Although the change was desirable for him, he also was much more nervous about it than he wished to acknowledge. While he knew that his feedback was intended with George's best interests in mind, he also was aware that he had developed a rewarding friendship with George. He was somewhat surprised that he was suggesting to George that they go their own ways.

There was some accuracy in what Gary wrote about George. But he also realized that some of what he wrote in his feedback also could be applied to himself. It was then that Gary took better ownership of his written feedback. He began to consider the symbols and phrases that he used in it. He used words like "being too much like me," "the belt," "being dependent," and "finding your own way." So he reflected on these elements. He especially looked at how it reflected his own hidden shadow and aura. He decided not to give his feedback to George until he could take better ownership of what he had written. He then personalized it in the following way:

> I have developed many wonderful skills for facilitating a group. But, I am afraid that I have become too entrenched in my own style; it pervades my being. I am anxious about making the transition to early retirement. I feel very uncertain whether my "black belt" of authority at the university will carry over to the things I now want to do. I worry that I have become too dependent upon the university. I want to find my own way, free of its security. But, I wonder if my style will work

well enough to succeed on the outside. And if others felt it didn't and rejected me for it, I would be very disappointed.

Gary looked closely at his feedback to George. He saw just how frightened he, himself, was of his own dependency needs and longings. He also realized how much he was discounting that his skills could be applied in a wide variety of settings. And he became more aware of just how valuable they really were. He also became aware of his disappointment that others might reject him and how he felt rejecting of them if they did.

With his early retirement coming soon, these particular needs were beginning to scream for attention. So it was easy for him to project them into his protégé, George. George was a natural screen for such projections, because in mentoring relationships, dependency needs and longings are inherent in those who

Our Contentious Inner Dialogue

assume the role of the protégé. Moving to early retirement clearly triggered Gary's terror of being overpowered by his own hidden fears. Some of his fears related to being unfairly rejected in a new work setting. He feared that others would be unjust and see his flaws over his own considerable competencies. The idea of this certainly disappointed him. But it also stirred his ire that he might not be appreciated. And this was also scary to him that others might see his anger and rage.

Gary kept his fears, his disappointment, and his ire in his shadow. He also realized just how much this life transition fueled his doubts over his buried talents. He was rejecting his own talents even before others could. And Gary contained his doubts and self-rejections in his aura. It was these self-rejections and fears that he placed in his feedback to George. In a sense, Gary, through his feedback, was imagining sending George out on a journey he may have been fearful to take himself—to leave the warmth of the womb and travel out into the world on his own.

Here's another example of how useful writing feedback can be in discovering what it may say about ourselves. Sarah felt compelled to speak her mind to her friend, Aidan. She liked Aidan for his quiet introspection and calm demeanor. He was single. And over the years, Sarah and her husband often went out with Aidan, accompanied by most of the new women he dated. Over the last few months, though, she found herself getting more impatient with him. She was now seeing his quiet and introspective nature as "quietly critical." It also seemed to her that he was revealing too many of his insecurities. She didn't like hearing him speak of wanting to find yet another new person to date. She also didn't like hearing that he wanted to find another employer. In order to better understand why she was getting so impatient with someone she had liked so well, Sarah elected to write some feedback to Aiden. As she put it,

> Aidan, I see you as a very wise person who seems very inwardly directed and shy. I see you searching for someone. But you seem to be afraid to commit to one person. I think that you worry too much about what other people think of you. I also think you feel

unsure of yourself and what you want in a partner. You are searching for something, but you're not sure what you're looking for. You want to be loved, but you are looking for someone else to validate your thoughts and feelings.

When Sarah looked into the cosmic mirror contained in her feedback, she personalized it as feedback to herself by writing,

I see myself as a very wise person who is very inwardly directed and shy. I am searching for someone, but I am afraid to commit to one person. I worry too much about what other people in my life think about me. I feel unsure of myself and what I want in a partner. I am searching, but I am not sure what I am searching for. I want to love and to be loved, but I am looking for someone to validate my thoughts and feelings.

As she reflected on what she wrote, Sarah sensed the truth that it revealed for her and began to examine her love life and her work life. There was something more that she longed for. She was turning fifty and had long buried a dream of hers to leave her company and set up her own practice as a consultant. She began to discover that what she was referencing in her feedback to Aidan was her own fear of committing to the independent side of herself who wanted to strike out on her own. She felt unsure she could even do it. When Aidan revealed his insecurities about his dating partners and about work, it struck a chord in her. Sarah realized that while the feedback may have carried some relevance for Aidan, it also clearly was a way for her to make contact with her own insecurities and the denied aura within herself.

Personal Mirror Reflection

See if you can involve someone you trust to write feedback to you along the lines of a personal note that would address the following four questions:

1. How do they experience your behavior?

2. What issues within you do they see are troubling you?

3. What they see as a strength within you that you bring to relationships with others?

4. What they would you like to encourage you to explore in future interactions with them?

They should write the feedback straight from their heart without editing it. You should also ask them if it would be alright for you to write feedback to them along the same lines.

When you have finished writing your feedback to the other person we want you to read through the feedback you have written and underline the parts that you know are also true *about you*. If they wish, the other person can do the same thing for their feedback to you. This is called *checking for projections*.

It would also be useful for you to write feedback to your self. Before you receive the feedback from your partner, write out what you imagine the other person might say to you. Sometimes, the best advice we can receive is what we imagine others will give us. Because you haven't yet heard what feedback the other person may have written to you, this self-feedback is comprised purely of projections and can contain invaluable insights about yourself.

When you have written your self-feedback and checked for projections in the feedback you wrote for your partner, exchange your feedback and discuss it with them. In your discussion, compare what you said to yourself with what your partner says about you—paying particular attention to your projections.

Looking closely at our own darkness is not easy. It is possible, though, that, through others, we can move beyond our projections to discover more about our self. Seeing our own inner light means tolerating our inner shadow and all of the flaws contained within it. We never fully achieve absolute wholeness. But we can continually evolve by discovering what is missing or unfinished in our own personal evolution. Throughout our lives, all of us are works in progress—learning is never-ending. In the next chapter, we will take a closer look at the full range of our emotions, what they mean, how we defend against feeling them, and how we can begin to see what is behind the cosmic mirror.

14

Uncovering the Emotional Side of the Cosmic Mirror

"People develop emotional problems not because of their emotions, but because they run away from them."

—*Thomas Fogarty*

At one time or another, all of us have received strong messages from others that have been intended to dampen or suppress our emotions. These messages may be explicitly or implicitly expressed. They are often passed off as if they are helpful guides to living a meaningful life. Examples of such messages are "Children are to be seen and not heard," "Don't make waves," "Big boys don't cry," "Never show your anger," "Don't let others know you are afraid," "It's better to suffer in silence," "Don't let others really know what you're feeling," "Others can't be trusted to take care of you", "Don't express affection by touching others," or "Nice girls don't do that."-These messages come from our

248

family, and they come from our culture. They are passed off as powerful rules, and many of us have unknowingly swallowed them whole without chewing them. Although well-intentioned, they operate within us like an inner judge. They dole out rulings in absolute terms that are rigidly cast as "shoulds" and "shouldn'ts". For example, an emotion-suppressing message you may have swallowed without consciously examining it is, "You are 'weak' for crying," or "You are 'mean' for expressing your anger."

As we follow these emotion-dampening messages, our feelings are less available for examination. When our feelings are suppressed we are not able to look at and render the breadth, depth, texture, and character of them. Subtleties and fine distinctions become blurred. In its extreme, what we are left with are merely categorical labels like "good" or "bad" that place judgments on our feelings. Like we did when we were very young, we split off our feelings into categories of "all good" or "all bad." Ingesting oversimplified messages launches a process that unknowingly leads us to think in a polarized and absolutist manner. Believing in emotion-suppressing messages entraps us. We begin to see people and events as simply "good" or "bad" while we submerge more complex ways of constructively analyzing them. These ways of coping with complex feelings and ideas are temporary, incomplete, and ineffective. This is true, because feelings that are submerged continuously push to make themselves known. Despite our attempts to keep them hidden, their voices grow louder and louder until they breaks through. To suppress our emotions is stifling to our growth and development and inevitably leads to needless emotional and physical distress.

One of the most prominent reasons we don't fully acknowledge and express our feelings to others is fear—

we are fearful because we have lived with and have been influenced by others who have critically judged us when we have done so. But you may have heard the aphorism, "If you can feel it, you can heal it." It implies that cathartically releasing our feelings helps us grow beyond our emotional blocks. We are told to "vent," "dump," or "get things off our chests." No doubt, this has some validity. However, it is insufficient to blindly expel our feelings without insight into the meaning those feelings hold for us. We grow by way of the insights we gain by taking ownership of our emotions. We also honor our self by acknowledging those emotions—both the ones we like and the ones we dislike. Healing from emotional pain comes by reflecting on the meaning of those emotions. And we grow by learning to constructively express those emotions to others—not simply when we are distressed but when we feel loving and are trying to truly connect with others. Stan Herman and Michael Korenich, noted Gestalt organization development consultants, poetically capture this idea this way:

> All that I withhold diminishes me and cheats you. All that you withhold diminishes you and cheats me. If we withhold ourselves for each other's sake, That is no service to us either one. We only collude in the weakening of us both.[1]

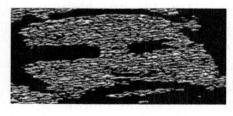

Exploring the Fear Within

As we become more skilled at identifying our hidden emotions and polarities, we are better able to manage our own personal demons. We enhance our ability to tap into and actualize our strengths and the power of our own potential.[2] As we do this, we move toward a level of consciousness not where fear is entirely absent but where we are experiencing a conviction and belief in our self that countermands the fear. Rather than being paralyzed by our fears, we are able to act despite them. By doing so, we assume responsibility for our life. We not only learn to appreciate our self, but we also learn to appreciate how to be of value to others in our life.

As we find and utilize more of our own emotional power we learn to better stand up for ourselves and others. Actualizing more of our abilities allows us to avoid shrinking from constructively confronting those who may disagree with us. Personal power, though, can be used for good or evil. For example, when many of us think of employing our own power, images of violence come to mind. Many people believe that looking at their own potential for violence leads them closer to *being* violent. Actually, the opposite is true. Understanding and recognizing our potential for violence *decreases* the likelihood that we will act on it. We can then learn how to constructively deal with the more volatile feelings within us. Using more of our own emotional power enables us to sense when confrontation is needed and when it is not. We are better able to recognize that we possess the skills to follow a path that comes from the innermost depth of our heart. Moreover, we discover how to find our courage to be our whole self and risk growing in unforeseen ways. What this takes is a healthy aggressiveness—an energized assertiveness that serves a healthy purpose within us. Thomas Moore and Douglas Gillette, internationally recognized Jungian psychoanalysts, paradoxically describe this unique type of aggressiveness:

> Aggressiveness is a stance toward life that rouses energies and motivates. It pushes us to take the offensive and to move out of a

defensive or "holding" position about life's
tasks and problems.[3]

Uncovering the emotional side of the cosmic mirror
also relates to our capacity to acknowledge and confront
our anxiety. Acknowledging our anxiety means to tolerate
it without defensiveness—without repression, denial,
projection, minimization, or other emotional defense
mechanisms. Confronting our anxiety means utilizing it
in a constructive way. To run from rather than face our
anxiety can leave us with a vapid, weak, unreal sense of
being. None of us can entirely escape the feeling of anxiety;
it is a part of the human condition. But while anxiety may
be unpleasant to experience, it is always in our best interest
to understand its message for us, because it is then that we
can discover our choices and options.

Looking into the cosmic mirror means stepping outside
of our comfort zone. It means learning to break the
emotional chains that bind us. Doing so also moves us past
settling for merely being passive or detached. It helps us
discover new boundaries and vistas in our lives. It allows
us to break through our self-imposed limitations. It helps
us carefully examine our pent-up and disowned feelings.
Becoming aware of our cosmic mirror involves seeing the
emotional box we place around ourselves. It also means
stepping out of it to explore new and potentially beneficial
actions. Once we are able to raise our awareness of the
feelings contained in our personal cosmic mirror, we can
then begin to own what we have been casting out onto
others. We can also then work through the fears we have
about those feelings. This is a powerful act. It helps us
appreciate and acknowledge who we are and who we are
becoming. It also enhances the recognition of our denied

positive potential. Testing a boundary like this is an act of courage—crossing it, a heroic act.

"Transformation isn't always about feeling comfortable – it's about learning new ways of being."

Identifying and disclosing our feelings is one of the most difficult tasks of living. Some psychotherapists believe the primary goal of therapy is to reach a point where the client can be entirely open about all their feelings—without censoring, without suppressing, without defending, or without hesitating. In each of us, some feelings are easily discussed. Other feelings seem much more risky. For example, many people are quick to anger, but it is much more difficult for them to express their sadness or fear. For others, expressing their fears or hurt is easy. But when it comes to expressing anger, they have immense difficulty.

Often, the first glimpse into the cosmic mirror is emotionally upending. It involves learning to see our own emotions and look at them head-on—without looking away or trying to rationalize them. Facing our own emotions honestly can be one of life's most difficult tasks. The ability required to look deeply within our self calls for confronting our fears, our rage, our despair, and our shame. It can feel like plunging into chaos—a deep, dark, and bottomless void. We can feel caught in an impasse or engulfed in an abyss. We may experience profound feelings of emptiness, pessimism, and despair. In entering this fearful abyss, we need to let go in spite of our fears and risk losing our self. It can feel like what has been metaphorically called "the dark night of the soul" or the death of the self.[4] As Fritz Perls put it,

"To suffer one's death and to be reborn is not easy." [5]

These chaotic feelings arise from suddenly discovering that our current way of being and relating is no longer desirable.

"Underneath the 'surface' self are the unconscious parts of ourselves that are waiting to be given a voice."

Simply being aware of an unpleasant feeling or undesirable action is not sufficient to change it. We don't know any other way to act. It's like a baby chick emerging from the safety of the eggshell saying, "What do I do next?" Although it may seem counter-intuitive, the way through the void is to allow ourselves to directly experience these deep but unsettling feelings. This is a formidable task—one marked by uncertainty, awkwardness, and tentativeness. To experience these uncomfortable feelings, though, is the very action that drives us to fill the vacuum of emptiness. Strangely, the void eventually becomes filled with constructive, life-enhancing thoughts, feelings, and behavior. This is because a true vacuum cannot exist over time; something must take its place. You can fill the emptiness with old or new defenses. Or you can progressively fill the emptiness with the evolving and complete self that lives behind both the shadow and the aura of the void.

Moving into "the dark night of the soul" can feel like jumping into the center of chaos—the unknown. However, within what is believed to be pure chaos is actually an intricate order. While we may feel we are falling apart, the reality is that we are going through a transformation phase. In time, the order within the chaos becomes apparent. In the physical sciences, *chaos theory* has taught us this. From within the chaos, a new order always emerges. A butterfly startlingly emerges from a caterpillar. It almost seems like a miracle. That's because with linear thinking, no one could predict such a transformation. From a linear perspective, the process within the chaos is irregular and unpredictable. And yet, just like in the physical universe, emotional patterns eventually take on a recognizable form. They operate by what might be called a *chaordic dynamic*. This is an order that exists within the chaos. Physicist Joseph Ford captures this dynamic when he describes chaos as,

> Dynamics freed at last from the shackles of order and predictability ... systems liberated to randomly explore their every dynamical possibility ... exciting variety, richness of choice, a cornucopia of opportunity.[6]

Finding order within chaos can occur with the emergence of any new thought, new idea, or new feeling. It can happen with a flash of insight. The Appalachian Expressive Arts Collective puts it this way:

> When a central idea has emerged, raw and formless, it is our job to allow and observe the wild, tender tendrils that shoot out from the central idea without trying to tame them or force them into shape. When they are ready, they will connect and order themselves. Our task is to maintain detached awareness. We are only the channels and witnesses for the process.[7]

The emotional chaos that comes with making transformational changes to our self can take two extreme forms. One form is like a pioneer. Pioneers are those who accept some discomfort as a necessary part of their journey. Another form is like a victim or prisoner. For them, the chaos is incarcerating. We can be victimized by the process or it can be a growth-producing learning experience. Getting through the emotional chaos enhances our ability to enter into, withstand, and better overcome confusion of any kind. As Carl Jung stated, "There is no birth of consciousness without pain." By going through the emotional pain associated with looking into the cosmic mirror, we emerge with a new consciousness.

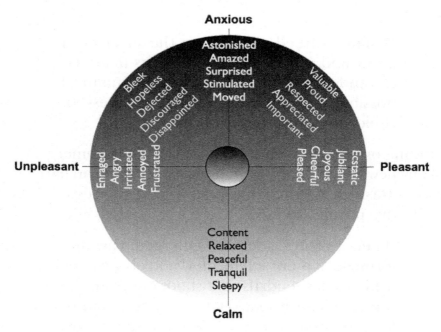

Anxious

Astonished
Amazed
Surprised
Stimulated
Moved

Bleek
Hopeless
Dejected
Discouraged
Disappointed

Valuable
Proud
Respected
Appreciated
Important

Unpleasant

Enraged
Angry
Irritated
Annoyed
Frustrated

Ecstatic
Jubilant
Joyous
Cheerful
Pleased

Pleasant

Content
Relaxed
Peaceful
Tranquil
Sleepy

Calm

Figure 14a: The Feelings Wheel

Take a look at figure 14a. Shown there is a spectrum of feelings that are placed on a wheel. See how the wheel is comprised of two dimensions: (1) whether the feeling that is being experienced is pleasant or unpleasant and (2) whether the feeling evokes an experience of tension or calmness.

For many people, calm and pleasant feelings—like feeling serene, still, and peaceful—are easy to experience. But feeling irritated, disgusted, or indignant are difficult. For others, sitting still is hard; raging and complaining are easy. How can we gain access to the denied, projected, or hidden emotions contained within our cosmic mirror? Gaining access to these minimized elements is based on several assumptions relating to the nature and structure of our feelings.

Assumption #1: Some of our thoughts, feelings, wishes, and fears are outside of our immediate awareness.

Assumption #2: When we experience a feeling as too uncomfortable, we guard against it by erecting *defenses* to push it out of our awareness. For example, we might pretend that the feeling doesn't exist—this is called denial. We also might believe that others have this feeling but not us—we have discussed this as projection. Or we might attack someone else that represents that feeling—this is called displacement. Or we might make an excuse for having that feeling—this is called rationalization. Or we might try and forget about the feeling— this is called repression. Or we try not let ourselves experience the feeling—this is called insulation.

Assumption #3: We can take responsibility for our feelings only with awareness of them. With awareness of a feeling, we can do three things: (a) we can experience the feeling, (b) we can reflect on it, or (c) we can express the feeling in words or actions. When we are aware of our feelings, the words we use or the actions we take are usually more constructive.

Personal Mirror Reflection

Throughout the book, we have referred to a variety of emotional defense mechanisms that we all employ from time to time. This *Personal Mirror Reflection* is designed to help you make contact with the defenses you may routinely use. Below is a list of commonly used emotional defenses. Think of a strong and unpleasant feeling you have experienced lately—perhaps it was fear or disgust or shame. What did you do to try to cope with it? When your feelings run strong, which defense mechanism(s) do you tend to use?

Denial:	I'll pretend the feeling doesn't exist.
Insulation:	I won't let myself feel the feeling.
Acting Out:	I'll just turn the feeling into behavior (like drugging or raging or withdrawing).
Projection:	I'll say others have the feeling ... but not me.
Displacement:	I'll attack something else that I use to represent the feeling (like punching the wall or scapegoating someone else).
Idealization:	I'll put the feeling (or person or ideal) on a pedestal.
Repression:	I'll try to forget about the feeling.

Devaluation:	I'll say that the feeling (or person or ideal) is worthless.
Introjection:	I'll swallow whole the feeling (or perception or rule) without thinking about it.
Intellectualization:	I won't feel the feeling—I'll lecture myself and others about it.
Rationalization:	I'll make an excuse for having the feeling.
Undoing:	I'll take back what I just said about the feeling or imagine that the event that triggered the feeling didn't take place.
Reaction Formation:	I'll reverse the feeling and turn the feeling into its opposite polarity, e.g., by saying, "It's all good."
Sublimation:	I'll transform the feeling into a socially acceptable form but not acknowledge it, e.g., by comfort eating or by taking a "sick day".
Fantasy:	I'll daydream about the feeling as if I am acting on it.

Karl Menninger proposed that when we experience a feeling that we have hidden from ourselves we first feel anxious. We feel uncomfortable with the feeling, and it feels unsettling and risky—even dangerous—for us to experience it. And when we get anxious or uncomfortable with a particular feeling we try to defend against it. We try to block it out. We try to push it away. Or we act out on it in the hope—albeit unknowingly—of discharging it. Menninger described this process by using a model he referred to as the *Triangle of Conflict*.[8] And this is shown in figure 14b.

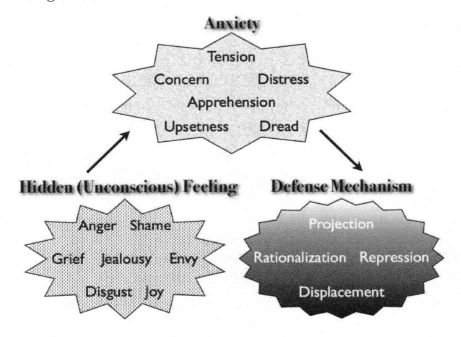

Figure 14b: Menninger's Triangle of Conflict

Here's how the Triangle of Conflict works. Consider for a moment that we have done something that we are ashamed of. (This is one of the *Hidden/Unconscious Feelings* that are listed in the bottom left panel of the figure.) It is likely that we would feel tense or apprehensive about it. (These are one of the feelings of *Anxiety* that are listed in the top panel of the figure.) As we discussed in the last *Personal Mirror Reflection*, these are *Defense Mechanisms*, and some of them are shown in the bottom right panel. We may use denial to try to block it out or we may use repression to try to forget about it. Let's say, though, that by circumstance, someone or something reminds us of our shame (*Hidden/Unconscious Feeling*). At that moment, the feeling is no longer hidden. It has seeped into our awareness. When this happens it makes us feel tense—we are reminded of it, and we don't like it. We might again try to push it out of our mind. We might irritably say, "Let's change the subject." Or we might try to displace our shame by shaming someone else. We might angrily snap at a person nearby us who brought it to mind. In this hypothetical example, we have used anger to shame someone else as a way of avoiding our anxiety. We have used anger to defend against our shame.

Defending against our feelings is a natural process that occurs throughout our day. In many ways, it's quite useful. If we could not set at least some of our feelings aside we could not sufficiently focus on the many tasks we need to accomplish? However, when defending becomes too commonplace for us, it isn't helpful. Those feelings repeatedly denied or projected or otherwise defended become part of our shadow or aura, and they never get fully examined.

How then can we change a pattern of excessive emotional defending? How can we look into what might be contained in our cosmic mirror? Using the feelings of anxiety, anger, and shame that we have just been discussing, five steps are needed:

1. We need to acknowledge that we are angry.

2. We need to look more closely at the tension that has triggered our angry defensive reaction. Before looking more closely at our anger (or our shame), it is easier to first admit that we are anxious about looking at it.

3. We need to take ownership for displacing our anger by recognizing that anger is our defense.

In this instance, anger is being used to cover up and avoid the more vulnerable, intense, and uncomfortable feeling of shame.

4. We need to recognize that our anger is being used to place shame in someone else. This is the essence of projection—we try to assign *our* shame into someone else.

5. We need to examine more directly the feeling of shame that underlie our defensiveness—where it come from, what it is about, and what it is doing to us and others.

Here's a real-life example of this process. Eugene was a doormat. His wife bullied him into doing things against his better judgment. He suffered from her constant hammering. He felt crippled in a marriage that wasn't working for him. As a result, he avoided others, but he also withdrew further into himself. Despite telling himself that he would not let it happen to him, Eugene he was depressed. He missed the special kind of relationship he and his wife had in the beginning of their marriage. For Eugene, the depression itself was his defense. It was his way of coping with feeling overwhelmed with tension. He feared that if he looked directly at his deeper feelings that he would either implode or explode. He was terrified of looking in the cosmic mirror.

But Eugene was able to overcome his fear and his depression. With help, he did so by allowing himself to risk experiencing and reflecting on what it meant to him to be depressed. Paradoxically, he stopped trying *not* to be depressed. He entered more fully into the chaotic void. Because he did so, he was able to examine more closely what was there. He squarely faced his fears of the inward journey. With the help of others, he discovered that underneath all the layers of his depression was resentment and anger at the way his wife was treating him. From the perspective of the cosmic mirror, Eugene projected his power, authority, and anger onto his wife—she being an unknowing receptacle for these feelings. As a consequence, he became more powerless, meek, and small. Once he was able to take ownership of his resentments, they did not overpower him, and they did not then get placed in his wife. He was able to regain his power without experiencing his dreaded fears. In doing so, he utilized his anger to constructively give voice to and assert his unmet needs.

"YOU MEAN YOUR BIG SMILE IS BOTTLED-UP AGGRESSION? MINE IS BOTTLED-UP HOSTILITY."

This has been a chapter about uncovering the emotions contained within the cosmic mirror. As family therapist Thomas Fogarty's quote at the beginning of the chapter implies, people become stuck in old and ineffective life scripts not *because* of their feelings but because they *avoid* them. We cannot transcend old patterns by suppressing our emotions. And yet, it takes courage to face them. How do we face and overcome our fears and learn how to express our feelings in a constructive and appropriate manner? This is, indeed, a puzzling undertaking—essentially because it has not been a part of our experience to do so. Take anger, for example. How do we constructively and appropriately deal with anger, especially when it is very strong? Do we throw dishes? Punch a pillow? Scream in our car? Run around the block? Count to 10? How can we better use our feelings as a guide into and out of our abyss? How can we forge new ways of seeing ourselves and others in a way that transforms us? How do we find the courage to take these steps? These are some of the topics that are covered in the next chapter.

15

Using Our Feelings to Guide Us

"Let your heart guide you. It whispers, so listen closely."

—*Anonymous*

Feelings are a part of every relationship. This is true whether or not we are aware of them or choose to openly express them. Every one of us has feelings. We feel angry; we feel powerful; we feel upset; we feel hurt; we feel grateful; we feel sad; we feel inspired; we feel rejected; we feel affirmed; we feel passionate; we feel discouraged; we feel alone; we feel inviting; we feel close; we feel fearful; we feel open. Many of

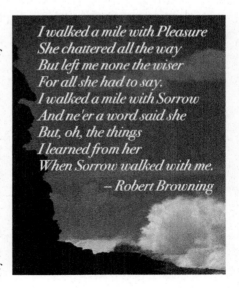

I walked a mile with Pleasure
She chattered all the way
But left me none the wiser
For all she had to say.
I walked a mile with Sorrow
And ne'er a word said she
But, oh, the things
I learned from her
When Sorrow walked with me.
– Robert Browning

265

us, though, have been brought up in families that have discouraged emotional closeness. There may have been silently implied disapproval when feelings were directly expressed. Many of us have been taught (indirectly or directly) to act as if we are being genuine when, in fact, we are not. In the film, *The Godfather,* Don Vito Corleone privately scolds his son, Sonny, by memorably telling him, "Never let anyone outside the family know what you are thinking again!" The message from others may have been that we are to wear a social mask—*a persona*— at the emotional surface to conceal who we are in our inner experience. The persona is designed to hide the inner world of our feelings. Its function is to act as a social wall to keep us from being known by others, knowing others, or knowing ourselves at a deep level.

Most of us falsely assume that we exercise complete control over what we reveal about ourselves. We make-believe that if we don't "let on," others will not see the parts of us we wish to keep hidden. The very idea that we have thoughts, feelings, and motives happening inside of us that are not in our immediate awareness—things that others may correctly infer from what they see—can feel quite threatening. That we are always aware and in control of what happens within us and between ourselves and others is clearly not the case.

The Mask We Wear

There are many cultural messages that are directed at us on how to present ourselves to others. Many of them encourage us to blunt or deaden ourselves from experiencing our feelings. Many of them discourage us from honoring our feelings as a vital life force within us. And many of them block us from directly expressing our feelings—messages like "Suffer in silence," "Never let anyone see you sweat," "Don't upset others." These messages dissuade us from experiencing our feelings and expressing ourselves in appropriate ways. Sometimes messages like these are explicit; sometimes they are quietly inferred.

When we don't recognize our feelings or we don't express them to others they often become distorted and go underground. Here are three examples of this. Jimmy sat through the meeting and listened to every word that was said. He knew he was angry with what he was hearing, but he was not going to bring himself to comment on anything. So he just "held his tongue." Knowing he could not stand being in the meeting another second, he politely excused himself. He got up. He went to the door. But as he walked out, he *slammed* the door shut. He then stuck his head back in to apologize.

Some recent consulting work we were doing for a department at a large university provides another illustration. While standing in their School of Management we overheard a secretary answer her telephone with an unintended slip—she said, "Good morning; *tools* of management." We later learned that she was feeling that management was not recognizing her worth and was very involved in establishing a union for secretaries. Finally, John had a reputation in his company for being a "result-oriented" autocrat. As he was being introduced to their new hire, Paul, John greeted Paul by saying, "Pleased to *beat* you." It was clear to Paul and those around him exactly what John had said—but John never realized he had said it.

Feelings always find an outlet for expression—*always*—even if not in direct or intended ways. Our feelings will always find a stage on which to be voiced. And the ways they are distorted can take many forms. We act out on them. We avoid them. We gossip about them. We scapegoat others. We throw a temper tantrum. We scheme with them. We manipulate others. We abuse a substance or engage in other addictive compulsions. They can take the form of rising fear, mistrust, apathy, boredom, disconnectedness, depression, loneliness, or feelings of alienation. Or they can become distorted through somatic symptoms like headaches, backaches, fatigue, poor sleep, ulcers, or stomach aches. Whatever form they assume, unprocessed feelings take their toll on our inner emotional life. Once they go underground we become disconnected from them. We lose touch with them. They are not available for us to manage in intentional ways. Sometimes people say they "feel nothing" or that they "don't know" what they feel. Typically, this means they have distanced themselves from their emotions. As a result, they have lost touch with constructive ways of dealing with them.

We might express our anger by telling someone, "You're a vindictive, game-playing phony." Despite what truth might be contained in such a statement, it is absolutist and one-sided. It is more of an emotional reaction than a rational evaluation and will probably not be constructive or helpful for you or for them. Name-calling is indirect and certainly not socially appreciated. It's destructive and dishonest in the sense that it's unbalanced. It's a play for power. And it is a non-constructive way of expressing anger and hurt. As the Buddha said, "Holding on to anger is like grasping a hot coal with the intent of throwing it at someone else—you are the one who gets burned." Hostility often begets hostility—it simply reinforces the belief that expressing all feelings is dangerous. Often, this is the motive behind why we hide our feelings. We are afraid of them. A common fear is that if we were to fully experience an uncomfortable feeling, it may lead to an automatically violent behavioral response—one that we cannot control. To manage the fear we might say to ourselves, "Don't tell them," "If I say anything they might hurt me," "I might harm them irreparably" or "They might leave me." We often believe we are protecting ourselves and others by hiding what we feel. Let's take an example.

Feeling rageful, we might *feel like* killing someone. To say that we "feel like" *doing* something is a common phrase. Feeling a feeling does not mean that we will act on it. Our fear in this example is that simply acknowledging that we *feel* rageful would, *in itself,* lead to uncontrollably rageful *actions.* Our fear is that if we allowed ourselves to experience rage we would inevitably release a savage monster from inside of us. Sometimes, it is difficult to know how to make the distinction between acknowledging a feeling and impulsively and inappropriately acting it out. Prisons are filled with those who have had difficulty making this distinction. It's a fact: some people *do have* poor impulse control. But impulses that are bottled up are *more likely* to lead to their escalation and to their expression in destructive ways. Awareness of our feelings should not be avoided.

Identifying Our Feelings

Being able to experience and identify our feelings as they occur moment-to-moment can be a very difficult task. However, avoiding feelings—being unable to fully experience and express our feelings—can take an even heavier personal toll. When we avoid or blunt fully experiencing a feeling, the feeling does not go away. If the feeling is repeatedly experienced and shunted it accumulates over time. In terms of feelings, what is resisted persists—albeit out of immediate awareness. Hidden in the background of our unconscious, the feeling does not disappear and can surface when we least expect it. The blocked or shunted feeling may come roaring out of us in a much more emotionally exaggerated form than the situation may call for. While such a release may be cathartic, it can be fraught with unintended consequences, further complicate situations, and have lasting effects on the relationships of the people involved. Blocking a feeling unintentionally reinforces a belief that fully experiencing it is dangerous. It also needlessly expends valuable energy— to truncate a feeling and keep it hidden takes effort.

People who have difficulty identifying their feelings are experiencing *alexithymia*. It is an ancient Greek word literally meaning "without words for emotions." Alexithymia is a personality trait that identifies a person who either has difficulty identifying the bodily sensations of emotional arousal or has trouble distinguishing between one feeling and another. Beyond a few limited adjectives such as "fine", "happy" or "OK," a person with alexithymia is unable to adequately describe their feelings to others. This contributes to the person's sense of detachment from themselves and makes it very difficult for them to feel connected to others in a meaningful way.[1]

As you might imagine, our family and cultural background each has a profound impact on how we suppress or encourage the acknowledgment and expression of our own emotions. We learn from our social context how to judge our feelings and attributes. Many of us have learned to see feelings and attributes as either "good" or "bad" or "right" or "wrong." In actuality, our feelings and attributes are much more than either of these polarities. To free ourselves from imposing judgment on them, we must complete three tasks:

1. We must identify *when* we are judging feelings

2. We must identify *how* we are judging feelings

3. We must learn *where* we began to make such judgments.

On their own, most children do not know how to talk about their feelings. They need help in naming their feelings and understanding them. However, obtaining such help depends on their parent's ability to identify and express feelings. Sometimes with words and sometimes by non-verbal cues, parents send messages to their child that they should suppress, eliminate, or refrain from talking about certain feelings. A parent may say, "Don't get angry at me young lady!" or "Quit that crying or I'll give you something to cry about!" or "No son of mine is going to be afraid!" Some of these messages reflect the dynamics of a family's own emotional legacy—that is, a parent's own experience passed down to their children from their observations of how their own parents expressed or did not express emotions. Some of these messages are gender based and come from the larger culture. Parents are early models for all of us in demonstrating how to manage our feelings. What we learn from them is deeply imprinted and shapes the way we deal with our feelings and emotions. Our family background forms the basis for our feelings of discomfort or sense of threat with certain feelings and sense of comfort with other feelings.

The ability to experience, decipher, acknowledge, and express our feelings is a skill. As a skill, we can work on it, refine it, and develop it. To experience our feelings and identify them in others is a multi-dimensional task in that there are differences and variations in vocal tones, facial expressions, gestures, and body language—we cry, we shout, we whisper, we smile, we frown, we tremble, we breathe in a shallow or deep manner, we grimace, our heart races, and many other manifestations.

Psychologist Paul Ekman has done considerable research on emotions and how they are expressed.[2] He argues that even impassive faces transmit emotions. His research suggests that with high accuracy, most people can identify basic emotions like fear and anger. Sometimes we are aware of our own reaction to others' emotional expression—sometimes not. There also seems to be an ingested cultural norm about avoiding openly discussing body language.[3] We can, however, develop our personal skill in identifying feeling responses in others as well as ourselves. Recent books and articles on "emotional intelligence" is testimony to the current interest in learning how to more accurately identify emotions in others and ourselves. Emotional intelligence refers to variations in the ability to accurately identify and constructive manage emotions in ourselves and others. Although identifying and observing emotions in others can make us more sensitive to how feelings are expressed it is not identical to experiencing our feelings first-hand—up close and personal. Neuroimaging studies of brain functioning have shown that putting the experience of our feelings into words reduces the intensity of unpleasant feelings. By labeling our feelings with words, we are *acknowledging* that we are experiencing them. This is an essential step in *fully* experiencing them. [4] This underscores the importance of us developing and practicing a rich and descriptive emotional vocabulary of feelings.

Of all the emotions, anger is one of the most avoided. Anger can be felt in varying degrees ranging from *mild* (which might be described as irritation or annoyance) to *strong* (which might be described as blinding or out-of-control rage). If the amount of our accumulated anger is relatively small, simply stating that we are angry maybe enough to achieve closure and allow us to let go of it. If, however, we have an excessive level of accumulated anger we may be hesitant to express it for fear we will open a floodgate of anger. We also may fear we may go "over the top" with anger and express it in a manner that does not match the situation at hand. Many people find their feelings of anger to be distasteful or frightening—in the sense that they fear experiencing their anger will lead to a loss of control. They confuse anger with violence. Violence is actually but one way—albeit a destructive way—of releasing pent-up anger. There are many other ways of releasing pent-up anger. Anger itself is only a feeling, not an action.

It may seem odd or surprising to hear that becoming more aware of how we are *breathing* is of considerable use in learning to fully experience and manage our feelings. The next time you are sad, notice how you hold your breath or are breathing in a shallow manner. This is a way of blunting or avoiding the full experience of your sadness. This may lead to you crying or releasing tears. When we deepen our breathing we allow our self to fully connect to the sadness. Sadness is released through tears when we allow ourselves to openly cry with our whole body. Shallow breathing also blunts the impact of fully experiencing other feelings—such as fear or anger. A useful technique for deepening our breathing is to inhale to the count of ten ... pause ... and, then, exhale to the count of five. Three or four such breaths increase the chances of fully experiencing what we find difficult.

How, though, do we "resolve" strong feelings? What does it mean to "work through" emotional issues? These are phrases that have been adopted into our cultural lexicon but that have not been fully defined or sufficiently understood. For example, when we grieve the loss of someone we love what is it that is happening within us that brings us to a place of resolution? When we are enraged with the cruelty of someone close to us how is it that we eventually arrive at a place of renewal where the strong emotional charge of our rage has diminished? How is it that people "come to grips" with their feelings in a constructive way, "metabolize" them, "let go" of them, or "move on" from them.

The essential process involved here is *resonance*. It is well known in physics that every object in the universe stores energy that vibrates at a frequency that is unique to itself. This is called its *resonance frequency*. It comes in many forms – it is the way guitar strings resound, children play on swings, clocks keep time, radio and TV stations broadcast their signals, and the earth revolves around the sun. It is also true about us—as feeling human beings. In popular language, we say, "We are on the same wave length" or "That resonates with me" or "I get 'bad vibes' from him" or "She was really 'in tune' with me." When we use these phrases we are describing the process of resonance. This is also the basis for how two people fall in love and is how we develop the capacity to become attuned to each other's inner emotional states.[5] Dating back to the

17th century, it has been observed that pendulum clocks placed in the same room will eventually vibrate together. The clocks become attuned with one another:

> [N]ature feels that it is more economical if two or any number of oscillators that vibrate at frequencies close enough to each other work together rather than insist on keeping their small differences[6]

Just as two people or objects can be attuned to one another, so can a person be *attuned to themselves.* We believe that when a person goes through an important life experience they absorb, come away with, or build up emotional energy from it. Psychoanalyst Donald Winnicott echoes this point:

> In a total psychology, being-stolen-from is the same as stealing, and is equally aggressive. Being weak is as aggressive as the attack of the strong on the weak.[7]

When we are robbed we feel the same rage that is often denied in our robber; when we lose someone we love a part of us dies with them, and we feel sadness and grief; when we witness the birth of our child something within us is born. If, however, we are too disconnected from our own experience we cannot release the feelings that might ordinarily resonate within us. And without this release, our experience is incomplete – *we do not allow our self to fully experience the feeling.*

Here's an example. Most of us have found the need to separate from an important but tempestuous romantic relationship. In doing so, it has been necessary to confront our shock, our anger, our sadness, our sense of loss, or our guilt over it. If we have not examined and experienced the full impact of these feelings our grieving process becomes constrained. We may have denied the experience by saying to ourselves, "It isn't so." Or we may have hoped beyond hope that the relationship could be revived. Or we may have tried to plead or bargain our way out of accepting the most profound and difficult feelings of loss. If, however, we have allowed ourselves to become attuned with and resonant with our own feelings—and we allow our self to fully experience them—with time our disquieting feelings subside.

The Sound of God Within Us

In Hinduism and other eastern religions, the vibration produced by chanting the word *Om* is believed to correspond to the primal vibration of the universe—to do so allows us to resonate with the vibration of God within us. In Shinto and Buddhist practices, the ringing of a gong or metallic bowl is believed to be the pathway to the divine, to one's spiritual power, and to the transformation of the self. As the bowl "sings" to us, we allow its vibrations to resonate within us. Religious rituals such as these are testimony to the wisdom of the ages that echoes the idea we must rejoice in our own natural vibrations.

Like the healing power of a sacred chant or mystical singing bowl, resonating with the natural and sacred sounds within us is also the way we work though our feelings. It is profoundly difficult, but when we fully embrace our sadness we simultaneously and paradoxically release it. And with time our sadness dissipates. We know it when it happens to us, because we feel it in our whole being We may sob unrelentingly for a time, but by doing so, we feel the freedom of cathartic release. We move on from our sadness or our anger or any other feelings when we no longer need to possess them. At the same instant that we allow ourselves to fully resonate with our feelings we become separate from them. We become aware that we are more than our feelings. It is in this process of getting in touch with and authentically resonating with our feelings that we more fully become who we are. With an authentic experience of the fullness of our feelings, we then can more fully allow our self to unfold rather than truncating or only partially experiencing our feelings.

To manage most of our feelings, it is not necessary to identify the object or target of the feeling. Simply taking ownership of the feeling makes it more available to intentionally manage. Here's what we mean by this. We could say to someone, "I am angry at you." To manage the feeling and move beyond it, it is first key to identify the core feelings from within the statement. The core feeling of the statement—"I am angry at you."—is *anger.* Initially, it only bogs us down to focus on where the anger is directed. It muddies the waters and makes it more difficult to manage the feeling. It does so because it pushes us to believe that the *other person* is involved or somehow responsible for *our* anger. They are not. *We* are responsible for *our own* feelings—no one else. The purest expression of this experience is to say, "I am angry" or "I feel angry." It is this elemental act of self-acknowledgment that is vital to work through the feeling. When we fully realize this, we take a huge step toward effectively managing the feeling. Giving ourselves permission to have the feeling goes a long way to resolving it.

Acknowledging our feelings is one thing. Expressing them is another. We often avoid talking about strong feelings in many of our relationships. We often believe that aside from being uncomfortable, it might be dangerous to do so. As we have said, not talking about what may be bothering us is likely to intensify our feelings. Fears of openly discussing feelings become reflected in sarcastic comments about being "touchy-feely" or "warm and fuzzy." And when couples argue it is often because feelings are being suppressed, and one partner believes they know what the other person is thinking or feeling. They cannot. And it's disrespectful for them to presume otherwise. Each of us must express our own feelings. No one can do it for us. There is much to gain from learning to identify our own feelings. In doing so, we then can better choose when and how to express them.

Hiding Who We Are

Ethan had lived a long and prosperous life. He was a successful banker and had many hobbies that he loved. After divorcing is fourth wife, he began to examine why his wives had all taken issue with his unwillingness to talk about his feelings. He always thought their insistence to talk about feelings was, as he put it, "bullshit." He saw himself as a "man's man." He couldn't deny, though, that he had been married four times and had not yet found marital happiness.

Ethan spoke to his mother regularly and had always maintained a good relationship with her. But she was ill, and he was very concerned, so he went to see her. At her bedside, he wanted to provide her emotional support. But because of the emptiness and confusion he was feeling in his life, he also needed some support from her. But when he was with her, she surprised him with something she said. He had never before heard her talk to him quite so forcefully. She said, "Why are you always asking me how I feel!?" Her starkness startled him but made him think of his marriages and the similar message he had almost uniformly given to his wives.

Later that day, Ethan reflected on his childhood. The family didn't speak to one another of their deeper or more vulnerable feelings. They simply buried these feelings deep within them or carried on in silence as if those feelings didn't exist. Their hidden family credo was "Suffer in silence." Ethan recalled how his mother and father debated and argued. But they never really realized or spoke directly to what feelings were beneath their hostile emotional tone. He wondered how this norm may have influenced him. Just then, something occurred to him. By watching his parents, could he have picked up on an underlying family message? Ethan wondered if he ingested their credo—feelings should not be openly discussed—without really understanding its implications. He wondered how this might have shaped how he related to each of his wives.

Intense emotions that emerge in relationships are not, in and of themselves, dangerous. Nor are they a sign of mental illness. They are part and parcel of our basic humanness. They are the voices within us that inform us about our own nature and the nature of our relationships. They tell us what needs of ours are being met and what needs may be going unmet. Detached from our feelings, we lose our capacity to manage our relationships in meaningful and competent ways. Moreover, like an unused muscle, with the passage of time, our capability to identify and give voice to our feelings will likely atrophy.

Coping with others expressing *their* emotions can also lead us to feel apprehensive or frightened. When others express their feelings it often triggers similar or mirrored hidden feelings in us. Some of us have never learned how to constructively deal with others' open emotional expression. Here's an example.

> *"Communicating our feelings is an inexact process ... at this, we are all prisoners of language."*

When Grace felt hurt and began to cry, Alexis became nervous. This was partly because it stirred up her own hurt and sadness and partly because she was not sure how to respond to Grace. With help, though, Alexis discovered one of the most important lessons of her life. She discovered that she did not have to do anything to "fix" Grace or stop her from crying. She realized that she simply had *to be with* Grace in a supportive way. She learned that Grace's crying would end when it was completed—that there were reasons that Grace was crying, even if she didn't know what they were. And those reasons needed to be honored. There was nothing Alexis needed to *do* but simply sit with her. Alexis feared that if Grace began to cry that her tears would never end. In fact, she was amazed to find that when Grace cried out her sadness, the tears eventually stopped, and both of them felt better about what had transpired.

In our attempt to communicate our interpersonal experience to one another, we search for words to describe it. The words we use are often inexact and unclear. Language is a symbolic attempt to convey our inner experience. We use words to express our sensations, intuitions, thoughts, emotions, perceptions, and internal images. It's not always easy to do this. There are many ways to express the experience of emotions. The words we use are often quite fuzzy. We may not always know what we want to say. And others can misinterpret what we are trying to say. For example, if someone does something to us that we don't like, we can label our experience as "irritated." We might also describe ourselves feeling "angry" or "annoyed" or "ticked off" or "pissed off" or "grumpy" or "sore" or "furious" or "resentful" or "rageful." As you can see, these feelings vary in their intensity. Being "pissed off" conveys a different tone and level of intensity than being "grumpy."

The experience of irritation is an *inner* sensation. The words we use, though, are only *outer* labels that describe that inner experience. Here's the problem. When we try to communicate our inner experience to someone else, almost without thinking about it we assume that the words we choose accurately describe that inner experience. We also assume that the words we use will mean the same thing to the other person as they do to us. These assumptions are too often misplaced.

From another perspective, expressing feelings through language is a murky pool. That's because some of our feelings are better expressed *without the use of words*—through nonverbal body expressions. Without translating them into language, a smile, an angry tone of voice, a trembling lip, a cold stare, or a defensive stance are all nonverbal ways to convey feelings. And there has

> *"When feelings are not acknowledged or expressed in relationships they tend to become distorted and go underground."*

been ample research showing that people pick up on and assign their own meaning to nonverbal cues. We give more weight to nonverbal cues. And we also assign meaning much more quickly and more often to nonverbal cues than we do to verbal ones.

In attempting to communicate our inner experience, we are all prisoners of language. The eighteenth century diplomat Charles Maurice de Talleyrand captured this well in his often-quoted remark,

> Language was given to man to conceal, not reveal, his true thoughts—a mask behind which man hides his true self.

This is the darker side of language. But at its best, language is also an exciting and dynamic art form to creatively express our inner self. There are often many ways to express a particular experience with words. Exploring new ways of communicating our feelings can feel awkward. But it also can unfold into an experience filled with excitement, pleasure, and the hope of new possibilities. Like building muscles, we can build strength, flexibility, and endurance in our use of feeling words. But it takes discipline and practice. Anybody who has been involved in physical exercise knows that stretching a muscle can be difficult or painful at first. But by sticking with it we can feel more vitality and vigor. This makes it worth the effort. Similarly, we may feel awkward, timid, or uncomfortable about experiencing and expressing our feelings at first. With practice, though, we will become more skilled at it. Here's the pay-off:

1. We can begin to appreciate that to experience our feelings is a natural process—that we do not need to be fearful of it—that any feeling is acceptable.

2. We can become open to experiencing the full range of our feelings—from the most painful negatives to the most exhilarating positives.

3. We can grow in our ability to listen, to understand, and to be empathetic to others' expression of feelings.

4. We can build truly meaningful relationships with others that last.

Personal Mirror Reflection

Building stronger and more intimate relationships with others requires developing our emotional vocabulary. This help us better describe our inner experience and communicate an understanding of our own inner life. Here's one way to begin to develop your emotional vocabulary. Take a look at the list of feelings shown in figure 15.

Select two or three feelings that you find difficult to experience or express. These are the feelings that may be contained in your shadow or aura. After selecting them, ask yourself, "What would be the *worst* possible thing that could happen to me if I experienced or expressed each of these feelings?" Also ask yourself what you think would be the *best* possible thing that could happen to you if you experienced or expressed each of the feelings? Take each of the feelings you listed, and state out load the following sentence:

Figure 15: Developing Your Emotional Vocabulary with a Partial List of Common Feelings

Excited	Appreciative	Threatened	Fearful
Open	Curious	Repulsed	Judged
Involved	Nurtured	Defensive	Blamed
Enthusiastic	Inspired	Embarrassed	Angry
Affirmed	Caring	Put Down	Annoyed
Connected	Hopeful	Suspicious	Manipulated
Creative	Powerful	Hopeless	Abandoned
Genuine	Competitive	Ignored	Closed
Proud	Powerful	Hurt	Disappointed
Supportive	Trusted	Overwhelmed	Vengeful
Connected	Valued	Vulnerable	Powerless
Stimulated	Close	Deceived	Empty
Eager	Optimistic	Disconnected	Skeptical
Animated	Affectionate	Helpless	Cynical
Energized	Peaceful	Apathetic	Trapped
Friendly	Grateful	Alone	Sad
Receptive	Inspired	Deceitful	Abused
Passionate	Imaginative	Lost	Betrayed
Optimistic	Tender	Lonely	Hostile
Encouraged	Loving	Rejected	Withdrawn
Resourceful	Warmhearted	Discouraged	Distrustful
Ingenious	Kindly	Insecure	Ridiculed
Euphoric	Humble	Remorseful	Bored
Joyous	Inviting	Distant	Rejected
Blissful	Cheerful	Guilty	Jealous
Capable	Confident	Ashamed	Inadequate
Secure	Supported	Contrite	Worthless
Poised	Rosy	Enraged	Useless
Affectionate	Calm	Furious	Sarcastic
Caring	Serene	Annoyed	Isolated
Content	Relaxed	Livid	Depressed
Pleased	Assertive	Isolated	Anxious
Ecstatic	Assured	Cross	Sorrowful
Delighted	Gentle	Outraged	Gloomy

"I am _____ (the feeling)." Repeat each feeling sentence five times. After you have completed this task, ask yourself what you are experiencing.

When you are done with this exercise, go to a trusted friend and ask them to listen to your feeling statement. Before stating your feeling sentence to them, ask them just to listen without responding. After you have stated your feeling sentence and you hear their silence, listen within the silence for what you imagine their reaction is. What do you hear in their silence? Was it praise? Criticism? What you hear in the silence may inform you about important messages you may be giving yourself. If you imagine the other person is criticizing what you said or if you feel a sense of guilt or shame in their silence, then you must examine it. It is in *their* silence that you have placed *your* projection. Now, ask your friend if they were actually thinking the critical thought. If they were not, then you know that it must have been your projection.

After you have checked it out with the other person, practice this exercise again until you feel more comfortable or centered within the other person's silence. Once you have done this, then you have begun to take full ownership of these formerly denied or minimized aspects of your own emotional life. You have begun to place what was formerly in your shadow or aura into your conscious awareness, where it is available to feel, express, and better understand.

Deflecting Mirror Reflections

Our defenses blind us from clearly seeing the image of ourselves that is reflected in our perception of the world.

Our defenses also keep us from making real contact with our own pain and the pain around us. They serve us in the sense that they help us manage our unpleasant thoughts and feelings. They help us temporarily distance ourselves from these thoughts and feelings. Our defenses are our "quick fix." In the long run, though, they hinder us.

Defenses prevent us from making deeper contact with ourselves and others. They keep us from connecting with more profound layers of understanding, meaning, and intimacy. We end up relating to ourselves and others through an impaired or constricted self. In doing so, we can become a stranger to our self. We also avoid our more difficult feelings that are necessary for emotional growth. We keep ourselves from the closeness with others that is available to us. As a result, we do not let others care for us in the ways that we truly need. We run away from available support and love. The following short story by Portia Nelson illustrates the challenges we experience in trying to acknowledge and work through our defenses.

> I walk down the street. There is a deep hole in the sidewalk. I fall in. I am lost. I am helpless. It isn't my fault. It takes forever to find a way out.

> I walk down the street. There is a deep hole in the sidewalk. I pretend I don't see it. I fall in. I can't believe I'm in the same place, but it isn't my fault. It will take a long time to get out.

Bidwiya

Seeing Ourselves in the Other

I walk down the street. There is a deep hole in
the sidewalk. I see it is there. I still fall in. It's
a habit. My eyes are open. I know where I am.
It is my fault. I get out immediately.

I walk down the street. There is a deep hole
in the sidewalk. I walk around it.

I walk down a different street.[8]

Learning new ways to deal with the difficulties of living
means forging new paths. Portia Nelson's story is a familiar
one to anyone who has been involved in twelve-step work.
Those attending Alcoholics Anonymous, Narcotics Anonymous, or Adult Children of Alcoholics support groups have
heard this story many times. Because it is both accurate
and supportive, it is told and retold to those struggling to
transform their lives in AA, NA, ACOA, and other support
groups. Trying on new behavior means letting go of seemingly soothing habits and ways of being. This is difficult,
and it takes time. Portia Nelson's story tells us that we
cannot learn without experience. In order to learn how to
avoid our missteps, we must travel, on a road where there
may be setbacks.

It is challenging work to uncover what is submerged
within us. There are feelings of discomfort involved. And it
takes effort to work through them. Much of those feelings
of discomfort come from unrealistic fears about what will
happen to us if we were to look into the mirror. Life has
love and joy, but life also has suffering and struggle. Both
are life-long. Our choice is to keep our joys and pain to
ourselves or share who we are with other people in our
lives. We can *decide* to involve others in our lives. Disclosing
our personal joys and struggles to others usually results in

them sharing their joys and struggles with us. Together, we can find meaningful ways to support each other.

Personal Mirror Reflection

One at a time, read each of the following sentence completion stems and fill in what is missing. After you have done this, repeat reading and completing each sentence stem four more times. In doing so, you may discover something about the way you experience or manage your feelings?

What I am fearful of …

What hurts me is …

What angers me is …

What saddens me is …

What I want in my life is …

_____

What I do with my fears is …

What I do with my feeling hurt is …

What I do with my anger is …

What I do with my sadness is …

What I do with my wants is …

When I don't get what I want I …

Once you have completed the stems, try revealing each of them to someone else. This will allow you to take even greater ownership for your feelings. What was it like for you to share your responses to each of the sentence stems? Talk about what it was like to share them with the other person.

Recently one of our daughters told us that her boyfriend of the moment had told her, "You have issues"—a vague and indirect term for psychological problems. She said that she calmly responded to him by saying,

> You're right. I do have issues. In fact, everyone has them. Even you. But what we often think is someone else's issue turns out to be our own issue. Let's talk about sorting that out.

She was grasping the edge of the cosmic mirror. She realized that whatever "issues" or "struggles" her friend was having with her first needed to be identified. Any projections needed to be worked through. Talking about their feelings was the only answer. She was aware that the problems we see in others might also be within ourselves— and the problems they see in us may also be a reflection of something inside of them.

How do we put all these perspectives to work for us? How do we begin to heal ourselves and repair our relationships with others? How do we risk knowing ourselves? How do we push through our own hypnotic haze and find the trusted others that we need to help us? This is what we will discuss in our final chapter—"Putting It All into Practice."

16

Putting It All into Practice

"To be what we are, and to become what we are
capable of becoming, is the only end of life."

—*Robert Louis Stevenson*

Earlier in the book, we discussed the idea of the magical illusion of healing. This is our tendency to believe that something outside of us might cure the emotional stress that is within us. We wish for and often depend on a pill, a lover, a guru, or a psychic to give us the answers. To some, it may seem almost impossible to begin a task as daunting as looking into their cosmic mirror without some kind of guide. Some of us may wish that we could leave it up to someone else to begin this process for us. And many of us unknowingly procrastinate and put it off with this rationale in mind. And we may stay stuck in a victim role asking ourselves, "Why do I have to do all this work on my own?" There is a very short parable, though, that might help us understand why no one else can do it for us.

> A man was thanking God for everything he had done for him. He then added: "But God, I have one question for you." "Why do you allow all the suffering in the world?" "Why don't you do something about it?" God answered him, "Oh, but I did. I created you!"

As much as we may think it is not fair and wish it wasn't the case, we are responsible for initiating the journey into our hidden, mysterious, unknown, and evolving self. Untangling and bringing into awareness our shadow, aura, projections, polarities, and magical thinking require a substantial emotional investment and commitment to our self. As Jung pointedly proclaims,

> One does not become enlightened by imagining figures of light, but by making the darkness conscious.[1]

Although it is not easy moving the dark reservoir of our unconscious into conscious awareness, it is possible when we commit to exploring it with an open heart and mind. As the Buddha is often quoted saying, "Conquering one's self is a greater task than conquering others."

Throughout this book, we have used the term *self* as if there were a common understanding of its meaning. There are many perspectives, though, on what constitutes the self. From the perspective of the cosmic mirror, we view it as the total set of polarities within a person—the polarities we know about and the ones we don't.[2] These polarities are fluid, evolving, and expanding attributes of our personality. They direct our attention to what is outside of us, and they direct our attention to what is inside of us. They are the many quiet—often silent—inner voices that influence us. Some of them are hidden and denied. Some are in full view. Some are only in partial view, knocking on the door of consciousness. Taken together, they are the driving emotional forces in our daily life. Whatever attribute we highly identify or associate to our self, the opposite attribute also exists in our unconscious and is waiting to be acknowledged. The more we are unable or unwilling to acknowledge it, the more it will push itself to be acknowledged or pull us into situations to make itself heard.

Being polarities, by definition, these opposite extremes can feel like they are at odds with each other. We can manage their inherent conflict, or we can let them manage us. Becoming aware of what Jung called the *law of opposites* in our daily life takes work. Handling these intrinsic incompatibilities first requires that they be brought into awareness. Once a given polarity has surfaced, we are able to address it in a more deliberate and intentional way. We can dialogue with each end of the polarity. Only then can we overcome the destructiveness of staying caught at one end of the polarity or the other.

For any change to be meaningful and sustaining, we need to *make friends* with our unknown polarities. Only by acknowledging our polarities and animating them—giving voice to them—can we transcend our current pattern of behavior. When we feel "stuck", bored, or empty, we are telling ourselves something that we need to hear—those feelings inform us that we may be avoiding squarely facing a polarity. The emptiness alerts us that something needs to be acknowledged. We feel "unbalanced" or "ungrounded." Until we listen to what we are telling our self from deep within, our life will continue to feel depleted. We will feel drained. We will lack vitality. And we will feel caught up in the "same old same old," doing what we have always done and getting nowhere. As Jung said,

> Once one has experienced a few times what it is like to stand judgingly between the opposites, one begins to understand what is meant by the self. Anyone who perceives his shadow and his light simultaneously sees himself from two sides and thus gets in the middle.[3]

We might hear someone explain a person's actions by saying something like, "Larry really showed his true colors" in betraying us. Or we might hear, "When Tom angrily yelled at me that was the *real* Tom coming out." Remarks like these are commonplace. The idea that we have a *true self* and a *false self* stems from the work of psychoanalyst Donald Winnicott. He believed that our spontaneous and uninhibited actions come from our "true self". He postulated that the layers of defenses that we use to create our polite and socially manicured persona stem from our "false self".[4] He was describing how we suppress our honest and uncensored feelings to accommodate to social demands. But the idea that there are aspects of our personality that are more valid or more real than others seems untenable. Despite having emotional defenses that may mask some of our deeper or more authentic feelings and thoughts, all aspects of our self are real—our persona is every bit as real as the emotional layers beneath it. Our emotional growth depends on us revealing our persona to ourselves—we must be aware of the mask we have created. Only then can we change it and discover our deeper self.

There are many facets of the self that are present in our everyday lives—despite the fact that some aspects of the self are more defended, filtered, or layered versions than others. As noted Gestalt therapist Erving Polster expresses,

> In spite of the attraction of a "real self," it is clearly an oversimplification of a person's existence. Though the real self is often a useful reference for what people would like to be or what they believe they once were, there is always a wider scope of personal options and development.[5]

Giving voice to our denied, polarized, and projected parts of our self—what we use the shadow and aura to contain— is a necessary step in freeing their contents and bringing them into our awareness. It is only then that they can be put to better use. What is essential is to animate—to give voice to—the concealed parts of the self. It is then that we can find the message contained within them. As Polster goes on to state,

> With the naming of each self, the self becomes an agent of the person—brightly; a spotlight on otherwise ephemeral existences; a banner, so to speak, around which the person rallies his psychological energies. Just as the novel creates human images that echo in the minds of its readers, the image of selves also comes alive, giving membership and coherence to otherwise disconnected parts of the person.[5]

Learning to label (or name) these evolving parts of our self and dialogue with them to find their message for us is a life-affirming skill that is waiting to be developed.

Surfacing Projections, Polarities, Magical Thinking, Shadow, and Aura

As we have discussed, we can learn how to identify our polarities and learn how to use creative dialogue to constructively reconcile them. You can begin exploring your polarities by paying attention to the strong emotional responses you have to people who irritate or enliven you. Similarly, whenever you find yourself emotionally over-reacting to an attribute or characteristic in someone that pushes your buttons, it is likely you have evoked an aspect of your shadow or aura. As we have advised earlier in the book, spotting the characteristic in others does not imply that it is an unacknowledged or under-acknowledged aspect of your self. We may be accurately and objectively observing the characteristic in them. But when the characteristic evokes a strong emotional reaction within you then it's a good bet that you are missing an important emotional aspect of it that is emanating from within your self. For example, if you over-react to someone's impatience, you may be overlooking the impatience within your self; if you are overly envious or admiring of someone else's leadership qualities you may be discounting similar characteristics within you. Its residence in your self is the basis for spotting it in others.

Discovering Reparation and Joy

When we are in situations where we feel especially vulnerable, inept, unprepared, embarrassed, irritated, hostile, fearful, or overly euphoric, it is likely that our shadow and aura are sending signals to us. When we are suddenly aware of surprisingly strong feelings within us or find our own behavior troubling in some way, it is more than likely that we are becoming aware that our shadow is surfacing unexpectedly. In previous chapters, we have presented exercises you can use to develop your skills in identifying your own projections, polarities, magical thinking, aura, and shadow. Using those exercises will serve you well in reclaiming and revitalizing yourself. As Jung so pointedly put it,

> If you imagine someone who is brave enough to withdraw all his projections, then you get an individual who is conscious of a pretty thick Shadow. Such a man has saddled himself with new problems and conflicts ... Such a man knows that whatever is wrong in the world is in himself, and if he only learns to deal with his own Shadow he has done something real for the world. He has succeeded in shouldering at least an infinitesimal part of the gigantic, unsolved social problems of our day. These problems are mostly so difficult because they are poisoned by mutual projections. How can anyone see straight when he does not even see himself and the darkness he unconsciously carries with him into all dealings? [6]

Dare to Know Yourself by Making Yourself Known to Others

In Greece, during the eighth century BC, the Oracle of Delphi proclaimed, "Know thyself." These words have since been echoed by countless poets, theologians, and philosophers. In *Hamlet*, Shakespeare wrote

> This above all: to thine own self be true.
> And it must follow, as the night the day.
> Thou canst not then be false to any man.

The cosmic mirror enables us to know ourselves at the deepest possible level. Just *wanting* to look deeply at the reflections of ourselves in the cosmic mirror is—in itself— the most crucial step in beginning the journey inward.

Knowing ourselves, however, is not just an individual task—it is also an interpersonal one. This is true because there is no identity, no self, no "I", without other people in our lives. We all have a fundamental need to relate, to connect—to *be with* others. Without that connection, we are less than our full self. We derive our sense of who we are by virtue of our life in our interpersonal world. What is needed is to understand ourselves *in the context of our relationships with others*. We derive our sense of who we are by the kind of life we live out with others. Somewhat paradoxically, we need the mirror provided by other people to see our self clearly. With this in mind, the Delphic Oracle's words "Know thyself" might be rearranged to read,

> Make thyself known, and then Thou wilt know thyself.[7]

Shakespeare's words then become more prophetic when reshaped to read,

> And this above all: to any other man be true.
> And thou canst not then be false to thyself.[7]

As humanistic psychologist Sidney Jourard poignantly puts it,

> No man can come to know himself except as
> an outcome of disclosing himself to another

person. This is the lesson we have learned in the field of psychotherapy. When a person has been able to disclose himself utterly to another person, he learns how to increase his contact with the real self, and he may then be better able to direct his destiny on the basis of this knowledge.[7]

There is considerable research indicating that self-disclosure of intimate information about oneself tends to promote self-disclosure in the listener. The greater the intimacy of the self-disclosure, the more the other person likes the self-disclosing person. What is profound about these findings is that you can affect and change the nature of your relationship with others by more personally disclosing what you are emotionally experiencing in the relationship. This is the meaning of intimacy in a relationship.[8]

Attempting to teach a topic is sometimes a way to discover what you don't know about it. In a similar way, we cannot truly know ourselves without telling others who we are. It takes a certain degree of risk to reveal ourselves to someone else. But this is essential for

Becoming You

us to see our deeper self. Like the glue that cements a joint, disclosure helps bond the connection with our newly emerging self. Contempt breeds ruin in relationships—so does insincerity. On the other hand, authenticity and empathy with others fosters the development of our own identity, our own integrity, our healing, and our growth.

Removing Our Mask

For many of us, the idea of talking to others about who we are can feel like an intimidating prospect. This is especially true when it comes to revealing our intimate, heartfelt, or mostly unrevealed self. How do we know that we can trust the other person? How do we know that they will not use our disclosures to harm us? To go beyond our persona and remove our mask around others— to speak what is typically unspoken, to voice what is unvoiced—takes an act of courage. We must overcome our worst fears about what will happen—checking out whether our fears are grounded in the facts about the current relationship or are merely echoes from our past. This is a constantly unfolding and lifelong path.

Too often at this stage, though, our process of self-discovery breaks down. Our fears intrude on us. They lead us into postponing the journey to the center of our self. We become hesitant. Reluctant. Skittish. And to deal with our hesitancy, we often do what we have done in the past—avoid, withdraw, fight, or flee. This, then, becomes a vicious cycle. Our avoidance is reinforcing. By avoiding our fears, they never get challenged. And we end up repeating what we have done over and over again. In trying to run away from facing ourselves, we only exhaust ourselves. We redo the very patterns that have undermined us. To break these patterns, we must identify the specific fears we have and acknowledge them. We must explore what we imagine would be the *worst* possible thing that could happen to us if we took that risk. We must also explore the *best* possible thing that could happen if we took the risk.

Everything starts with awareness—awareness of what we are experiencing and what we are doing. Awareness that unhealthy patterns are influencing our life breaks the cycle and allows us to make healthier choices for our evolving self. The building of the self takes raising our level of awareness of what we are doing and experiencing right now, from moment to moment, and on a daily basis. Without awareness, we can take no intentional action. We are not able to choose what we do. Emotional awareness of ourselves helps us better see what we project into others and what others project into us. It is only through awareness that we can begin to take ownership of our projections and discover our polarities. As noted psychiatrist R. D. Laing has written in this short poem,

> The range of what we think and do
> Is limited by what we fail to notice.
> And because we fail to notice that we fail
>   to notice
> There is little we can do to change
> Until we notice how failing to notice
> Shapes our thoughts and deeds.[9]

What assists our learning is listening from deep within our heart and speaking from deep within our heart. Doing so helps us examine whether or not the feedback we are hearing from others is valid about us or simply *their own* projection. It also helps us see what we may be projecting. Learning to make these distinctions is not an easy task. Here are some questions that might help you on your path:

~ Can you hear the depth and humanity in your own disclosures?

~ Can you hear the love in the other person's voice and message?

~ Can you hear their anger or sadness without defensively reacting to it?

~ Can you be with them without judgment or derision?

Awareness and Acknowledgment of Feelings and Emotions

Crucial in allowing ourselves to unfold and blossom is identifying and acknowledging our feelings and emotions on a daily basis. Developing a vocabulary of feelings and emotions to describe our inner experience is vital to our development. As we have previously mentioned, learning to label our feelings and emotions and communicate them to our self or others is an art form that we can only develop through practice.

Learning the language of feelings and emotions is similar to building physical muscles—repetition and practice builds strength, flexibility, and endurance. Stretching the muscles can at first seem difficult and painful, but as we build them, our enhanced sense of vitality rewards us. So initially, while we feel awkward, timid, and uncomfortable with experiencing, labeling, and expressing our newly explored feelings and emotions, daily practice will help us become more skillful and foster our enjoyment in being more emotionally expressive. Like driving a high performance car or using a new mechanical tool, it eventually becomes second-nature to us. As we practice our new emotional skills, we begin to acknowledge that experiencing all of our feelings is a natural process that we can give ourselves permission to experience.

Expressing our deeper feelings is a choice we must make and requires using our intellect as a guide. This helps us make our verbal expression constructive rather than destructive. *Although we are responsible for what we do with our feelings it is not our choice to have them.* We are not responsible for acquiring our defenses—only for what we choose to do with them once we become aware of them. With the freedom from judging our feelings, we become open to experiencing the full continuum of them. In doing so, we can also develop our ability to listen, identify, and understand the verbal and nonverbal expression of emotions by others.

Awareness of Past Influences on Present Behavior

We are not born knowing how to see ourselves and how to see the world—we are taught. As children and adults, we learn from our cultural matrix. Our current actions and feelings are significantly influenced by our past family dynamics. Paradoxically, while our past is unmanageable we are unwittingly managed by it—but only until we become aware of its influences on what we do and the way we are in the world. Knowingly and unknowingly, we have learned from our parents and the way they emotionally dealt with us, themselves, and others in their world. In so many ways, we are created in their image. In our early development, they were our mirrors.

At some point, many of us are able to break away from those teachings and see the world through our own eyes. But, this is never purely the case. To some degree, our learning—good and bad, healthy and unhealthy—is carried with us wherever we go. Breaking the hypnotic spell of our programming, though, can free us to discover more of our unfolding self. And to be free from such programming, it is necessary to routinely examine our own beliefs. We must ask ourselves,

~ Do *I* really believe this? Have I *chosen* to believe this or have I been *taught* to believe it without closely examining it?

~ Have I swallowed whole what I have been fed by others? Or have I first chewed on it and spit out the parts that I didn't want, because they didn't have (or no longer have) any nurturing value for me?

Again, Sidney Jourard offers us guidance here:

We begin life with the world presenting itself to us as it is. Someone—our parents, teachers, analysts—hypnotizes us to "see" the world and construe it in the "right" way. These others label the world, attach names and give voices to the beings and events in it, so that thereafter, we cannot read the world in any other language or hear it saying other things to us. The task is to break the hypnotic spell, so that we become undeaf, unblind, and multilingual, thereby letting the world speak to us in new voices and write all its possible meaning in the new book of our existence.[10]

Using the *Personal Mirror Reflection* exercises—especially the ones in the chapter on mothers and fathers—can be powerful tools for you in identifying how your emotional past is influencing you in your current life. You can explore how each parent—or the absence of them—has influenced the development of your shadow and aura as well as acknowledge attributes or characteristics you may have projected into them.

Creating a Cosmic Mirror Learning System

It is difficult enough to learn about the many submerged parts of our self, but it is almost impossible to do it all by ourselves. Teachers, mentors, and guides are important to find, but as the ancient Chinese proverb says,

> *"It is important to remember that at first blush, going sane feels just like going crazy."*
> *—Julia Cameron*

"Teachers open the door, but you must enter by yourself." We have discussed how overreliance on these guides can itself be problematic, but under-reliance on them can also inhibit our growth. For those of us who have trouble finding and identifying those guides, they *are* out there waiting for us, wanting to help us. It is often said in Zen Buddhist circles, "When the student is ready the teacher appears." If we are open to learning, wisdom will make itself available to us. The following story further illustrates this point:

> This guy's walking down the street when he falls in a hole. The walls are so steep he can't get out. A doctor passes by and the guy shouts up, "Hey you. Can you help me out?" The doctor writes a prescription, throws it down in the hole, and moves on.

Then a priest comes along and the guy shouts up, "Father, I'm down in this hole can you help me out?" The priest writes out a prayer, throws it down in the hole, and moves on.

Then a friend walks by, "Hey, Joe, it's me can you help me out?" And the friend jumps in the hole. Our guy says, "Are you stupid? Now we're both down here." The friend says, "Yeah, but I've been down here before and I know the way out."[11]

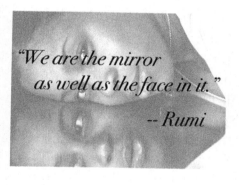

"We are the mirror as well as the face in it."

-- Rumi

We all need an emotional *holding environment.* By this, we mean an environment where others are available to provide emotional support and guidance to us. None of us can go it alone. For a child, a safe and loving home nurtures them. It fosters their mental and physical health. For adults, a nurturing holding environment is one that makes us feel genuinely cared for, safe, understood, encouraged, and loved. A holding environment helps us increase our self-awareness. It evokes our spontaneous self. It assists us in overcoming and transcending our fears. It enhances our sense of independence. And it fosters the feeling of being more fully alive. We can seek out others who trigger or instill these feelings in us. And we can treat ourselves in the same way. As physician and internationally known expert in conscious living and inner transformation Richard Moss asserts,

Being present and attentive to our feelings without collapsing into them, and not

> identifying with our suffering, is analogous
> to the way a loving, empathic mother relates
> and responds to her baby.[12]

With a strong and supportive holding environment, almost anything is possible. With the appropriate kind of support, we can grant ourselves permission to be the way we want to be in the world. We all have the right to our own experience. And we have the right to experience our unfolding self—without disparaging it, without criticizing it, and without belittling it.

With the help of the people you bring into your holding environment, you can learn much about your shadow, aura, magical thinking, polarities, and projections. You can practice being more self-disclosing with others and practice soliciting meaningful feedback from them—especially, about your "blind" spots. With the people you invite into your inner life, you can practice the exercises we have presented throughout this book. You can periodically write feedback to the people you elect to bring closer to you and discuss it openly. You can also watch yourself closely when receiving any feedback from others—especially if you find yourself too quickly saying "I'm never like that."

If you find yourself feeling hurt or severely criticized, pay close attention—chances are your defenses have been evoked and with further reflection you may realize that you may have unknowingly revealed your shadow to another person. Remember: we have a tendency to project our shadow and aura onto people who more openly display the attributes, feelings, and wants that our contained in them. We see the unwanted attribute in another, and we believe that we have found a "resting place" for our own unwanted attribute. The feedback, advice, excessive praise, or criticisms we give others may also say something about us. At the same time, the feedback we receive from others may also be saying something about them.

The people in our holding environment are the ones with constructive intent. This is true because the people we trust show us that they are willing to work through difficult issues with us in a constructive and creative way. Think of what it might be like to your own growth and development if you were to bring those trusted others together in the same room. You might think of it as a cosmic mirror learning group. Deepen your understanding of yourself through one of our cosmic mirror learning events posted on our website—www.thecosmicmirror.org—or start your own.

Staying with It

To look at one's hidden self in the cosmic mirror is not easy. Attaining anything of real and sustainable value, though, seldom is. Since time eternal, those embarking on this inner journey have searched for a quick path to becoming a fully-functioning and socially constructive human being. But there is no easy path. There is no quick fix. As Fritz Perls put it,

> The growth process is a process that takes time. We can't just snap our fingers and say, "Come on, let's be gay! Let's do this" ... You don't have to be on a couch or in a Zendo for twenty or thirty years, but you have to invest yourself, and it takes time to grow.[13]

We hope you invest yourself in exploring "*you*" in depth and take the time you need to grow and unfold.

To confront our own reflection in the cosmic mirror means honesty examining the way we actual are in our world—without illusions. It means paying attention to the strong positive and negative emotional charges we feel toward others. This helps us identify what we are projecting into others. We are often afraid to admit certain things about ourselves as if it were dangerous to become conscious of our self. There is no real danger. Although there is a wish to know the depth of ourselves there is also a fear of actually knowing it. But as novelist Marcel Proust has said, "We are healed from suffering only by experiencing it to the fullest."

Thinking that we have something to fear that we cannot overcome or that we would be better off not knowing is a false and misguided belief. At times, to fully experience ourselves seems like it may be a chaotic venture. But, like all things, the chaos doesn't last if we allow ourselves to flow with it. The way *out* of it is going *through* it. It means trusting the process of change that this experience brings with it. As mathematician and Pulitzer Prize winner Douglas Hofstader says,

> It turns out that an eerie type of chaos can lurk just behind a facade of order ... and yet, deep inside the chaos lies an even eerier [*and more wondrous*] type of order.[14]

It's not easy to look deeply at our reflections in our personal cosmic mirror. It requires some degree of risk-taking. But it does not end there. We must overcome our fears over and over again and repeatedly step outside of our comfort zone. But just like anything else that is strange or new or mysterious, with practice, it becomes less difficult. We adapt. And with that, we grow. While at one time we feared the unfamiliar and found it threatening, we learn to see it as a source for our creativity and imagination. We then learn one of the most profound teachings of a lifetime: we learn that we have a choice. We can face our fear and move forward toward growth or we can withdraw into what feels familiar and safe but keeps us shackled in an unsatisfying or unworkable routine.[15] "Feel the fear and do it anyway" seems a useful adage.

Most of us live in settings that encourage the maintenance of the status quo. This norm is all around us. It can be inhibiting—it can be stifling. You might say, "Well, how can I grow in an environment like that?" Or you might ask, "Shouldn't I use what others are doing as my own yardstick?" Or you might say to yourself, "If everyone else is going along with things just the way they are, doesn't that tell me that what they are doing is normal?" These are questions that challenge us all. But how can we separate what is commonplace or widely accepted from what may be unhealthy?[16] How are we to make distinctions like these *before* we act or react? Philosopher Jiddu Krishnamurti helps us answer this when he says,

> It is no measure of health to be well adjusted
> to a profoundly sick society.

This is the fundamental dilemma for us all. Do we go with the flow, not make waves? Or do we honor ourselves and stand up for what we believe in? Do we permit ourselves to express ourselves to others in the way we may most want or need? These are important questions.

If we wish to change ourselves or influence others, we must first acknowledge what is true about ourselves and others. We need to acknowledge the way *we are* in the world—and the way *others are* in the world. We need to be vigilant that out of spite, anger, shame, pain, or hurt, we do not condemn ourselves or condemn others. Self-contempt and the contempt of others frees no one to change—it only oppresses as it blocks real and constructive change.

The central message of the cosmic mirror is that the things we believe we see in our outer world often are reflections of what we carry inside of us. Furthermore, not only do we shape the world by our actions, but we also shape our own lives by the expectations we have of ourselves and others. As Carl Jung puts it,

> If we do not fashion for ourselves a picture of the world, we do not see ourselves either, who are the faithful reflections of that world. Only when mirrored in our picture of the world can we see ourselves in the round. Only in our creative acts do we step forth into the light and see ourselves whole and complete. Never shall we put any face on the world other than our own, and we have to do this precisely in order to find ourselves.[17]

We tend to underestimate the amount of joyous and profound meaning and exuberance that we could experience in our lives. We discount how many exciting things we have yet to discover and to embrace in our self. By underestimating ourselves, we fail to see the full power within our aura. Nevertheless, it is available to us. Artist, poet, playwright, composer, novelist, filmmaker, and journalist Julia Cameron captures it well when she says,

> All of us are far richer than we imagine. None of us possess a life devoid of magic, barren of grace, divorced from power. Our inner resources, often unmined and even unknown

or unacknowledged, are the treasures we carry.[18]

> "There is no end to the journey;
> it is an endless pilgrimage.
> You are always arriving,
> and arriving, and arriving,
> but you never arrive."
>
> ~ Osho, a spiritual teacher

It is our fervent hope that the framework we have presented to you in the cosmic mirror provides you with a powerful tool that you can use to mine the unrecognized treasures within you. Learning to use the cosmic mirror takes courage and practice. But it also takes kindness towards ourselves and patience with ourselves. We wish you well on your sojourn.

~ Gary and George

Glossary

ACKNOWLEDGE: To admit the existence, reality, or truth of projected attributes, feelings, or behavior.

ACTING OUT/ACTING IN: To unknowingly change a thought or feeling into an action. That action is focused either toward the world outside of us or the one inside of us. We *act out* by translating thoughts and feelings into actions without fully knowing why we are doing so or without wisely planning it. It is usually impulsive or reactive. *Acting in* refers to taking those unknown motivations and internally turning them on ourselves. Instead of having an impact on what is outside of us, we hold those thoughts and feelings inside of us—we unknowingly direct them inward.

ANIMUS: Unconscious stereotypical male attributes, feelings, and behavior in females.

ANDROGYNY: A healthy mix of stereotypically male and female social qualities—the best of being male blended with the best of being female.

ANIMA: Unconscious stereotypical female attributes, feelings, and behavior in males.

ARCHETYPE: A universal and collective image that is common across people and across cultures. The image has widespread meaning but the reason it has such meaning is not entirely in our immediate awareness. Archetypes include images of the hero, the wise man, the shadow, a locked door, a mountaintop, a heart, or open and outstretched arms.

AURA: Constructive attributes, talents, feelings, and behavioral qualities of the self that are submerged, denied, and projected. We are attracted to the targets—people, objects, or ideals—toward which we send these projections.

AWARENESS: Consciousness of our self and our environment gained through our senses or by means of information. Self-awareness is the acknowledgement and recognition of our feelings and emotions.

CHANGE: To transform a fundamental aspect of our self. It is to alter or modify a longstanding or undiscovered part of ourselves and thereby create something new within us. It can take place gradually or in a flash of insight.

CHOICE: One of the most powerful aspects of our lives. Choice is an awareness of options. It is the basis of our power, our rights, and our opportunity to guide our own life. It is the prospect of new possibility and alternative.

CONFORMITY: Action that we unknowingly take in order to adhere to others' attitudes and standards of conduct. It is deeply imprinted conventionality. When we conform we often diminish our own personal standards and values.

CONSCIOUSNESS: A state of awareness of what is happening inside the self and outside in the environment.

CONSTRUCTIVE AGGRESSION: Marshalling our energies to deliberately and wisely act on our environment (and the people in it) in a way that honors our own needs (but does not dishonor others' needs).

CONSULTANT or FACILITATOR: A person who is skilled at interpersonal relations who assists a person, a group, or an organization to access the contents of their shadow and aura.

COSMIC MIRROR: The people and objects in our daily environment that reflect the hidden parts of ourselves and others. The mirroring process is cosmic in the sense that its presence is universal. It extends across people and across cultures. It is also cosmic in the sense that mirroring is vast; it's ubiquitous; and it's extensively employed in the process of creating ourselves. Mirroring is also cosmic because it follows an orderly pattern of development and consistently fits into the larger system of our thoughts and actions. Mirroring extends beyond our conscious awareness to include what is unseen, what is unfamiliar, and what is unexplored.

COUNTERTRANSFERENCE: A mental state within the psychotherapist where the therapist strongly feels that their client is experiencing an emotion when, in fact, they are not. The therapist is often unconsciously compelled to act out their own unresolved issue with their client.

DEFENSES: Unconscious processes that are aimed at reducing the pain and anxiety associated with emotionally unacceptable thoughts, feelings, attributes, or behavior.

DELUSION: A persistent and false belief. Although the term is used in psychiatry to imply a psychotic state of mind we are using the word delusion to mean any belief that we adopt, that we surrender to, and that we accept without challenging or questioning. A delusion can be patently obvious to others or it can be subtle and hidden.

DENIAL: A process of removing from consciousness painful attributes, feelings, thoughts, and behavior. It is a refusal to admit to one's self the truth—the reality—of aspects of the self.

DIALOGUE: To speak to the polarities within ourselves. It is a conversational process by which we increase our awareness of ourselves. To dialogue with our inner polarities is to pretend that each end of a polarity is a person who can talk and think and express themselves. Each end of a polarity is given a voice and asked to speak openly and out loud.

DISOWN: To refuse to acknowledge an attribute, feeling, or thought that is part of ourselves. We see ourselves as if we do not possess a quality when the truth is that we do. Disowning is a means of defending against an awareness of the contents of our shadow or our aura.

GOOD OBJECTS/BAD OBJECTS: A term coined by child psychologist Melanie Klein. It refers to a mental state that begins in early infancy where the child's perceptions of their inner and outer world is divided into separate and distinct categories. Everything in their universe—including their thoughts, feelings, wishes, and fears—first becomes identified as an object of love or an object of hate, an object of pain or an object of pleasure.

HARMONY ILLUSION: A phase in a group's development where the group has embraced their own exaggerated goodness and has denied the undesirable qualities about themselves. The harmony illusion is often accompanied by a sense of group superiority and by the projection of the group's rage and inferiority onto a perceived enemy group.

HONORING: The highest level of respect we can place on feelings. It is the absolute recognition of their worth.

What we honor can be pleasant or unpleasant (e.g., we can honor our talents or our anger or our shame). The act of honoring our feelings always connects us to our self.

ICON: An enduring symbol of great importance. We are using the term to represent something outside of ourselves—a person or an object—onto which we project our own denied inner talents contained in our aura. It is a symbol to which we attach great devotion but at the cost of diminishing an important aspect of ourselves.

INTIMACY: A close emotional moment in a relationship. It involves us sharing our most important feelings. Those feelings can be pleasant or unpleasant, but in either case, they are shared with authenticity and genuineness. With true intimacy, all defenses are stripped away.

MAGICAL ILLUSION OF HEALING: we are using the term to mean the excessive and unwarranted belief that something outside ourselves can exclusively heal us without us needing to take the necessary actions on our own to assist ourselves in the healing process.

MAGICAL THINKING: A normal developmental phase in childhood where the child believes that thoughts, feelings, objects, and events relate to each other when they do not. In adulthood, magical thinking takes the form of superstitions, charms, and curses. But it also takes shape in the notion that our thoughts and feelings cause others to act, that our wishes can come true without action, and that our fears are true because we experience them.

MIRROR-ROLE: A term coined by psychoanalyst Donald Winnicott to mean the role taken by a parent or caretaker that allows the child to see their own goodness mirrored back to them. Through loving gazes and gestures, the parent enacts the role. Mirroring provides the basis for the child's self-esteem.

OWNING: Refers to the process of recognizing emotions, projections, and other defenses and acknowledging them as belonging to one's self.

PARADOX: A statement that seems false or self-contradictory but in reality expresses a truth. One example of this is the idea that we can let a feeling go only by fully embrace it.

PERCEPTION: A process of attending, interpreting, and organizing in a meaningful pattern what we observe in our environment. It is our internal understanding of something external to us.

PERSONA: The image or mask one presents in public. It is our public image as distinguished from our inner self, which may be at odds with the image we show to others.

POLARITY: Two opposite extremes in attributes, feelings, or behavior. One extreme usually has a pleasant or positive emotional charge while the other extreme has a painful or negative emotional charge.

PROJECTION: Externalizing outward one's attributes, thoughts, feelings, or inclinations into or onto someone else or some object in the environment. What feels emotionally unacceptable in our self is rejected and attributed to other people or objects.

REENACTMENT: A process where the past—with all its problems and conflicts—is unknowingly brought into the present. Reenactment can take the form of perceiving that others are treating us or judging us in a way that is similar to or reminds us of how we were treated in the past—whether others are actually doing so or not. It can also take shape if we were to act on a belief or memory from our past as if it were true in the present moment.

REPARATION: The process of healing longstanding and painful emotional wounds. The process is often slow and frequently uncomfortable. Significant time and effort are usually involved. Like other wounds, we measure the process of healing by how much more flexible and useful the wounded area has become when we try to look at it or use it.

ROLE: A defined set of thoughts, feelings, and actions that follow an identifiable script or image. Examples include the "macho role," the "victim role," the "follower role," the "role of the phony" and the "role of the healer." They are a limited or constrained set of behaviors. This can make them extremely useful in some task situations. But in relationships where intimacy and closeness are essential, rigid emotional roles can cripple.

SELF: The center of our being—that which we respect and accept within us—the part of us where all life-energy emanates. It is also the sum of all the resolved polarities within us.

SELF-LOATHING: A condition in which a person acts on their anger and rage at the outside world by turning it on themselves.

SHADOW: Submerged, denied, and projected attributes, thoughts, feelings, and behavior that we consider unacceptable in our self. We are prone to project these undesirable aspects of the self onto others and are simultaneously repulsed by those we have targeted with our own shadowy projections.

STEREOTYPE: An exaggerated and oversimplistic label given to a person or a group. Stereotypes are a way to defend against thinking about the complexities in the world and in ourselves. It is an extreme way of characterizing others that includes only a select set of features or qualities and excludes other characteristics that may limit, qualify, or contradict those that have been identified.

TRANSFERENCE: A state in which a client in psycho-therapy feels compelled to act out unresolved emotional conflicts with their therapist. It's normal, and when interpreted by the therapist and clearly understood by the client leads to growth and healing.

UNCONSCIOUS: Feelings, thoughts, images, memories, and behavior of which we are not directly or fully aware at a conscious level. It influences our behavior even though we are not aware of the underlying influence. It is what lies behind the curtain of consciousness.

WHOLENESS: A state of being where all of the parts to the self are acknowledged and honored—where polarities within the self are integrated and accepted. It is a condition where we feel an order and acceptance of the darkness and the illuminating light within us—where our aura and shadow are revealed and loved.

Appendix

The Karl Menninger Letter to Thomas Szasz

October 6, 1988

Dear Dr. Szasz:

I am holding your new book, *Insanity: The Idea and Its Consequences*, in my hands. I read part of it yesterday and I have also read reviews of it. I think I know what it says but I did enjoy hearing it said again. I think I understand better what has disturbed you these years and, in fact, it disturbs me, too, now. We don't like the situation that prevails whereby a fellow human being is put aside, outcast as it were, ignored, labeled and said to be "sick in his mind." If he can pay for care and treatment, we will call him a patient and record a "diagnosis" (given to his relatives for a fee). He is listened to and then advised to try to relax, consider his past sins to be forgiven, renounce his visions or voices or fits, quit striking his neighbor's windows with his cane, or otherwise making himself conspicuous by eccentric behavior. He tries.

For this service we charge, now. Doctors were once satisfied with a gift, or token, or sometimes just an earnest verbal expression of gratitude. Even if the treatment given was not immediately curative, the doctor had done the sagacious and difficult task of having approached the crazy subject and listened to him and given the condition a NAME, and a prognosis. (In fact, the latter was what he was a specialist in; treatment was really secondary.) You and I remember that there didn't use to be any treatments, just care and prognosis, "fatal," "nonfatal," "serious," "committable," "nonpsychotic." Gradually empirical and chemical agents were discovered, which seemed to alter something in the organism which was reflected in the customer's changed behavior. We accumulated a few methods that seemed to relieve the suffering of these customers, our "patients." We used prolonged baths, cold sheet packs, diathermy, electric shock, and there were all those other treatments of whipping, strapping down, giving cold douches and sprays. King George III of England was slapped and punched by the fists of one of his "nurses" who later bragged that he even knocked his patient, the King, to the floor "as flat as a flounder." And the King ultimately recovered but those treatments weren't outlawed. Added to the beatings and chaining and the baths and massages came treatments that were even more ferocious: gouging out parts of the brain, producing convulsions with electric shocks, starving, surgical removal of teeth, tonsils, uteri, etc.

Next someone discovered some chemicals that had peculiar effects on people who swallowed them. Alcohol was already well known and opium and morphine and heroin and cocaine; but Luminal was introduced and "Seconal" and similar pharmaceutical concoctions given names ending in "al" or "ol" (as in Demerol). These were regarded as therapeutically useful because they did dispel some of the symptoms and they made the patient feel better (briefly). No baths, no brain operations, no chemicals, no electric shocks, no brain stabbing.

Long ago I noticed that some of our very sick patients surprised us by getting well even without much of our "treatment." We were very glad, of course, but frequently some of them did something else even more surprising.

321

They kept improving, got "weller than well" as I put it, better behaved and more comfortable or reasonable than they were before they got into that "sick" condition. We didn't know why. But it seemed to some of us that kind of the "sickness" that we had seen was a kind of conversion experience, like trimming a fruit tree, for example.

Well, enough of those recollections of early days. You tried to get us to talk together and take another look at our material. I am sorry you and I have gotten apparently so far apart all these years. We might have enjoyed discussing our observations together. You tried; you wanted me to come there, I remember. I demurred. Mea culpa.

Best wishes.
Sincerely,
Karl Menninger, M.D.

Thomas Szasz's Response to Karl Menninger

October 12, 1988

Dear Dr. Menninger:

I was deeply touched by your generous and moving letter. Thank you for writing it. As you must have felt and known, I have always had the deepest respect for you—for your sincerity, your integrity, last but not least because I realized that you wanted to hold on to the values of free will and responsibility and were struggling to reconcile them with psychiatry.

For myself, I felt sure, long before I switched my residency from medicine to psychiatry, that this was impossible, that psychiatry was basically wrong (because "mental illness" was existential, not medical). I thought there was something worthwhile in psychoanalysis, and there is, though one must dig it out from the rubble in which the psychoanalytic bureaucracy has buried it.

I will always treasure this letter. It is, of course, a piece of psychiatric history. Because it is, I am prompted to ask if you would grant me the permission, and the privilege, to cite it, in whole or in part. (I have no specific occasion in mind, at the moment.) I will respect your no, of course; in the meanwhile I will treat the letter as the personal correspondence it is.

I enclose a few small items, which I hope you will find of interest.

With affection and best wishes,
Cordially,
Thomas S. Szasz, M.D.[1]

Notes

Notes to Chapter 1

1. Muktananda (1993). *God is with you.* South Fallsburg, NY: SYDA Foundation, 34.

2. Jung, C. G., & Hull, R. E. C. (1977). *CG Jung speaking.* Princeton, NJ: Princeton University Press.

3. Rizzolatti G., & Craighero L., (2004). The mirror-neuron system. *Annual Review of Neuroscience, 27,* 169-192.

4. Terje Falck-Ytter, T., Gredebäck, G., & von Hofsten, C. (2006). Infants predict other people's action goals. *Nature Neuroscience, 9,* 878-879.

5. Dobbs, D. (April/May 2006). A revealing reflection: mirror neurons are providing stunning insights into everything from how we learn to walk to how we empathize with others. *Scientific American Mind,* 22-27.

6. Gallese, V., Eagle, M. N., & Migone, P. (2007). Intentional attunement: mirror neurons and the neural underpinnings of interpersonal relations. *Journal of the American Psychoanalytic Association, 55,* 131-176.

7. Iacoboni, M. (2008). *Mirroring people: the new science of how we connect with others.* New York: Farrar, Straus and Giroux, p. 134.330.

8. Watts, A. (1972). *The book: on the taboo against knowing who you are.* New York: Vintage, 19.

9. Lewin K. (1951). *Field theory in social science: selected theoretical papers.* New York: Harper & Row, 169.

Notes to Chapter 2

1. Jung, C. G. (1968). Archetypes of the collective unconscious. In Carl Jung, *The Collected Works of C. G. Jung, (Volume 7) The Archetypes of the Collective Unconscious* (G. Adler and R. F. C. Hull., Trans.). Princeton University Press. (Original work published in 1916)

2. See Klein, M. (1937). Love, guilt, and reparation. In M. Klein & J. Riviere (Eds.), *Love, hate, and reparation* (pp. 306-343). New York: Norton. Also see Klein, M. (1946). Notes on some schizoid mechanisms. *International Journal of Psychoanalysis, 27,* 99-100.

3. Jung, C.G. (1975). Psychology and religion. In *The Collected Works of C.G. Jung, Volume 11, Alchemical Studies.* Princeton, NJ: Princeton University Press. (Original work published 1938), 131.

4. Murdoch, R. (2009, February 24). Statement from Rupert Murdoch. *New York Post.* Retrieved from http://www.nypost.com

5. Jung, C. G. (1963). *Memories, dreams, and reflections.* New York: Pantheon.

6. Perls, F. S. (1977). *Gestalt therapy verbatim.* New York: Bantam.

Notes to Chapter 3

1. Klein, M. (1946). Notes on some schizoid mechanisms. *International Journal of Psychoanalysis, 27,* 99-100.

2. Jung, C. G. (1958). Flying saucers: a modern myth of things seen in the sky. In *The Collected Works of C. G. Jung, (Volume 10) Civilization in Transition* (G. Adler, M. Fordham,

W. Mcguire, and H. Read, Eds.), Princeton, NJ: Princeton University Press.

3. Newcott, B. (September/October 2007). Life after death. *AARP: the magazine*, pp. 58ff.

4. Muktananda (1993). *God is with you*. South Fallsburg, NY: SYDA Foundation.

5. Maslow, A. H. (1968). The Jonah complex. In Warren Bennis, et al. (Eds.), *Interpersonal dynamics: essays and readings on human interaction* (pp. 714-720). New York: Dorsey Press, 193, 119.

6. Plato (P. Shorey, Trans.) (1930). *The Republic*. London: W. Heinemann.

7. Fromm, E. (1941). *Escape from freedom*. New York: Holt, Rinehart and Winston.

8. Lerner B. H. (October 22, 2002). Cases: the doctor, the patient, the funeral. *New York Times*.

9. Nuland, S. (1993). *How we die: reflections on life's final chapter*. New York: Vintage.

10. Chen P. (2007). *Final exam: a surgeon's reflections on mortality*. New York: Knopf.

11. Hesse, H. (1999). *Siddhartha*. New York: Penguin Books. (Original work published 1922), 102.

12. Kornfield, J. (1994). *Buddha's little instruction book*. New York: Bantam, 53.

13. Watts, A. (1972). *The book: on the taboo against knowing who you are*. New York: Vintage, 9.

14. We invite you to examine Maslow, A. (1970). *Religions, values, and peak-experiences.* NY: Viking Press. One of the early contributions to the study of transpersonal psychology, Maslow's book focuses on the transformational experiences of self-actualized people. He also was instrumental in establishing the *Journal of Transpersonal Psychology*, which is still considered to be the leading journal in that field. He continued to focus his work and writings on transpersonal psychology until his death in 1970. His work is still influencing people in this field. Maslow believed there was an innate drive in all of us toward the transpersonal.

15. Welwood, J. (2000). *Toward a psychology of awakening: Buddhism, psychotherapy, and the path of personal and spiritual transformation.* Boston, MA: Shambhala Publications, 207.

16. Storm, H. (1972). *Seven arrows.* NY: Valentine Books, 4-5.

Notes to Chapter 4

1. Einhäuser, W., Martin, K. A. C., & König, Peter (2004) Are switches in perception of the Necker cube related to eye position?. *European Journal of Neuroscience, 20,* 2811-2818.

2. Thomas, W. I., & Thomas, D. S. (1928). *The child in America: behavior problems and programs.* New York: Knopf, 572.

3. Rosenthal, R. & Jacobson, L. (1992). *Pygmalion in the classroom: teacher expectation and pupils' intellectual development.* New York: Irvington Publishers.

4. Jersey, B, & Friedman, J. (Producers/Directors) (1987). *Faces of the enemy*. Broadcast nationally on PBS: A Quest Production.

Notes to Chapter 5

1. Fodor, N., Gaynor, F., & Reik, T. (Eds.), (1950). *Dictionary of psychoanalysis*. New York: Philosophical Library.

2. Pronin, E., Gilovich, T. D., & Ross, L. (2004). Objectivity in the eye of the beholder: divergent perceptions of bias in self versus others. *Psychological Review, 111*, 781-799.

3. Freud, S. (1962). The neuro-psychoses of defense. In J. Strachey (Ed. and Trans.), *The Standard Edition, Vol. I* (pp. 59-75). London: Hogarth Press. (Original work published 1894)

4. Klein, M. (1955). On identification. In M. Klein, P. Heimann, & R. E. Money-Kyrle (Eds.), *New directions in psycho-analysis* (pp. 309-345). New York: Basic Books.

5. Jersey, B, & Friedman, J. (Producers/Directors) (1987). *Faces of the enemy*. Broadcast nationally on PBS: A Quest Production.

6. Tuttle, L. (personal communication, June 26, 2007). Lori Tuttle is an expressive arts therapist living in Yellow Springs, Ohio. You can find her on the web at www. LoriTuttle.com.

7. Storrs, A. (1997). *Feet of clay*. New York: Free Press Paperbacks.

8. Zimbardo, P. G., Haney, C., Banks, W. C., & Jaffe, D. (April 8, 1973). The mind is a formidable jailer: a Pirandellian prison. *New York Times Magazine*, pp. 36ff. See

also Haney, C., Banks, W. C. and Zimbardo, P. G., (1973). A study of prisoners and guards in a simulated prison. *Navel Research Review, 30,* 4-17.

Notes to Chapter 6

1. Hutson, M. (March/April2008). Magical thinking. *Psychology Today Magazine, 41,* 88-95.

2. Winnicott, D. W. (1971a). Transitional objects and transitional phenomena. In D. W. Winnicott (Ed.), *Playing and reality (pp. 1-25). London: Tavistock.*

3. Winnicott, D. W. (1971b). Mirror role of mother and family in child development. In D. W. Winnicott (Ed.), *Playing and reality* (pp. 111-118). London: Tavistock.

4. Fairbairn, W. R. D. (1952). *Psychoanalytic studies of the personality.* London: Routledge & Kegan Paul, 66.

5. Byrne, R. (Producer) (2006). *The Secret.* Melbourne, Australia: Prime Time Productions. Cambridge, MA: MIT Press.

6. della Cava, M. R. (2007, March 28). Secret history of 'The Secret'. *USA Today [Electronic Version].* Retrieved November 10, 2007, from http://www.usatoday.com/ life/ books/news/2007-03-28-the-secret-churches_N.htm

Notes to Chapter 7

1. Winnicott, D. (1956). Primary maternal preoccupation. In *Collected Papers: Through Paediatrics to Psycho-Analysis* (pp. 300-305). New York: Basic Books, 111, 112.

2. Law, D. L. (1969, April 27). *New York Times Book Review,* 47.

Notes to Chapter 8

1. University of Montreal (2009, October 21). Women outperform men when identifying emotion. *Science Daily.* Retrieved from http://www.sciencedaily.com

2. Powell, G. N. (1988). *Women and men in management.* Newbury Park, CA: Sage.

3. Jung, C. G. (1968). Archetypes of the collective unconscious. In Carl Jung, *The Collected Works of C. G. Jung, (Volume 7) The Archetypes of the Collective Unconscious* (G. Adler and R. F. C. Hull., Trans.). Princeton University Press. (Original work published in 1916)

4. Sanford, J. A.(1980). *The invisible partners.* New York: Paulist Press.

5. See, for example, Aries, E. (1985). Male-female interpersonal styles in all male, all female and mixed groups. In A.G. Sargent (Ed.), *Beyond Sex Roles* (pp. 403-410). St. Paul, MN: West. Also see Heilman, M. E. (1983). Sex bias in work settings: the lack of fit model. In L. L. Cummings and B. M. Staw (Eds.) (1983). *Research in Organizational Behavior - Vol.* 5 (pp. 269-298). Greenwich, CT: JAI Press.

6. Jacobi, J. (1959). *Complex, archetype, symbol.* Princeton, NJ: Princeton University Press.

7. See, for example, Hendrix, H. (1988). Getting the love you want: a guide for couples. New York: Henry Holt and Company. Scharff, D. E. (1982). *The sexual relationship.* London: Routledge.

8. Sanford, J. A.(1980). *The invisible partners.* New York: Paulist Press, 55.

9. Alapack, R, Blichfeldt, M. F., & Elden, A. (2005). Flirting on the Internet and the hickey: a hermeneutic. *Cyberpsychology & Behavior, 8,* 52-61.

10. Money, J. (1986). *Lovemaps.* New York: Irvington Publishers.

11. Lacan, J. (1977). The mirror stage as formative of the function of the I as revealed in psychoanalytic experience. In Jacques Lacan's, *Ecrits: a selection* (Alan Sheridan, Trans.) (pp. 1-7). New York: W.W. Norton. (Original work published 1949)

12. Hendrix, H. (1988). *Getting the love you want: a guide for couples.* New York: Henry Holt and Company.

13. Gemmill, G, & Schaible, L. (1991). The psychodynamics of female/male role differentiation within small groups. *Small Group Research, 22,* 220-239.

Notes to Chapter 9

1. See, for example, Pronin, E., Gilovich, T. D., & Ross, L. (2004). Objectivity in the eye of the beholder: divergent perceptions of bias in self versus others. *Psychological Review, 111,* 781-799.

2. Scheidlinger, S. (1982). On scapegoating in group psychotherapy. *International Journal of Group. Psychotherapy, 32,* 131-143.

3. Becker, E. (1973). *The denial of death.* New York: Free Press.

4. Gemmill, G. (1989). The dynamics of scapegoating in small groups. *Small Group Behavior, 20,* 406-418.

5. The following three references are classic studies from the social psychology of conformity, group processes, and obedience to authority: (1) Asch, S. E. (1951). Effects of group pressure upon the modification and distortion of judgment. In H. Guetzkow (ed.), *Groups, leadership and men*. Pittsburgh, PA: Carnegie Press. (2) Janis, I. (1972). *Victims of groupthink*. Boston, MA: Houghton Mifflin. (3) Milgram, S. (1963). Behavioral study of obedience. *Journal of Abnormal and Social Psychology, 67,* 371-378.

6. Eagle, J., & Newton, R. (1981). Scapegoating in small groups: an organizational approach. *Human Relations, 34,* 283-301.

7. de Saint-Exupéry, A. (R. Howard, Trans.) (2000). *The little prince*. Ft. Washington, PA: Harvest Books. (Original work published 1943)

Notes to Chapter 10

1. See, for example, Hall, J. & Williams, M. (1970). Group dynamics training and improved decision making. *Journal of Applied Behavioral Science, 6,* 39-68.

2. See, for example, Gemmill, G. (1986). The mythology of the leader role in small groups. *Small Group Behavior, 17,* 41-50. Also see Gemmill, G., & Kraus, G. (1988). Dynamics of covert role analysis in small groups. *Small Group Behavior, 19,* 299-311. Also see Gemmill, G. & Oakley, J. (1992). Leadership: an alienating social myth. *Human Relations, 45,* 113-129. Also see Pedigo, J. M., & Singer, B. (1982). Group process development: a psychoanalytic view. *Small Group Behavior, 13,* 496-517.

3. Kopp, S. (1972). *If you meet the Buddha on the road, kill him! The pilgrimage of psychotherapy patients.* Palo Alto, CA: Science and Behavior Books.

4. Kopp, S. (1978). *An end to innocence: facing life without illusions.* New York: Bantam, 85.

5. Asch, S. E. (1951). Effects of group pressure upon the modification and distortion of judgment. In H. Guetzkow (ed.), *Groups, leadership and men.* Pittsburgh, PA: Carnegie Press.

6. Berns, G. S., Chappelow, J., Zink, C. F., Pagnoni, G., Martin-Skurski, M. E., & Richards, J. (2005). Neurobiological correlates of social conformity and independence during mental rotation. *Biological Psychiatry, 58,* 245-253.

7. Milgram, S. (1963). Behavioral study of obedience. *Journal of Abnormal and Social Psychology, 67,* 371-378, xii.

8. Freud, S. (1963). *Psychoanalysis and faith: Dialogues with the Reverend Oskar Psister.* NY: Basic Books, 61-62.

9. *Ghandi.* (1982). Director: Richard Attenborough. Performers: Ben Kingsley, Candice Bergen, Edward Fox, John Gielgud, Trevor Howard, John Mills, Martin Sheen.

Notes to Chapter 11

1. Brewer, M. (1986). The role of ethnocentrism in intergroup conflict. In S. Worchel and W. Austin (Eds.), *Psychology of intergroup relations* (pp. 88-102). Chicago, IL: Nelson-Hall.

2. The original citation for this poem is not available but the following letter appeared in a *Dear Abby* column on October 25, 1999:

DEAR ABBY: My husband, James Patrick Kinney, wrote the poem "The Cold Within" in the 1960s. It is gratifying to know he left something behind that others appreciate. He submitted it to the Saturday Evening Post; however, it was rejected as "too controversial" for the times. Jim was active in the ecumenical movement. His poem was sent in to the Liguorian, a Catholic magazine. That was its first official publication to my knowledge. Since then, it has appeared in church bulletins, teaching seminars and on talk radio, listed as "Author Unknown." If that was done for legal protection, I understand. My family is always happy to see it appear, but we do think the true author should be given credit. Jim died at 51 of a heart attack on May 23, 1973, after retiring to Sarasota, Fla. My second marriage was to Homer Kenny, a Sarasota widower, so I became ... Mrs. James Kinney-Kenny.

3. Gemmill, G., & Elmes, M. (1993). Mirror, mask, and shadow psychodynamic aspects of intergroup relations. *Journal of Management Inquiry, 2,* 43-51.

4. Stein, H. F., (1982). Adversary symbiosis and complementary group disassociations. *International Journal of Intercultural Relations, 6,* 55.

5. Keen, S. (1986). *Faces of the enemy: reflections of the hostile imagination.* San Francisco: Harpers, 21.

6. Kirschenbaum, H. & Henderson, V. (Eds.), (1989). *The Carl Rogers Reader.* NY: Houghton Mifflin, 18.

Notes to Chapter 12

1. Cartwright, S. A. (1851). Report on the diseases and physical peculiarities of the negro race. *The New Orleans Medical and Surgical Journal*, May, 691-715.

2. In 1974, the decision to create a new revision of the DSM was made by the American Psychiatric Association, and Robert Spitzer was selected as chairman of the task force. The quote is Spitzer's and can be found in Mayes, R. & Horwitz, A. V. (2005). DSM-III and the revolution in the classification of mental illness. *Journal of the History of Behavioral Sciences, 41*, 249–67.

3. Monroe S. M., & Simons, A. D. (1991). Diathesis-stress theories in the context of life stress research implications for the depressive disorders. *Psychological Bulletin, 110*, 406-425.

4. Szasz, T. S. (1974). *The myth of mental illness: foundations of a theory of personal conduct*. New York: Harper & Row.

5. Laing, R. D. (1967). *The politics of experience*. Baltimore: Ballantine Books

6. Fromm, E. (1955). *The sane society*. New York: Fawcett Premier Books. Also see Foucault M. (1988). *Madness and Civilization: A History of Insanity in the Age of Reason*. New York: Vintage.

7. Rosenhan, D. (1973). On being sane in insane places. *Science, 179*, 250-258.

8. American Psychiatric Association. (1994). *Diagnostic and statistical manual of mental disorders. 4th edition*. Washington, DC : American Psychiatric Association.

9. Buruma, I. (January 3, 2005). *Final cut: how one man revolutionized psychiatry*. The New Yorker.

10. Widiger, T. A., & Trull, T. J. (2007). Plate tectonics in the classification of personality disorder: shifting to a dimensional model. *American Psychologist, 62*, 71-83.

11. Torrey, E. F. (1986). *Witchdoctors and psychiatrists: the common roots of psychotherapy and its future.* New York: Harpers.

12. Helmchen, H. H. (1994). The validity of diagnostic systems for treatment. In J. E. Mezzich, Y. Honda, and M. C. Kastrup (Eds.), *Psychiatric diagnosis: a world perspective* (pp. 217-227). New York: Springer-Verlag, 217.

13. See, for example, Arean, P. A., & Cook, B. L. (2002). Psychotherapy and combined psychotherapy/pharmacotherapy for late-life depression. *Biological Psychiatry, 52*, 293-303.

14. Heuzenroeder, L., Donnelly, M., Haby, M. M., Mihalopoulos, C., Rossell, R., Carter, R. et al. (2004). Cost-Effectiveness of psychological and pharmacological interventions for generalized anxiety disorder and panic disorder. *Australian and New Zealand Journal of Psychiatry, 38*, 602-612.

15. This story has appeared in many forms. The quote here is by Father Cavanaugh to President Jed Bartlet from the television show *The West Wing*, in an episode entitled "Take This Sabbath Day," which first aired February 9, 2000.

16. Lee, R. R., & Martin, J. C. (1991). Psychotherapy after Kohut: a textbook of self psychology. Hillsdale, NJ: The Analytic Press, 8.

17. Frank, J. (1963). *Persuasion and healing.* New York: Schocken.

18. Fournier, J. C., DeRubeis, R. J., Hollon, S. D., et al. (2010). Antidepressant drug effects and depression severity: a patient-level meta-analysis. *Journal of the American Medical Association, 303,* 47-53.

19. Campbell, C. H. (1957) *Induced delusions: the psychopathy of freudism.* Chicago, IL: Regent House, 18.

Notes to Chapter 13

1. Beisser. A. (1970). The paradoxical theory of change. In J. Fagan and I. L. Shepard (Eds.), *Gestalt therapy now: theory, techniques, applications.* Palo Alto, CA: Science and Behavior, 77.

2. Hirschhorn, L. (1988), *The workplace within: the psychodynamics of organizational life.* Cambridge, MA: MIT Press, 8.

3. Argyris. C. (1982). *Reasoning, learning, and action: individual and organizational.* San Francisco: Jossey-Bass. See also Argyris, C. (1990). *Overcoming organizational defenses: facilitating organizational learning.* Boston, MA: Prentice Hall.

Notes to Chapter 14

1. Herman, S., & Korenich, M. (1977). *Authentic management: a gestalt orientation to organization and their development.* Reading, MA: Addison-Wesley, 38.

2. Millman, D. (2000). *Way of the peaceful warrior: a book that changes lives.* Novato, CA: H. J. Kramer—New World

Library. See also, Castaneda, C. (1972). *Journey to Ixtlan: the lessons of don Juan*. New York: Pocket Books.

3. Moore, R., & Gillette, D. (1990). *King, warrior, magician, lover: rediscovering the archetypes of the mature masculine*. San Francisco, CA: HarperSanFrancisco, 79. Also see, Kraus, G. (1997). The psychodynamics of constructive aggression in small groups. *Small Group Research, 28,* 122-145.

4. Saint John of the Cross (2002). *Dark night of the soul* (Mirabai Starr, Trans). New York: Riverhead Books.

5. Perls, F. S. (1977). *Gestalt therapy verbatim*. New York: Bantam. From the Inscription.

6. Gleick, J. (1987). *Chaos: Making a New Science*. New York: Penguin Books, 306.

7. Appalachian Expressive Arts Collective (2003). *Expressive arts therapy: creative process in art and life*. Boone, NC: Parkway Publishers.

8. Menninger, K. (1958). *Theory of psychoanalytic technique: Menninger clinic monograph series no. 12*. New York: Basic Books.

Notes to Chapter 15

1. Mattila, A. K., Poutanen, O, Koivisto, A-M. et al. (2007). Alexithymia and life satisfaction in primary healthcare patients. *Psychosomatics, 48,* 523-529.

2. Ekman, P. (2003). Emotions revealed: recognizing faces and feelings to improve communication and emotional life. New York: Henry Holt.

3. Goleman, D., (1998). Working with emotional intelligence. New York: Bantam Books.

4. For more on the neuroscience of emotions, see the following references: Tabibnia, G., Lieberman, M., and Craske, M. (2008). The lasting effects of words on feelings: Words may facilitate exposure effects to threatening images, *Emotions*, 8, 307 – 317. Lieberman, M., Eisenberger, N., Crockett, M., Pfeifer, J., and Way, B. (2007), Putting feelings into words: affect labeling disrupts amygdala activity to affective stimuli. *Psychological Sciences, 18*, 421-428.

5. Lewis, T, Amini, F, & Lannon, R. (2000). *A General theory of love*. New York: Random House.

6. Bentov, I. (1977). *Stalking the wild pendulum: on the mechanics of consciousness*. Rochester, VT: Destiny Books. The quote of from page 38.

7. Winnicott, D.W. (1950/1992). Aggression in relation to emotional development. In *Through paediatrics to psycho-Analysis* (pp. 204-218). New York: Brunner Manzel. The quote is taken from page 204.

8. Nelson, P. (1994). *There's a hole in my sidewalk (2nd ed.).* New York: Atrin Books

Notes to Chapter 16

1. Jung, C.G. (1970). Good and evil in analytical psychology. In *The Collected Works of C.G. Jung, Volume 10, Civilization in Transition*. Princeton University Press, 872.

2. See, for example, Kolak, D., & R. Martin, R. (Eds.) (1991). *Self & identity: contemporary philosophical issues*. New York: Macmillan. Also see Mansfield, N. (2000). *Subjectivity:*

theories of the self from Freud to Haraway. New York: New York University Press. Also see McCarthy, J. (1997). *The whole and divided self: Bible and theological anthropology.* New York: Crossroad Publishing.

3. Jung, C.G. (1983). The philosophical tree. In *The Collected Works of C.G. Jung, Volume 13, Alchemical Studies.* Princeton, NJ: Princeton University Press, 335.

4. Winnicott, D. W. (1965). Ego Distortion in Terms of True and False Self. In *The maturational process and the facilitating environment: studies in the theory of emotional development* (pp. 140-152). New York: International Universities Press. (Original work published 1960).

5. Polster, E. (1995). *A population of selves: a therapeutic exploration of personal diversity.* San Francisco: Jossey-Bass, 28, 59.

6. Jung, C.G. (1975). Psychology and religion. In *The Collected Works of C.G. Jung, Volume 11, Alchemical Studies.* Princeton, NJ: Princeton University Press. (Original work published 1935), 83.

7. Jourard, S. M. (1964). *The transparent self: self-disclosure and well-being.* New York: Van Nostrand Reinhold, 5.

8. Collins, N.L. & Miller, L.C. (1994). Self-disclosure and liking: A meta-analysis review. *Psychological Bulletin, 116,* 457-475.

9. Laing, R. D. (1971). *Knots.* London: Penguin.

10. The quote was made by Sidney Jourard, but an original citation is unavailable. See, however, Peltier, B. (2001). *The psychology of executive coaching: theory and applica*tion. London: Brunner-Routledge, 22.

11. This quote is by Leo McGarry to Josh Lyman from the television show *The West Wing*, in an episode entitled "Noël," which first aired December 20, 2000.

12. Moss, R. (2007). *The mandala of being: discovering the power of awareness*. Novato, CA: Awareness New World Library, 135.

13. Perls, F. S. (1969). *Gestalt therapy verbatim*. Lafayette, CA: Real People Press, 2.

14. Gleick, J. (1987). *Chaos: Making a New Science*. New York: Penguin Books. The quote is from the back cover. We have added the phrase "and more wondrous" to the quote.

15. Gemmill, G., & Wyncoop, C. (1991). The psychodynamics of small group transformation. *Small Group Research, 44*, 4-23.

16. Maslow, A. (1970). *Religions, values, and peak-experiences*. NY: Viking Press.

17. Jung, C. G. (1970). Analytical psychology and weltanschauung. In Carl Jung, *The Collected Works of C. G. Jung*, Volume 8, The Structure and Dynamics of the Psyche. Princeton, NJ: Princeton University Press. (Original work published 1928), 737.

18. Cameron, J. (1997). *The vein of gold*. New York: Tarcher.

Notes to the Appendix

1. The letters that were exchanged between Karl Menninger and Thomas Szasz are in the public domain and can be found at http://www.szasz.com/menninger.html

References

A Civil Action. (1998). Director: Steven Zaillian. Performers: John Travolta, Robert Duval, Tony Shaloub, William H. Macy, Kathleen Quinlan, and John Lithgow. Touchstone Pictures.

Alapack, R, Blichfeldt, M. F., & Elden, A. (2005). Flirting on the Internet and the hickey: a hermeneutic. *Cyberpsychology & Behavior, 8*, 52-61.

American Beauty. (1999). Director: Sam Mendes. Performers: Kevin Spacey, Annette Benning, Wes Bentley, Thora Birch, Mena Suvari, and Chris Cooper. DreamWorks.

American Psychiatric Association. (1994). *Diagnostic and statistical manual of mental disorders. Fourth edition.* Washington, DC : American Psychiatric Association.

Arean, P. A., & Cook, B. L. (2002). Psychotherapy and combined psychotherapy/pharmacotherapy for late-life depression. *Biological Psychiatry, 52*, 293-303.

Argyris, C. (1990). *Overcoming organizational defenses: facilitating organizational learning.* Boston, MA: Prentice Hall.

Argyris. C. (1982). *Reasoning, learning, and action: individual and organizational.* San Francisco: Jossey-Bass.

Aries, E. (1985). Male-female interpersonal styles in all male, all female and mixed groups. In A. G. Sargent (Ed.), *Beyond Sex Roles* (pp. 403-410). St. Paul, MN: West

Asch, S. E. (1951). Effects of group pressure upon the modification and distortion of judgment. In H. Guetzkow (ed.), *Groups, leadership and men.* Pittsburgh, PA: Carnegie Press.

Becker, E. (1973). *The denial of death.* New York: Free Press.

Beisser. A. (1970). The paradoxical theory of change. In J. Fagan and I. L. Shepard (Eds.), *Gestalt therapy now: theory, techniques, applications.* Palo Alto, CA: Science and Behavior.

Bentov, I. (1977). *Stalking the wild pendulum: on the mechanics of consciousness.* Rochester, VT: Destiny Books.

Berns, G. S., Chappelow, J., Zink, C. F., Pagnoni, G., Martin-Skurski, M. E., & Richards, J. (2005). Neurobiological correlates of social conformity and independence during mental rotation. *Biological Psychiatry, 58,* 245-253.

Brewer, M. (1986). The role of ethnocentrism in intergroup conflict. In S. Worchel and W. Austin (Eds.), *Psychology of intergroup relations* (pp. 88-102). Chicago, IL: Nelson-Hall.

Buruma, I. (January 3, 2005). Final cut: how one man revolutionized psychiatry. *The New Yorker.*

Byrne, R. (Producer) (2006). *The Secret.* Melbourne, Australia: Prime Time Productions. Cambridge, MA: MIT Press.

Cameron, J. (1997). *The vein of gold.* New York: Tarcher.

Campbell, C. H. (1957) Induced delusions: the psychopathy of freudism. Chicago, IL: Regent House.

Cartwright, S. A. (1851). Report on the diseases and physical peculiarities of the negro race. *The New Orleans Medical and Surgical Journal, May,* 691-715.

Castaneda, C. (1972). *Journey to Ixtlan: the lessons of don Juan.* New York: Pocket Books.

Chen P. (2007). *Final exam: a surgeon's reflections on mortality.* New York: Knopf.

Collins, N.L. & Miller, L.C. 1994. Self-disclosure and liking: A meta-analysis review. *Psychological Bulletin, 116,* 457-475.

Cooley, C. (1902). *Human nature and the social order.* New York: Charles Scribner's Sons.

Dalai Lama (1998). *The four noble truths.* New York: Thorsons.

della Cava, M. R. (2007, March 28). Secret history of 'The Secret'. USA Today [Electronic Version]. Retrieved November 10, 2007, from http://www.usatoday.com/life/books/news/2007-03-28-the-secret-churches_N.htm

de Saint-Exupéry, A. (R. Howard, Trans.) (2000). *The little prince.* Ft. Washington, PA: Harvest Books. (Original work published 1943)

Dobbs, D. (April/May 2006). A revealing reflection: mirror neurons are providing stunning insights into everything from how we learn to walk to how we empathize with others. *Scientific American Mind*, 22-27.

Drop Dead Fred. (1991). Director: Ate de Jong. Performers: Rik Mayall, Phoebe Cates, Marsha Mason, Tim Matheson, and Carrie Fisher. New Line Cinema.

Eagle, J., & Newton, R. (1981). Scapegoating in small groups: an organizational approach. *Human Relations, 34*, 283-301.

Ekman, P. (2003). Emotions revealed: recognizing faces and feelings to improve communication and emotional life. New York: Henry Holt.

Einhäuser, W., Martin, K. A. C., & König, Peter (2004). Are switches in perception of the Necker cube related to eye position?. *European Journal of Neuroscience, 20*, 2811-2818.

Ellenberger, H. F. (1970). *The discovery of the unconscious: The history and evolution of dynamic psychiatry*. New York: Basic Books.

Fairbairn, W. R. D. (1952). *Psychoanalytic studies of the personality*. London: Routledge & Kegan Paul.

Fisher, L. (2009, April 20). Perez Hilton 'floored' by Miss California. ABC News. Retrieved from http://abcnews.go.com

Fodor, N., Gaynor, F., & Reik, T. (Eds.), (1950). *Dictionary of psychoanalysis*. New York: Philosophical Library.

Fournier, J. C., DeRubeis, R. J., Hollon, S. D., et al. (2010). Antidepressant drug effects and depression severity: a patient-level meta-analysis. *Journal of the American Medical Association, 303*, 47-53.

Frank, J. (1963). *Persuasion and healing*. New York: Schocken.

Freud, S. (1963). *Psychoanalysis and faith: dialogues with the Reverend Oskar Psister*. NY: Basic Books.

Freud, S. (J. Strachey, Ed. and Trans) (1961). *Civilization and its discontents*. New York: Norton. (Original work published 1930)

Freud, S. (1962). The neuro-psychoses of defense. In J. Strachey (Ed. and Trans.), The Standard Edition, Vol. I) (pp. 59-75). London: Hogarth Press. (Original work published 1894)

Fromm, E. (1955). *The sane society*. New York: Fawcett Premier Books.

Fromm, E. (1941). *Escape from freedom*. New York: Holt, Rinehart and Winston.

Gallese, V., Eagle, M. N., & Migone, P. (2007). Intentional attunement: mirror neurons and the neural underpinnings of interpersonal relations. *Journal of the American Psychoanalytic Association, 55,* 131-176.

Gemmill, G. (1986). The mythology of the leader role in small groups, *Small Group Behavior, 17,* 41-50.

Gemmill, G. (1989). The dynamics of scapegoating in small groups. *Small Group Behavior, 20,* 406-418.

Gemmill, G., & Elmes, M. (1993). Mirror, mask, and shadow psychodynamic aspects of intergroup relations. *Journal of Management Inquiry, 2,* 43-51.

Gemmill, G. & Oakley, J. (1992). Leadership: an alienating social myth. *Human Relations, 45,* 113-129.

Gemmill, G, & Schaible, L. (1991). The psychodynamics of female/male role differentiation within small groups. *Small Group Research, 22,* 220-239.

Gemmill, G., & Wyncoop, C. (1991). The psychodynamics of small group transformation. *Small Group Research, 44,* 4-23.

Gleick, J. (1987). *Chaos: making a new science.* New York: Penguin Books.

Goleman, D., (1998). Working with emotional intelligence. New York: Bantam Books.

Hall, J. & Williams, M. (1970). Group dynamics training and improved decision making. *Journal of Applied Behavioral Science, 6,* 39-68.

Haney, C., Banks, W. C. and Zimbardo, P. G., (1973). *A study of prisoners and guards in a simulated prison.* Navel Research Review, 30, 4-17.

Heilman, M. E. (1983). Sex bias in work settings: the lack of fit model. In L. L. Cummings and B. M. Staw (Eds.) (1983). *Research in Organizational Behavior* (Vol. 5, pp. 269-298) Greenwich, CT: JAI Press.

Helmchen, H. H. (1994). The validity of diagnostic systems for treatment. In J. E. Mezzich, Y. Honda, and M. C. Kastrup (Eds.),

Psychiatric diagnosis: a world perspective (pp. 217-227). New York: Springer-Verlag.

Hendrix, H. (1988). *Getting the love you want: a guide for couples.* New York: Henry Holt and Company.

Herman, S., & Korenich, M. (1977). *Authentic management: a gestalt orientation to organization and their development.* Reading, MA: Addison-Wesley.

Hesse, H. (1999). *Siddhartha.* New York: Penguin Books. (Original work published 1922)

Heuzenroeder, L., Donnelly, M., Haby, M. M., Mihalopoulos, C., Rossell, R., Carter, R. et al. (2004). Cost-Effectiveness of psychological and pharmacological interventions for generalized anxiety disorder and panic disorder. *Australian and New Zealand Journal of Psychiatry, 38,* 602-612.

Hirschhorn, L. (1988). *The workplace within: the psychodynamics of organizational life.* Cambridge, MA: MIT Press.

Iacoboni, M. (2008). *Mirroring people: the new science of how we connect with others.* New York: Farrar, Straus and Giroux.

Jacobi, J. (1959). *Complex, archetype, symbol.* Princeton: Princeton University Press.

Janis, I. (1972). *Victims of groupthink.* Boston, MA: Houghton Mifflin.

Jersey, B, & Friedman, J. (Producers/Directors) (1987). *Faces of the enemy.* Broadcast nationally on PBS: A Quest Production.

Jourard, S. M. (1964). *The transparent self: self-disclosure and well-being.* New York: Van Nostrand Reinhold.

Jung, C.G. (1983). The philosophical tree. In *The Collected Works of C.G. Jung, Volume 13, Alchemical Studies.* Princeton, NJ: Princeton University Press.

Jung, C.G. (1975). Psychology and religion. In *The Collected Works of C.G. Jung, Volume 11, Alchemical Studies.* Princeton, NJ: Princeton University Press. (Original work published 1935)

Jung, C.G. (1970). Good and evil in analytical psychology. In *The Collected Works of C.G. Jung, Volume 10, Civilization in Transition.* Princeton University Press.

Jung, C. G. (1970). Analytical psychology and weltanschauung. In Carl Jung, *The Collected Works of C. G. Jung, Volume 8, The Structure and Dynamics of the Psyche.* Princeton, NJ: Princeton University Press. (Original work published 1928)

Jung, C. G. (1968). Archetypes of the collective unconscious. In Carl Jung, *The Collected Works of C. G. Jung, Volume 9. The Archetypes of the Collective Unconscious.* Princeton University Press. (Original work published in 1916)

Jung, C. G. (1963). *Memories, dreams, and reflections.* New York: Pantheon.

Jung, C. G. (1958). Flying saucers: a modern myth of things seen in the sky. In *The Collected Works of C. G. Jung,* (Volume 10) *Civilization in Transition* (G. Adler, M. Fordham, W. Mcguire, and H. Read, Eds.), Princeton, NJ: Princeton University Press.

Jung, C. G., & Hull, R. E. C. (1977). *CG Jung speaking.* Princeton, NJ: Princeton University Press.

Keen, S. (1986). *Faces of the enemy: reflections of the hostile imagination.* San Francisco: Harpers.

Kirschenbaum, H. & Henderson, V. (Eds.), (1989). *The Carl Rogers reader.* NY: Houghton Mifflin.

Klein, M. (1964). Love, guilt, and reparation. In M. Klein and J. Riviere,. *Love, hate and reparation* (pp. 57-119). New York: Norton. (Original work published 1937)

Klein, M. (1955). On identification. In M. Klein, P. Heimann, & R. E. Money-Kyrle (Eds.), *New directions in psycho-analysis* (pp. 309-345). New York: Basic Books.

Klein, M. (1946). Notes on some schizoid mechanisms. *International Journal of Psychoanalysis, 27,* 99-100.

Klein, M. (1937). Love, guilt, and reparation. In M. Klein & J. Riviere (Eds.), *Love, hate, and reparation* (pp. 306-343). New York: Norton.

Kolak, D., & R. Martin, R. (Eds.) (1991). *Self & identity: contemporary philosophical issues.* New York: Macmillan.

Kopp, S. (1978). *An end to innocence: facing life without illusions.* New York: Bantam.

Kopp, S. (1972). *If you meet the Buddha on the road, kill him! The pilgrimage of psychotherapy patients.* Palo Alto, CA: Science and Behavior Books.

Kornfield, J. (1994). *Buddha's little instruction book.* New York: Bantam.

Kraus, G. (1997). The psychodynamics of constructive aggression in small groups. *Small Group Research, 28*, 122-124.

Lacan, J. (1977). The mirror stage as formative of the function of the I as revealed in psychoanalytic experience. In Jacques Lacan's, *Ecrits: a selection* (Alan Sheridan, Trans.) (pp. 1-7). New York: W.W. Norton. (Original work published 1949)

Laing, R. D. (1971). *Knots.* London: Penguin.

Laing, R. D. (1967). *The politics of experience.* Baltimore, MD: Ballantine Books

Law, D. L. (1969, April 27). *New York Times Book Review*, 47.

Lee, R. R., & Martin, J. C. (1991). *Psychotherapy after Kohut: a textbook of self psychology.* Hillsdale, NJ: The Analytic Press.

Lerner B. H. (October 22, 2002). Cases: the doctor, the patient, the funeral. *New York Times.*

Lewin K. (1951). *Field theory in social science: selected theoretical papers.* New York: Harper & Row.

Lewis, T, Amini, F, & Lannon, R. (2000). *A General theory of love.* New York: Random House.

Lieberman, M., Eisenberger, N., Crockett, M., Pfeifer, J., and Way, B. (2007), Putting feelings into words: affect labeling disrupts amygdala activity to affective stimuli. *Psychological Sciences, 18*, 421-428.

Malancharuvil, J. M. (2004). Projection, introjection, and projective identification: a reformulation. *American Journal of Psychoanalysis, 64*, 375-382.

Mansfield, N. (2000). *Subjectivity: theories of the self from Freud to Haraway.* New York: New York University Press.

Maslow, A. H. (1971). *The further reaches of human nature.* New York: Viking Press.

Maslow, A. (1970). *Religions, values, and peak-experiences.* NY: Viking Press.

Maslow, A. H. (1968). The Jonah complex. In Warren Bennis, et al. (Eds.), *Interpersonal dynamics: essays and readings on human interaction* (pp. 714-720). New York: Dorsey Press.

Maslow, A. H. (1963). The need to know and the fear of knowing. *Journal of General Psychology, 68,* 111-125.

Mattila, A. K., Poutanen, O, Koivisto, A-M. et al. (2007). Alexithymia and life satisfaction in primary healthcare patients, *Psychosomatics, 48*: 523-529.

May, R. (1967). *Psychology and the human dilemma.* Princeton, NJ: Van Nostrand.

May, R. (1958). Contributions of existential psychotherapy. In Rollo May, Ernest Angel, and Henri Ellenberger (Eds.), *Existence* (pp. 37-91). New York: Basic Books.

Mayes, R. & Horwitz, A. V. (2005). DSM-III and the revolution in the classification of mental illness. *Journal of the History of Behavioral Sciences, 41,* 249–67.

McCarthy, J. (1997). *The whole and divided self: Bible and theological anthropology.* New York: Crossroad Publishing.

Menninger, K. (1958). *Theory of psychoanalytic technique.* New York: Basic Books.

Milgram, S. (1963). Behavioral study of obedience. *Journal of Abnormal and Social Psychology, 67,* 371-378.

Millman, D. (2000). *Way of the peaceful warrior: a book that changes lives.* Novato, CA: H. J. Kramer—New World Library.

Money, J. (1986). *Lovemaps.* New York: Irvington Publishers.

Moore, R., & Gillette, D. (1990). *King, warrior, magician, lover: rediscovering the archetypes of the mature masculine.* San Francisco, CA: HarperSanFrancisco.

Moss, R. (2007). *The mandala of being: discovering the power of awareness.* Novato, CA: New World Library.

Muktananda (1993). *God is with you.* South Fallsburg, NY: SYDA Foundation.

Murdoch, R. (2009, February 24). Statement from Rupert Murdoch. *New York Post*. Retrieved from http://www.nypost.com

Nelson, P. (1994). *There's a hole in my sidewalk* (2nd ed.). New York: Atrin Books

Newcott, B. (September/October 2007). Life after death. *AARP: the magazine*, pp. 58ff.

Nuland S. (1993). *How we die: reflections on life's final chapter.* New York: Vintage.

Peck, M. S. (1977). *The road less traveled: a new psychology of love, traditional values and spiritual growth.* New York: Simon and Schuster.

Pedigo, J. M., & Singer, B. (1982). Group process development: a psychoanalytic view. *Small Group Behavior, 13,* 496-517.

Perls, F. S. (1977). *Gestalt therapy verbatim.* New York: Bantam.

Plato (P. Shorey, Trans.) (1930). *The Republic.* London: W. Heinemann.

Polster, E. (1995). *A population of selves: a therapeutic exploration of personal diversity.* San Francisco: Jossey-Bass.

Powell, G. N. (1988). *Women and men in management.* Newbury Park, CA: Sage.

Pronin, E., Gilovich, T. D., & Ross, L. (2004). Objectivity in the eye of the beholder: divergent perceptions of bias in self versus others. *Psychological Review, 111,* 781-799.

Rizzolatti G., & Craighero L., (2004). The mirror-neuron system. *Annual Review of Neuroscience, 27,* 169-192.

Rosenhan, D. (1973). On being sane in insane places. *Science, 179,* 250-258.

Rosenthal, R. & Jacobson, L. (1992). *Pygmalion in the classroom: teacher expectation and pupils' intellectual development.* New York: Irvington Publishers.

Saint John of the Cross (2002). *Dark night of the soul* (Mirabai Starr, Trans). New York: Riverhead Books.

Sanford, J. A.(1980). *The invisible partners.* New York: Paulist Press.

Scharff, D. E. (1982*). The sexual relationship.* London: Routledge.

Scheidlinger, S. (1982). On scapegoating in group psychotherapy. *International Journal of Group. Psychotherapy, 32*, 131-143.

Schopenhauer, A. (E. F. J. Payne, Trans.) (1998). *On the basis of morality*. Indianapolis, IN: Hackett Publishing. (Original work published 1840)

Stein, H. F., (1982). Adversary symbiosis and complementary group disassociations. *International Journal of Intercultural Relations, 6*, 55-83

Stevenson, R. S. (1991). *The strange case of Dr. Jekyll and Mr. Hyde*. Mineola, NY: Dover Publications. (Original work published 1886)

Storm, H. (1972). *Seven arrows*. NY: Valentine Books.

Storrs, A. (1997). *Feet of clay*. New York: Free Press Paperbacks.

Szasz, T. S. (1974). *The myth of mental illness: foundations of a theory of personal conduct*. New York: Harper & Row.

Tabibnia, G., Lieberman, M., and Craske, M. (2008). The lasting effects of words on feelings: Words may facilitate exposure effects to threatening images, *Emotions, 8*, 307 – 317.

Terje Falck-Ytter, T., Gredebäck, G., & von Hofsten, C. (2006). Infants predict other people's action goals. *Nature Neuroscience, 9*, 878-879.

The Breakfast Club (1985). Director: John Hughes. Performers: Anthony Michael Hall, Ally Sheedy, Emilio Estevez, Molly Ringwald, Judd Nelson, and Paul Gleason. A & M Films.

Thomas, W. I., & Thomas, D. S. (1928). *The child in America: behavior problems and programs*. New York: Knopf.

Torrey, E. F. (1986). *Witchdoctors and psychiatrists: the common roots of psychotherapy and its future*. New York: Harpers.

Tuttle, L. (personal communication, June 26, 2007). Lori Tuttle is an expressive arts therapist living in Yellow Springs, Ohio. You can find her on the web at www. LoriTuttle.com.

University of Montreal (2009, October 21). Women outperform men when identifying emotion. *Science Daily*. Retrieved from http://www.sciencedaily.com

Watts, A. (1995). *The Tao of philosophy: the edited transcripts*. Boston: Tuttle Publishing.

Watts, A. (1972). *The book: on the taboo against knowing who you are*. New York: Vintage.

Welwood, J. (2000) *Toward a psychology of awakening: Buddhism, psychotherapy, and the path of personal and spiritual transformation*, Boston, MA: Shambhala Publications

What About Bob?. (1991). Director: Frank Oz. Performers: Bill Murray, Richard Dreyfuss, Julie Hagerty, Charlie Korsmo, Kathryne Erbe. Touchstone Pictures.

Widiger, T. A., & Trull, T. J. (2007). Plate tectonics in the classification of personality disorder: shifting to a dimensional model. *American Psychologist, 62*, 71-83.

Winnicott, D.W. (1992). Aggression in relation to emotional development. In *Through paediatrics to psycho-Analysis* (pp. 204-218). New York: Brunner Manzel. The quote is taken from page 204. (Original work published in 1950)

Winnicott, D. W. (1971a). Transitional objects and transitional phenomena. In D. W. Winnicott (Ed.), *Playing and reality* (pp. 1-25). London: Tavistock.

Winnicott, D. W. (1971b). Mirror role of mother and family in child development. In D. W. Winnicott (Ed.), *Playing and reality* (pp. 111-118). London: Tavistock.

Winnicott, D. W. (1965). Ego distortion in terms of true and false self. In *The maturational process and the facilitating environment: studies in the theory of emotional development (pp. 140-152)*. New York: International Universities Press. (Original work published 1960)

Winnicott, D. (1956). Primary maternal preoccupation. In *Collected Papers: Through Paediatrics to Psycho-Analysis* (pp. 300-305). New York: Basic Books.

Yeung, K-T, & Martin, J. L. (2003). The looking glass self: an empirical test and elaboration. *Social Forces 81*, 843-879.

Zimbardo, P. G., Haney, C., Banks, W. C., & Jaffe, D. (April 8, 1973). The mind is a formidable jailer: a Pirandellian prison. *New York Times Magazine*, pp. 36ff.

Biographies

Gary Gemmill, PhD, is Professor Emeritus of Organizational Behavior at Syracuse University and a doctoral faculty mentor at Walden University. He has been certified as a Professional Group Development Consultant by the International Association of Applied Social Scientists and is recognized as both a Personal Growth Consultant and Group Development Consultant by the Association for Creative Change in Religious and Other Social Systems. Dr. Gemmill leads intensive programs in personal growth, leadership dynamics, and team dynamics around the world and has written many professional articles on the psychodynamics of personal growth and group development. He has a postgraduate diploma in Gestalt Therapy from the Gestalt Training Center of San Diego, where he studied with Erv and Miriam Polster.

George Kraus, PhD, ABPP is a clinical and consulting psychologist in private practice with Layh and Associates in Yellow Springs, Ohio. He specializes in the care of older adults, especially those suffering from Alzheimer's and other dementias. Dr. Kraus has published in a variety of professional journals and is the author of *At Wit's End: Plain Talk on Alzheimer's for Families and Clinicians*, released in 2006 by Purdue University Press. He is board certified in clinical psychology by the American Board of Professional Psychology, and he is on the graduate faculty of the School of Professional Psychology at Wright State University. Dr. Kraus is also on the editorial board of *Aggression and Violent Behavior: A Review Journal*. To learn more about Dr. Kraus and his practice, visit him at www. GeorgeKrausPhD.com.

CPSIA information can be obtained
at www.ICGtesting.com
Printed in the USA
BVOW10s0439260817
493144BV00012B/131/P